Regional Development Poles and the Transformation of African Economies

T0300182

This book argues that the development of capital goods manufacturing industries in four relatively large African economies will create regional development poles, from which industrialization will spread to the smaller African countries.

In this book, Benaiah Yongo-Bure explains the need for capital goods industries in Africa and shows how manufacturing can transform economies. He outlines the roles of the Democratic Republic of Congo (DRC), Ethiopia, Nigeria, and South Africa as potential regional development poles, showing how the existing economies, natural resources, and populations of these countries make them ideal candidates, while also considering possible challenges to industrialization. Finally, the author assesses what major infrastructural development is needed to link the countries and regions to increase the spread effects of economic growth.

This book will be of interest to scholars and policymakers in economic development and regional development in Africa.

Benaiah Yongo-Bure is Associate Professor of Economics at Kettering University, USA.

Routledge contemporary Africa series

Africa's Elite Football
Structure, Politics, and Everyday Challenges
Chuka Onwumechili

Social Licensing and Mining in South Africa
Sethulego Matebesi

The Everyday Life of the Poor in Cameroon
The Role of Social Networks in Meeting Needs
Nathanael Ojong

Introduction to Rwandan Law
Jean-Marie Kamatali

State Fragility and Resilience in Sub-Saharan Africa
Indicators and Interventions
John Idriss Lahai and Isaac Koomson

Press Silence in Postcolonial Zimbabwe
News whiteouts, Journalism and Power
Zvenyika E. Mugari

Urban Planning in Rapidly Growing Cities
Developing Addis Ababa
Mintesnot G. Woldeamanuel

Regional Development Poles and the Transformation of African Economies
Benaiah Yongo-Bure

For more information about this series, please visit: www.routledge.com/ Routledge-Contemporary-Africa/book-series/RCAFR

Regional Development Poles and the Transformation of African Economies

Benaiah Yongo-Bure
Kettering University Flint, MI, USA

Routledge
Taylor & Francis Group

LONDON AND NEW YORK

First published 2020
by Routledge
4 Park Square, Milton Park, Abingdon, Oxon OX14 4RN
605 Third Avenue, New York, NY 10017

First issued in paperback 2023

Routledge is an imprint of the Taylor & Francis Group, an informa business

British Library Cataloguing-in-Publication Data
A catalogue record for this book is available from the British Library

Library of Congress Cataloging-in-Publication Data
A catalog record has been requested for this book

ISBN: 978-1-03-257095-2 (pbk)
ISBN: 978-0-367-44440-2 (hbk)
ISBN: 978-1-003-02480-4 (ebk)

DOI: 10.4324/9781003024804

Typeset in Bembo
by Apex CoVantage, LLC

Publisher's Note
The publisher has gone to great lengths to ensure the quality of this reprint but
points out that some imperfections in the original copies may be apparent.

Contents

Figures and tables

Preface and acknowledgment

The structures of virtually all African economies are not consistent with the patterns of consumption of the populations. Like people elsewhere in the world, Africans' demand is mostly for manufactured goods, most of which are imported from outside the continent. This situation is heightened with the sources of production inputs, especially of machinery and equipment. Most of the modern manufacturing carried out within Africa is concentrated on consumer goods, assembling from imported components, and processing of primary products. These subsectors of manufacturing are not technologically dynamic; have limited backward and forward linkages to the domestic economies; and are import- and foreign exchange-intensive. They cannot lead a country to self-sustaining development.

The manufacture of capital goods is the key to initiating a self-sustaining economy. Capital goods industries can supply the economy with a variety of productive inputs. They are technologically dynamic as technology is embodied in capital goods. Capital goods industries enable an economy to be flexible in adjusting to changing demand and production patterns.

Machinery and other capital goods are on what all African countries spend their inelastic foreign exchange. During times of depressed world market commodity prices, most African countries can hardly meet their requirements for imports, including imports of capital goods. Consequently, they cannot fulfil their development programs nor even carry out maintenance and repair of their existing productive capacities.

As technological progress takes place in the technologically advanced countries, African economies are forced to either replace their existing machinery or lag behind technologically. They may have to scrap still-useful productive capacities because of lack of spare parts or replacement inputs. Therefore, instead of increasing their capital stocks, such countries are tied to replacement of the same capital stock.

However, given the limited sizes of their domestic markets and resources not all African countries can manufacture large capital goods. Only a few African countries are large enough to sustain the manufacture of most capital goods. The few large African countries will have to undertake the establishment of heavy manufacturing machinery. The establishment of integrated infrastructure networks will facilitate cheaper diffusion of the capital goods among African countries.

Acknowledgment

This work is to a large extent a result of my teachers and colleagues in development economies during both my undergraduate and graduate studies. I have pondered over the years as I reflect on the role of development economics on African development. I also wish to thank the anonymous reviewers of the manuscript, especially the one who suggested to include the impact of the Belt and Road Initiative in the analysis. The staff of Routledge, especially Leanne Hinves, Henry Strang, and Aruna Rajendran, have done a professionally excellent job in preparing the book for publication. Thanks also go to my son, Jame, for taking over the running of the family errands while I prepared the manuscript for publication.

Abbreviations

AfDB	=	African Development Bank
AMU	=	Arab Maghreb Union
ASM	=	Artisanal and Small Scale Mining
AU	=	African Union
AUC	=	African Union Commission
BRI	=	Belt and Road Initiative
CAR	=	Central African Republic
CENSAD	=	Community of Sahel-Saharan States
COMESA	=	Common Market for Eastern and Southern Africa
CSR	=	Corporate Social Responsibility
DRC	=	Democratic Republic of Congo
EITI	=	Extractive Industries Transparency Initiative
ECA	=	East African Community
ECCAS	=	Economic Community of Central African States
ECOWAS	=	Economic Community of West African States
HEPC	=	Heavily Indebted Poor Countries
IGAD	=	Intergovernmental Authority on Development
NEPAD	=	New Partnership for Africa's Development
OAU	=	Organization for African Unity
OHADA	=	Organization for the Harmonization of Business Law in Africa
PIDA	=	Program for Infrastructure Development in Africa
PIDA-PAP	=	PIDA Priority Action Plan
SADC	=	Southern African Development Community
SNEL	=	Societe Nationale d'Electricite
UNECA	=	United Nations Economic Commission for Africa
UNEP	=	United Nations Environmental Program

Abbreviations

1   Capital goods and economic transformation

Introduction

Economic transformation requires the diversification and industrialization of an economy. The industrial sector includes a number of subsectors such as mining, manufacturing, construction, electricity, water, and gas. However, of all these, manufacturing is the most transformative subsector of industry. But not just any kind of manufacturing is sufficient to transform an economy. Distinction must be made among the three subsectors of manufacturing, namely manufacturing of consumer goods, intermediate goods, and capital goods.

Consumer goods industries produce goods that are ready for final use. These are the factories that process food, clothing, footwear, beverages, and the thousands of other ready-for final-use products. The machinery they use is produced by capital goods industries. Intermediate goods are inputs used in the manufacture of both consumer goods and capital goods. These include industries manufacturing bolts and joints, spare parts, industrial inputs, ingredients such as sugar used in the manufacture of confectionery, and many other inputs. The machinery for making all types of manufactures originates from the capital goods industries.

As can already be seen, capital goods are the manufactured goods that are used to produce all machinery, plus those used in machinery's own production. It is a diverse sector used to manufacture machinery and equipment used in various types of manufacturing. They include engineering and construction machineries, agricultural, transportation, energy generation, and equipment, and so many types of machinery and equipment for various sectors. They have profound impact on various sectors of the economy. They are also the subsector where most technological innovations take place.

The embodiment of technology in capital goods industries makes the subsector the most dynamic. Once a country establishes a substantial size of the capital goods subsector, it can supply many of its own industries with machinery and equipment, and it can guide much of its own technological advancement. Hence, the establishment of large capital goods manufacturing within Africa is crucial for African economic transformation. This is because Africa needs large-scale plants for the manufacture of strategic capital goods such as energy generation and transmission equipment, agricultural processing plants, chemical plants, transport machinery and equipment, mining machinery, and many other various manufacturing machinery and equipment.

Capital goods manufacturing is also characterized with economies of scale as many indivisibilities and high-skilled labor are involved in their construction and operation. Capital goods manufacturing is the most dynamic subsector. It supplies itself as well as the other two manufacturing subsectors with inputs. Capital goods industries are technologically dynamic; their regular supplies to all sectors of the economy ensure regular capacity utilization and technological flexibility in the whole economy. With flexible and rapidly changing technology, as consumer demand changes, the economy's capacity to adjust to the changing demand patterns will instantaneously adapt, ensuring fairly stable adjustments in the economy.

Metal processing and manufacturing is an important component of the capital goods industry. According to the International Standard for Industrial Classification, the metal industry consists of basic metal and engineering industry. The engineering industries can be further grouped into: manufacture of basic iron and steel; manufacture of fabricated metal products except machinery and equipment; manufacture of machinery and equipment; and manufacture of motor vehicles, trailers, and semi-trailers.[1]

The engineering subsector

Machinery and equipment needed in manufacturing are products of the engineering subsector. This subsector embodies most technologies in the machinery and equipment it makes and uses. It comprises elements such as engineering design and development, tool engineering and production, production engineering, materials engineering, and maintenance engineering. Together these subsectors translate science and technological innovations and developments into new, more efficient and more economical machines, plants, and equipment. The engineering industry has the capacity to design, adapt, and manufacture the components of new technical systems as well as repair, modify, and rehabilitate existing industrial plants and equipment. Therefore, the engineering industry, drawing from the basic metals and metal-working industries, constitutes the central pillar of an industrial economy (Agbu 2007). Hence, industrialization and technological development are not just a matter of importing more efficient equipment and installing it. It must be linked with fundamental development of scientific knowledge and capital goods industry and the capability to adapt them flexibly into an evolving economy. This process must be internalized within the domestic economy for dynamic and flexible economic transformation to take place.

In view of foreign exchange constraints for importing machine tools, the need to achieve a level of self-reliance in this strategic subsector through the local manufacture of machine tools is a precondition for self-sustaining development, not only of the engineering industry, but also of industry in general and the rest of the economy. Capability in the manufacture and use of machine tools would also contribute to the repair and maintenance of machinery and equipment used in various socio-economic activities. Machinery and equipment are what absorbs most of African foreign exchange as virtually all of them are imported far from outside the continent. Given the necessity of capital and intermediate goods in all industrial activities, shortage of foreign exchange means a predominantly importing economy comes to a halt. This was what happened to most African economies from the 1970s when the prices of petroleum and machinery rose considerably beyond the prices of African exports. This led to the International Monetary Fund's (IMF) structural adjustment programs, the debt crises, and the two lost decades of African development of the 1980s and 1990s.

Establishment of the capital goods subsector would make technological adaptation and innovation in Africa flexible. New technological capital goods and spare parts would be more easily acquired through acquisition of the currencies of the capital-goods–producing African countries in the neighborhood.

Foreign trade cannot be relied upon permanently for self-sustaining development or as an engine of growth and transformation. Foreign trade led to the establishment of the current structures of African economies. As foreign demand changes, the performances of African economies responded accordingly. African economies boomed as foreign demand for African primary products rose during the colonial period; and in the early post-colonial periods of the 1960s and early 1970s. The post-Second World War boom, due to reconstruction in the west and the boom of the 1960s, helped African economies boom temporarily. However, the prolonged difficulties in the world economy, from the 1970s, pushed the dependent African economies to the lost decades of the 1980s and 1990s.

Africa's positive economic performance in the 2000s relied mainly on the demand for African oil and minerals from China, India, and other newly industrializing economies. African economies withstood or recovered fast from the Great Recession of 2007–2009 because of the changes in the continent's direction of trade to China and India. However, as China's growth rate slowed, African oil and mineral exporters began to experience economic difficulties. Africa must use the enormous export earnings it brings in during foreign demand booms to transform its economies so that when the foreign demand declines, the continent is able to sustain its economies largely through internal African demand. The huge potential African market must be developed through integrated and transformed African economies.

The strategy of *commodity-based industrialization* of the United Nations Economic Commission for Africa and the African Union Commission (UNECA and AUC 2013a) is a necessary prelude and ingredient of the capital goods industrialization strategy (UNECA 2013b). Commodity industrialization will boost the African market and skills, and contribute to African integration as it will promote intra-industry trade. It will also promote rural development and expand the African market. Most of the intra-African trade is in manufactured goods rather than in raw agricultural products[2] (Linder 1961).

The consumption of many raw agricultural products is more culturally specific than that of manufactured products. Processed and manufactured agricultural exports will earn Africa more foreign exchange, which will help in capital goods industrialization. However, massive exportation of similar manufactured agricultural products to the world market may lead to worsening of African terms of trade as such massive increase in exports will flood the world market and depress commodity export prices.

As Table 1.1 shows, the more industrialized African countries have more intra-African exports than imports. These include Cote d'Ivoire, Kenya, and South Africa. South Africa, being the most industrialized African country, exports manufactured goods to virtually all African countries. Cote d'Ivoire and Kenya are among the relatively more industrialized African countries. They export substantial manufactures mostly to their neighbors. Hence, intra-African trade should generally increase as manufacturing and transformation progress in African economies.

Nigeria's higher exports and imports are explained by its export of petroleum to many African countries. South Africa's large value of intra-African imports results mainly from its imports of petroleum, particularly from Angola and Nigeria. Ethiopia's low value of intra-African trade can partly be explained by the classification of some of its major African markets, such as Djibouti and Somalia, as Middle Eastern markets. The high level of Cote d'Ivoire's intra-African imports reflect manufactures from South Africa and other fairly industrialized economies in West Africa such as Ghana and Senegal. Cote d'Ivoire also imports oil from Angola, Cameroon, Equatorial Guinea, Gabon, and Nigeria.

Technology and development

Technology is critical in economic transformation. Together with efficiency, technology improves the productivity of all factors of production, releasing resources for an ever-higher level of output. However, technology is not only the scientific and machine-tool knowledge, and tools and machines. It also encompasses the country-specific human understanding, skills, education, and training essential for making use of this knowledge, machines, and tools. Thus, technology is specific to each economy or similar economies. It has different effects on productivity in different economies or even firms since the tools are combined with labor forces in each economy with specific accumulated skills operating within a larger institutional and organizational framework.

The more rapidly technological knowledge can be adapted and put to work in an economy, the more rapid will be the pace of economic growth. This requires that workers and entrepreneurs have hands-on experience using such ideas in the act of producing. The more such machines and equipment are domestically produced, the more familiar the local workers are to their operations and adoptability to different industrial needs and uses.

Technology and human capital are fundamental complementary inputs affecting the rate of economic growth and the level of per capita income.

Table 1.1 Industrialization and intra–African trade

Country	Year Items	2005	2006	2007	2008	2009	2010	2011	2012	2013	2014	2015
DR Congo	**Exports**	126.1	97.3	202.0	568.4	530.0	1,259.4	1,370.5	1,266.0	1,801.7	1,455.1	1,075.8
	Imports	742.9	1,115.5	1,696.4	2,477.3	1,703.5	2,224.5	2,807.8	3,586.1	4,110.0	3,580.8	3,101.6
Cote d'Ivoire	**Exports**	2,087.4	2,284.7	2,405.0	3,009.0	2,947.2	3,123.5	3,251.8	3,623.6	5,936.6	4,104.8	3,271.4
	Imports	1,606.9	1,784.0	1,948.2	2,647.5	1,765.2	2,387.1	1,906.4	2,920.6	4,086.0	2,875.4	3,047.7
Ethiopia	**Exports**	4.1	2.8	4.4	5.1	21.7	24.1	25.0	33.3	30.8	37.7	34.1
	Imports	26.5	56.4	35.8	28.7	105.5	105.7	104.3	141.3	153.4	169.4	182.4
Kenya	**Exports**	1,144.0	1,201.0	1,446.0	1,612.0	1,573.0	1,673.0	2,038.0	2,121.0	1,989.0	2,029.0	2,390.0
	Imports	719.0	191.0	1,077.0	1,315.0	1,184.0	1,147.0	1,390.0	1,272.0	1,346.0	1,319.0	1,332.0
Nigeria	**Exports**	3,810.0	4,800.0	5,921.0	7,719.0	5,712.0	7,126.0	8,645.0	10,176.0	10,170.0	11,173.0	9,450.0
	Imports	1,446.0	1,580.0	1,810.0	2,339.0	2,001.0	2,123.0	2,303.0	2,660.0	2,733.0	2,557.0	2,208.0
South Africa	**Exports**	6,795.0	7,229.0	8,922.0	11,976.0	10,098.0	22,781.0	14,053.0	26,939.0	26,691.0	27,096.0	23,046.0
	Imports	2,013.0	3,260.0	5,298.0	6,657.0	4,693.0	7,641.0	7,356.0	11,467.0	11,343.0	12,416.0	8,447.0

Source: International Monetary Fund (IMF). Direction of Trade Statistics, 2010, 2012, 2016.

Technological knowledge in use is economy specific as a result of differences in the capacity of end-users to apply knowledge in the production process. There is need to focus on social investment in specific human capital and organizational inputs if such knowledge is to be utilized to its full effect. There are gaps among economies and each economy must develop its own relatively unique *technological base*. Investment in complementary inputs is very important, particularly in education and research and development (R&D), which contribute over time to each country's specific capability to effectively make use of the world's supply of technological knowledge.

Without continuous technological change, economic growth slows and eventually development falters. Rapid economic growth and transformation cannot be achieved without continuous technological investment. The successful introduction of technology into the domestic production process in any country requires a domestic scientific establishment capable first of understanding, adopting, and adapting new, often foreign-created, technological knowledge to the specific needs of the domestic economy. Machines and tools often have to be customized to fit local conditions; that is, technology is "borrowed" from the world supply and made to fit the local economy. *But borrowing cannot be in perpetuity. Efforts have to be made to indigenize the technology through domestic investment and innovation.* This needs the building of substantial domestic economic capability. *Neighboring countries, at approximately similar cultural levels of development, have more relevant experiences to share.*

Virtually all the manufacturing industries set up in Africa at independence were consumer goods industries. They were capital-intensive, imported from the former colonial powers. This made their operations hinge on availability of foreign exchange; otherwise the plants would operate at very low capacity or even be closed down for want of foreign exchange to import spare parts, raw material, or replacement machinery and equipment. There is no dynamism in such industries. Hence, they cannot be the basis of transforming African economies.

The sizes of African economies and markets

The Appendix shows various indicators of the sizes, capacities, and indices of human development of virtually all African economies as of 2015, relative to the rest of the world. These indices include land areas, populations, national income and per capita incomes, infant mortality and life expectancy, and the development of education at various levels.

The small fragmented markets of most individual African economies cannot support the establishment of capital goods industries. Unless established on regional basis, such industries would be underutilized in most individual African countries. Moreover, in many cases, technology designed for developed countries are not suited for African countries at present stages of development.

While the initial capital goods can be imported from the established industrial countries, reliance on importation should not be continued indefinitely.

Development of domestic capital goods industries must be established so that over time the national economy will largely depend on domestic capital goods industries so as to ensure sustainable supplies of machinery and equipment, spare parts, and other inputs to its various sectors. Capacity utilization and further growth of the economy may be frustrated by constraints in the importing capacity of the economy for foreign inputs. Such constraints may arise from shortage of foreign exchange. For example, inability of a country to import may arise from uncertainty in the international market for its exports, rendering a country unable to import vital inputs for its economy. This may lead the economy to operate much below its full capacity. Even old machinery and equipment may not be replaced, leading the economy to stagnate or operate very inefficiently.

But if the capital goods were domestically manufactured, or at least made in the neighborhood, their acquisition may be easier as the currencies of the neighboring countries are easier to obtain than those of the farther away countries with hard currencies. In the absence of domestic capital goods or capital goods in the neighborhood, domestic savings cannot be converted into capital goods unless it is changed to a hard currency. For example, the small neighboring countries of South Africa can easily acquire their industrial and mining inputs from South Africa by using the South African rand even if they do not have sufficient dollars, euros, or yen. However, this is not the case for most African countries.

Regional integration would provide African countries with the opportunity to pool their markets and resources. By establishing these industries in Africa, technological progress will be internalized in Africa; in the long-run, this will introduce flexibility into African industry as technological progress will be internally generated and machinery and equipment designs will keep pace with the required changes in manufacturing as the structure of demand changes with development.

However, there are a few large African countries with large resources and potential domestic markets that can go a long way in establishing large manufacturing sectors from which industrialization can diffuse to the neighboring countries. Given the slower rate of regional integration in Africa, the few large single African political entities could be developed into major *regional development poles* from which industrialization can more easily diffuse to the rest of the continent.

Table 1.2 shows that there were seven African countries in 2015 that had populations of approximately 50 million and above. By 2030 and 2050, this number of countries will increase to ten and twenty-two respectively. However, these countries have different resource endowments. Some are arid, while others will soon be densely populated. Hence, they offer different potentials for individual self-sustaining industrialization. By 2050, Nigeria is projected to have the world's fourth-largest population.

From the projected world population on Table 1.2, many African countries will have over forty million people each by 2050, which constitute a sizable domestic market. Educated and trained, such numbers of young people would

Table 1.2 Projections of Africa's population to 2050 (thousands)

No	Country	2015	2030	2050
0	**World**	**7,349,472**	**8,500,966**	**9,725,148**
00	**Africa**	**1,186,000**	**1,679,000**	**2,478,000**
1	Algeria	39,667	48,274	56,461
2	Angola	25,022	39,351	65,473
3	Burkina Faso	18,106	27,244	42,789
4	Cameroon	23,344	32,947	48,362
5	Côte d'Ivoire	22,702	32,143	48,797
6	Dem. Rep. of Congo	**77,267**	**120,304**	**195,277**
7	Egypt	**91,508**	**117,102**	**151,111**
8	Ethiopia	**99,391**	**138,297**	**188,455**
9	Ghana	27,410	36,865	50,071
10	Kenya	**46,050**	**65,412**	**95,505**
11	Madagascar	24,235	35,960	55,294
12	Malawi	17,215	26,584	42,155
13	Mali	17,600	27,370	45,404
14	Morocco	34,378	39,787	43,696
15	Mozambique	27,978	41,437	65,544
16	Niger	19,899	35,966	72,238
17	Nigeria	**182,202**	**262,599**	**398,508**
18	South Africa	**54,490**	60,034	65,540
19	Sudan	40,235	56,443	80,284
20	Tanzania	**53,470**	**82,927**	**137,136**
21	Uganda	39,032	61,929	**101,873**
22	Zambia	16,212	25,313	42,975

Source: United Nations, Department of Economic and Social Affairs, Population Division. 2015. *World Population Prospects: The 2015 Revision*. New York, NY: United Nations.

constitute a large labor force. With equitable national development that widens their individual national markets, the countries with large natural resources could pursue viable industrialization programs, with substantial establishment of capital goods industries. While all African countries can pursue the strategy of *commodity-based industrialization* for raising general living conditions for the majority of the African population, *manufacture of capital goods in Africa is a prerequisite for establishing self-sustained development in the continent*. The commodity-based industrialization will raise the general living conditions of the populations, greatly reducing unemployment and underemployment, poverty, and inequalities as well as expanding the national markets for further industrialization. But they will need continuous importation of capital goods from afar, outside Africa. Availability of foreign exchange has always been a major impediment, limiting African imports from outside the continent.

Population dynamics and economic transformation

Africa is a youthful continent and the demographics of adolescents and youth will largely shape the future social and economic development prospects of the continent. Africa's share of the world population will increase from 13 percent in 2012 to 24 percent in 2050. Africa's median age was 19.7 in 2012 and will increase to 25.4 in 2050. This is in contrast to median age of 30.4 for the world, which is projected to reach 37.9 in 2050 (Janneh 2012).

Approximately 85 percent of all the people in Africa in 2012 were below age 45 while only 5 percent of them were aged 60 or more. As these ratios are not expected to change much by 2050, Africa will continue to be youthful for the foreseeable future. Young people below age 30 will increase from about 729 million in 2012 to 1.2 billion in 2050. Within the same period, adolescents aged 10 to 19 will increase from 237 million to 416 million, and youth aged 15 to 24 will increase from about 212 million to 391 million (Janneh 2012).

These people need to be provided for so that they will be productive and contribute positively to society. If left to grow in poverty, the situation will only get worse. Investment in food, housing, health, and education are a must for a brighter future. These investments will make the future more productive. Although youth literacy has increased, and gender disparities in education attainment have narrowed, many countries still have very low enrollment of less than 5 percent in tertiary education. There is need to extend progress made in achieving universal primary education to secondary and tertiary levels. Besides improving the knowledge and skills levels, investment in secondary and tertiary education will promote the contribution of youth and adolescents to productivity and competitiveness of the African economies.

Youth in Africa face the challenge of high unemployment and poverty, and low productive jobs mainly in the informal sector. Many African youth perish in the Sahara Desert and the Mediterranean Sea while trying to travel in search of job opportunities in Europe. This unfortunate situation will continue to be perpetuated unless major transformational development policies are initiated within Africa. Therefore, there is an urgent need for addressing youth unemployment in Africa. Economic diversification and transformation will create employment opportunities for the African youth entering the labor market every year.

Economic growth and development will also simultaneously address the problems of poverty and inequality and create stability in societies. Significant investment in health, education, and employment will enable African countries to reap high economic returns from the large and rapidly increasing number of youth and adolescents. They will supply the labor market and constitute the rising market of African middle class.

With lack of opportunities in the rural areas, most youth are pushed to the urban areas. The urban areas are where open unemployment and glaring inequalities are much more dangerous to individual and national security. Hence, urbanization is one of the most significant population trends and problems in Africa. And as education expands, the rate of rural–urban migration will accelerate. Without dynamic industrial economies, economic, social, and political problems will intensify in the continent. To reap any demographic dividend, Africa must first massively invest in its youth.

Urban population growth is increasing rapidly in virtually all African countries, driven both by natural increase in urban areas and widespread rural-urban migration. The process of urbanization can provide countries with enormous opportunities to achieve sustainable development, including economic growth, poverty reduction, and service provision via agglomeration economies of scale. At the same time, rapid urbanization can bring with it significant challenges depending on government capacity, planning, and response, such as slum growth, inadequate provision of services and infrastructure, poor health and quality of life, and environmental degradation. In Africa, at present, the negative aspects of urbanization by far outweigh the positives. This trend needs urgent reversal through economic transformation.

Although Africa is the least urbanized continent, its rate of urbanization is the fastest in the world. Urban inhabitants grew from 33 million persons in 1950 to 414 million in 2011, 471 million by 2015, and are expected to reach 744 million by the year 2030, that is 47.7 percent of the population (UNECA and AUC 2013b).

Rapid urbanization implies that the urban settlements will progressively absorb the population growth in Africa. The continent will therefore witness an increase in population concentration in urban areas. An industrial economy absorbs more population than a more predominantly primary producing economy.

Table 1.3 Top 20 fastest-growing African cities

No	City	Country	Population (Thousands)	
			2010	2025
1	Lagos	Nigeria	10,578	15,810
2	Kinshasa	D. R. Congo	8,754	15,041
3	Cairo	Egypt	11,001	13,531
4	Luanda	Angola	4,772	8,077
5	Abidjan	Cote d'Ivoire	4,125	6,321
6	Nairobi	Kenya	3,523	6,246
7	Dar es Salaam	Tanzania	3,349	6,202
8	Alexandria	Egypt	4,387	5,648
9	Kano	Nigeria	3,395	5,060
10	Addis Ababa	Ethiopia	2,930	4,757
11	Dakar	Senegal	2,863	4,338
12	Ibadan	Nigeria	2,837	4,237
13	Johannesburg	South Africa	3,670	4,127
14	Casablanca	Morocco	3,284	4,065
15	Cape Town	South Africa	3,405	3,824
16	Ekurhuleni	South Africa	3,202	3,614
17	Algiers	Algeria	2,800	3,595
18	Accra	Ghana	2,342	3,497
19	Durban	South Africa	2,879	3,241
20	Douala	Cameroon	2,125	3,131

Source: African Development Bank. *Tracking Africa's Progress in Figures*, 2014.

At present, rapid urbanization entails high levels of urban poverty. Most studies reveal that between 15 and 65 percent of African city dwellers are living in poverty, very often in informal settlements with limited access to infrastructure, poor health and environmental conditions, and few social or urban services (UNECA and AUC 2013b). While cities continue to attract significant numbers of rural-to-urban migrants, primarily for economic opportunities, indicators for the urban poor in Africa are often the same or potentially worse than their rural counterparts. Inadequate infrastructure and high crime rates threaten poorer parts of cities. Well-informed and sound policies are needed to meet the demands of the growing numbers of urban poor, particularly to secure for them the benefits of urban living. A booming manufacturing economy would considerably overcome these challenges. It would substantially contribute to the reduction of unemployment, poverty, and inequalities.

Rural development and encouragement of growth of medium-sized cities in the regions would decongest the single large cities, usually the capital city of each country. These programs will be possible with a dynamic self-sustaining industrial economy coupled with a deliberate public policy to promote development in the national regions instead of leaving the backwash effects of the colonial pattern of development to dominate national economic policy.

African industrialization strategies since independence

Conscious industrialization policy in Africa, as in most other underdeveloped countries, began in the post–World War II period. Since the developed countries were industrialized, while the underdeveloped countries were primary producers, economic development came to be identified with industrialization. While prices of industrial exports persistently increased relative to those of primary products, prices of exported primary products were unstable and tended to decline or at best stagnate over time (Prebisch 1950; Singer 1950). As markets for primary products stagnated, and as synthetics were increasingly substituted for primary products, underdeveloped countries turned to industrialization as a strategy for economic growth and development.

Having decided to industrialize, the underdeveloped countries planned to substitute their industrial imports with local production. This was the strategy of *import substitution industrialization*. It was thought that underdeveloped economies would progress from the simpler level of manufacturing consumer goods to intermediate goods and eventually to the manufacture of capital goods.

Import substitution was expected to improve the balance of payments of underdeveloped countries as more manufactured imports would be produced domestically. Tariffs were imposed to protect the infant industries from foreign competition. But these tariffs became progressively higher with higher stages of processing. Foreign firms were encouraged to establish "tariff factories" to circumvent the protective tariffs. Their use of capital-intensive technologies resulted in limited employment opportunities. Frustrations with foreign firms led to their nationalization and/or the establishment of national public development corporations. However, neither proved viable in most underdeveloped countries.

The capital-intensive consumer industries themselves required more imports of spare parts, raw materials, and replacement capital goods, thus requiring more foreign exchange to service them. Consequently, more resources were being devoted to these urban industries than to the agricultural sector and rural development. Moreover, rural development was just understood in a narrow sense as just being agricultural development. Rural-urban migration increased, but because the capital-intensive industries created few jobs, open urban unemployment increased. While the urban unemployment did not generate much instability because the migrants were gullible peasants who largely blamed themselves for their misfortune, this is no longer the attitude of many of the urban poor as they have increasingly come to consist of school-leavers. Soon the majority of the urban poor will come to consist of university graduates who will not fear to directly challenge those wielding political and military power. The dire economic situation will lead to more serious social and political problems and confrontations between the authorities and unemployed who will increasingly come to consist of the politically conscious educated. With increases in university enrollments and output, the numbers and sophistication of the politically conscious unemployed is greatly increasing. Only expanding opportunities through viable self-sustaining economic development will greatly minimize socio-political instability.

Because of the limitations of import-substitution industrialization, underdeveloped countries changed their industrialization strategy to manufacturing for export. The *export-of-manufactures strategy* was recommended particularly for small economies with limited domestic markets. At the early stages of manufacturing, most underdeveloped countries produced similar products and could not absorb much of each other's products. Tariffs in the more industrially developed economies progressively increased with the degree of value added of manufactured imports from the underdeveloped economies unless an underdeveloped country was a satellite of a major industrial country[3] (Todaro and Smith 2015: 588–614; Krugman and Obstfeld 2006: 243–258).

Given the barriers to export of manufactures, underdeveloped countries intensified efforts on promoting *regional integration* so as to pool their markets. But while the cooperating and integrating countries could see the joint benefits of integration, they could not easily agree on equitable sharing of these potential benefits. The partner states were at different low levels of industrialization, and each partner wanted to accelerate its own rate of industrialization and development. Hence, agreements on the location of industries among members of an integrating group became almost impossible. This outlook toward economic integration has not changed much, and hence the slow pace of regional integration in Africa.

Regional and continental integration

The economic problems of the 1970s and 1980s led African countries to revert to the economic policies of market fundamentalism being expounded by conventional free market institutions such as the International Monetary Fund (IMF). But these were the bases of the colonial economic policies that had left Africa in the dependent economic position it was in at independence. Hence, there is no wonder that since the implementation of structural adjustment policies in Africa, poverty on the continent became more widespread and deepened. As dissatisfactions with the IMF structural adjustments became widespread, African countries renewed their determination for regional and continental integration with greater vigor. There was realization that African integration is a strategy for African development. It is intended not to follow development but to precede it; or both integration and industrialization must be pursued simultaneously. The argument that each country should solve its problems before entering into integration is spurious because lack of capacity is an integral part of the failure to develop. If each country could achieve its development on its own, then why integrate?

The intensification of efforts towards regional integration resulted in the adoption of the Lagos Plan of Action by the African Heads of State and Government in 1980. This step culminated in the signing of the Abuja Treaty of 1991 promulgating the African Economic Community (AEC), which came into effect in 1994. The agreement to establish the AEC Free Trade Area was signed in Kigali in March 2018. However, the full establishment of the AEC is to be phased out in six stages[4] (Yongo-Bure 2011). The establishment of a continent-wide common market, the African Common Market (ACM), is aimed at realization by 2023. The continent-wide economic and monetary union is to be achieved by the end of 2028. The transitional period, during which all these structures are to be established, would end by 2034 at the latest.

But as much as African leaders seem to appreciate the importance of collective African self-reliance, their political rhetoric on African integration has so far not been accompanied by commensurate results. Consequently, multiple regional groupings have been established all over the continent, many of which have overlapping memberships. This duplication and overlapping of membership in the regional integration blocs in Africa has hampered the progress of regional integration instead of facilitating it, thereby perpetuating Africa's vulnerability to global economic forces.[5]

Many countries have joined a number of groupings for political and strategic reasons. Economic reasons rank low. Duplication of membership hinders integration programs related to trade facilitation and market integration. Lack of harmonized market integration schemes means that each regional economic community has its own rules of origin or its own certification process. This limits trade between communities. The duplication and overlapping of membership contribute to the underfunding of the communities as members find it difficult to pay all their dues to multiple communities. There is also the problem of adequately staffing the many RECs with their various levels of technical needs. Declarations by the African Summit of July 2007 indicated a strong desire to rationalize the existing RECs and reflect a decision not to recognize more RECs than the eight then existing as the main pillars of the AEC (UNECA, Vol. 3: 30).

The acceleration of African regional and continental integration since the signing of the Abuja Treaty is a clear manifestation of African leaders' recognition of the need for larger economic units in the continent to achieve viable development in the current global economic environment. However, the processes of realizing the RECs and the AEC will be slow and long. In the meanwhile, technological changes will not wait for African integration. Such a situation will perpetuate Africa's follower status in regard to the challenges of globalization. For Africans to have an impact and influence on the direction of globalization, and thus on the continent's destiny, African countries must internalize the processes of technological progress within a shorter time frame. *The greater challenge of internalizing substantial technological changes within Africa can be undertaken by the large African countries that should be able to muster the political leadership to turn their potentials into regional development poles in the continent.* Development emanating from these regional poles (or "African industrial workshops") will diffuse faster to the rest of the continent, thus enabling the smaller economies to transform faster than when depending on economic diffusion from outside the continent.

The Regional Development Poles Strategy

The strategy of *Regional Development Poles* (*RDPs*) places emphasis on accelerating the economic transformation of the few large African countries that *can largely industrialize on their own efforts,* based on their tremendous natural and human resources, and large domestic markets (Yongo-Bure 2014). The creation of *"regional development poles"* within Africa could lead *to the establishment of diversified industrial economies on the continent,* which may in *turn lead to faster diffusion of economic development to the surrounding African countries.* The building of intra-African highways, railways, long-distance power transmission lines, ports, and direct communications links could accelerate this diffusion, making it cheaper and faster for the rest of the smaller African countries to import development inputs from the *neighboring development poles.* The need to earn foreign exchange from the established hard currencies will be less desperate than at present, as it will become relatively easier to acquire the currencies of the *neighboring development poles* and import from them. And as African economies become increasingly more industrialized, diversified, and integrated, and intra-industry trade becomes significant, even smaller economies will be able to establish capital goods industries.

The strategy of regional development poles draws lessons from the strategies of big push or balanced growth and unbalanced growth of the 1960s.

It advocates large investment in capital goods industries on the premises that lack of capital goods industries or inability to import them because of bottlenecks with foreign exchanges frustrates development efforts of most African countries. The structures of African industry have been unbalanced with bias towards the manufacture of consumer goods. This imbalance in industry has to be urgently addressed. But since most African countries are so small such that all cannot establish such large industries characterized with indivisibilities, the few large African economies with huge natural and financial resources as well as large potential domestic markets should undertake such manufactures. Combined with intra-African transportation networks, the few large African capital goods manufacturing countries will act as *African Industrial Workshops*. The cost of supplying capital goods to most African countries from within Africa will be less than the importation of capital goods from outside the continent. Moreover, both formal and informal importation from neighboring countries is possible given ease of contacts and acquisition of foreign currencies of neighboring countries. For example, South Africa's neighbors can easily acquire the *rand* and import from South Africa.

While the arguments against Rosenstein-Rodan's big push (1943) and Nurkse's balanced growth (1953) were based on the subsistence stages of the economies at their earlier stages of development, this is no longer the case with many African economies (Chapter 3). Moreover, African countries have reactivated the development of intra-African infrastructure as reflected in regional infrastructure development programs and the Program of Infrastructure Development in Africa (PIDA, Chapter 8). What will be taking place will be replacement of some capital goods from outside Africa with African manufactures. Hence, the African demand is available. Supply is feasible as many African countries such as Nigeria have been generating large investable resources from oil since the 1960s. Since the beginning of the twenty-first century, Ethiopia has been generating huge resources and investing in massive energy generating programs. The Democratic Republic of Congo has all the resources a country needs for a massive industrial development. What is lacking is a developmental political leadership.

While Hirschman (1958) believed that the preferable unbalanced path is the one led by investment in directly productive activities (DPAs) so that social infrastructure responds to pressure created by excess capacity of DPAs, many African countries and the African Union Commission are investing in infrastructure. Moreover, most African countries have already substantial amounts of human capital and can quickly train more from the many university and secondary school graduates. However, it is important to encourage DPAs along the infrastructure networks. Presence of infrastructure does not mean that DPAs will spontaneously sprout along the network. Action has to be taken to encourage productive activities along the infrastructure networks. Hence, the regional development poles strategy will mainly focus on creating the capital goods industries, although in many cases it will have to create some infrastructure, especially in the field of energy development.

What the regional development poles strategy really advances is a new import substitution strategy focusing on manufacture of capital goods rather than the earlier strategy that concentrated on manufacture of consumer goods. Capital goods manufacturing has more impactful backward and forward linkages than the manufacture of consumer goods. Moreover, the supply and demand constraints African countries experienced at independence have been substantially reduced. Experience has been gained and lessons can be learned from similar recently underdeveloped but now industrializing economies such as Brazil and South Korea.

Concluding remarks

To fundamentally transform an economy, a country needs to establish an appropriate industrial infrastructure, develop research and development (R&D) capability, and internalize technology. A dynamic industrial economy usually comprises numerous strategic industries such as basic metals, chemicals, metal working, and engineering. The basic metals include iron and steel and non-ferrous metals such as aluminum, copper, tin, zinc, lead, and nickel. It involves mining, metallurgy, rolling, extrusion, and drawing that produce intermediate goods. These goods serve as inputs into the metal-working industry and constitute the basic capital goods industries, essential for self-sustaining economic growth and transformation.

Capital goods industries are usually large and depend on the exploitation of economies of scale. They have beneficial external effects in the surrounding countries as they have large-spread effects in the neighborhood. In light of the slow processes of regional integration, the small African economies will benefit from the establishment of such industries in the large African countries. The African Union, the New Partnership for African Development (NEPAD), the United Nations Economic Commission for Africa, and the African Development Bank, among other African organizations, together with the elites of the large African countries, should lead in the establishment of the viable development poles in the continent. Self-sustaining development of the rest of the countries on the continent will spread from the regional development poles. The establishment of diversified industrial economies, financial systems, and convertible currencies in the regional development poles will further facilitate industrialization in the smaller neighboring economies.

Regional integration is a slow process and cannot be the sole reliance on African economic transformation. The present regional groupings are riddled with duplication and overlapping membership, which results in a scattering of resources and efforts. Politicians make fine speeches on the need for African collective self-reliance, but they are loath to concede any of their vaunted sovereignty to a supranational body. Thus, while African countries should continue efforts toward achieving collective action to support development, those that are large enough to go it alone should spearhead a process to speed up transformation from their own economies. *The regional development poles strategy will reinforce regional integration through greatly increased intra-industry African trade.*

To maximize the spread effects of such a strategy, there is need to build intra-African infrastructure, especially transport networks, ports, energy, and ICT. The state will also have to play a crucial role in this process as has been the case throughout histories of national economic transformations. A developmental state endowed with tremendous natural and human resources can succeed more easily and faster than one lacking in both factors. Cooperation and collaboration with neighbors can help, but effective coordination of development policy by different political entities can be difficult and very slow, clouded with uncertainties, especially where legalistic sovereignty is overemphasized.

Notes

1 United Nations Department of Economic and Social Affairs. 2008. *International Standard Industrial Classification of All Economic Activities Revision 4.* New York, NY: United Nations.
2 Linder's hypothesis is that countries begin to export manufactures to markets with *similar demand patterns.*
3 While import duties in industrial countries for manufactures from developing countries increase with the degree of processing, export of Western corporations located in their satellite in the underdeveloped countries had free access to Western markets. Western ships and cargo planes returning from delivering military supplies to Far East countries also needed return cargo; this need necessitated transportation of Far Eastern manufactured products to the West duty free.
4 For details on the phases of realizing the African Economic Community, see Yongo-Bure 2011, 69–87.
5 The African Union has recognized only eight regional economic communities (RECs) as the bases of the African Economic Community. These are the Economic Community of West African States (ECOWAS), the Economic Community of Central African States (ECCAS), the Southern African Development Community (SADC), the East African Community (EAC), the Common Market for Eastern and Southern Africa (COMESA), the Inter-Governmental Authority on Development (IGAD), the Arab Maghreb Union (UMA), and the Community of Sahel-Saharan States (CENSAD).

Bibliography

Agbu, Osita. 2007. *The Iron and Steel Industry and Nigeria's Industrialization: Exploring Cooperation with Japan Institute of Developing Economies.* Osaka: Japan External Trade Organization.
Alemayehu, Makonnen. 2000. *Industrializing Africa: Development Options and Challenges for 21st Century.* Trenton and Asmara: Africa World Press, Inc.
Balassa, Bela. 1989. "Outward Orientation." In *Handbook of Development Economics, Vol. 2,* eds. Hollis Chenery and T. N. Srinivasan. Amsterdam: North Holland Publishers: 1645–89.
Burton, Harry. 1989. "Import Substitution." In *Handbook of Development Economics, Vol. 2,* eds. Hollis Chenery and T. N. Srinivasan. Amsterdam: North Holland Publishers: 1601–44.
Chenery, Hollis. 1979. *Structural Change and Development Policy.* New York, NY: Oxford University Press.
Chenery, Hollis and Moshe Syrquin. 1975. *Patterns of Development 1950–1970.* Oxford: Oxford University Press.

Cornwall, John. 1977. *Modern Capitalism: Its Growth and Transformation.* London: Martin Robertson.

Cypher, James M. and James L. Dietz. 2009. *The Process of Economic Development.* New York, NY: Routledge; Taylor & Francis Group.

Hirschman, Albert A. 1958. *Strategy of Economic Development.* New Haven, CT: Yale University Press.

Janneh, Abdoulie. 2012. *A Statement on Demographics of Adolescents and Youth in Africa.* Addis Ababa: UNECA.

Krugman, Paul R. and Maurice Obstfeld. 2006. *International Trade: Theory and Policy.* New York, NY: Pearson Addison Wesley.

Lewis, Arthur W. 1954. "Economic Development With Unlimited Supplies of Labor." *Manchester School of Economics and Social Studies* 22: 139–91.

Lewis, Stephen R. Jr. 1989. "Primary Exporting Countries." In *Handbook of Development Economics, Vol. 2,* eds. Hollis Chenery and T. N. Srinivasan. Amsterdam: North Holland Publishers: 1542–600.

Linder, Staffan B. 1961. *An Essay on Trade and Transformation.* New York, NY: John Wiley & Sons.

Myrdal, Gunnar. 1957. *Economic Theory and Underdeveloped Regions.* London: Duckworth.

Nurkse, Ragnar. 1953. *Problems of Capital Formation in Underdeveloped Countries.* New York, NY: Oxford University Press.

Prebisch, Raul. 1950. *The Economic Development of Latin America and Its Principal Problems.* New York, NY: United Nations.

Rosenstein-Rodan, Paul N. 1943. "Problems of Industrialization of Eastern and South-Eastern Europe." *Economic Journal* 53, no. 2 (June–September): 202–11.

Singer, Hans. 1950. "The Distribution of Gains between Investing and Borrowing Countries." *American Economic Review* 40: 473–85.

Todaro, Michael P. and Stephen C. Smith. 2015. *Economic Development.* New York, NY: Pearson Addison Wesley.

United Nations Economic Commission for Africa (UNECA). 2015. *Economic Report of Africa 2015: Industrializing Through Trade.* Addis Ababa: UNECA.

———. 2014. *Frontier Markets in Africa: Misperceptions in a Sea of Opportunities.* Addis Ababa: UNECA.

United Nations Economic Commission for Africa (UNECA) and African Union Commission (AUC). 2013a. *Making the Most of Africa's Commodities: Industrializing for Growth, Jobs and Economic Transformation.* Addis Ababa: UNECA.

———. 2013b. *Policy Brief No 3: Urbanization and Development Transformation in Africa.* Addis Ababa: UNECA.

———. 2011a. *Economic Report on Africa 2011: Governing Development in Africa: The Role of the State in Economic Transformation.* Addis Ababa: UNECA.

———. 2011b. *Africa Youth Report 2011: Addressing the Youth Education and Employment Nexus in the New Global Economy.* Addis Ababa: UNECA.

———. 2011c. *Policy Brief No 6: Unleashing Africa's Potential as a Pole of Global Growth.* Addis Ababa: UNECA.

———. 2011d. *Minerals and Africa's Development: The International Study Group Report on Africa's Mineral Regimes.* Addis Ababa: UNECA.

United Nations Economic Commission for Africa (UNECA), African Union Commission (AUC), and African Development Bank (AfDB). 2017. *Assessing Regional Integration in Africa VIII: Bringing the Continental Free Trade Area About.* Addis Ababa: UNECA.

————. 2016. *Assessing Regional Integration in Africa Vol. VII: Assessing Regional Integration in Africa VII: Innovation, Competitiveness and Regional Integration.* Addis Ababa: UECA.

————. 2015. *Africa Region Report on the Sustainable Development Goals: Summary.* Addis Ababa: UNECA.

————. 2013. *Assessing Regional Integration in Africa Vol. VI: Assessing Regional Integration in Africa (ARIA VI): Harmonizing Policies to Transform the Trading Environment.* Addis Ababa: UNECA.

————. 2012. *Assessing Regional Integration in Africa Vol. V: Assessing Regional Integration in Africa (ARIA V): Towards an African Continental Free Trade.* Addis Ababa: UNECA.

————. 2010. *Assessing Regional Integration in Africa Vol. IV: Assessing Regional Integration in Africa IV: Enhancing Intra-African Trade.* Addis Ababa: UNECA.

————. 2008. *Assessing Regional Integration in Africa Vol. III: Towards Monetary and Financial Integration in Africa.* Addis Ababa: UNECA.

————. 2006. *Assessing Regional Integration in Africa Vol. II: Rationalizing Regional Economic Communities.* Addis Ababa: UNECA.

————. 2004. *Assessing Regional Integration in Africa Vol. 1: Policy Research Report.* Addis Ababa: UNECA.

United Nations, Department of Economic and Social Affairs, Population Division. 2015. *World Population Prospects: The 2015 Revision.* New York, NY: United Nations.

Woldemichael, Andinet, Adeleke Salami, Adamon Mukasa, Anthony Simpasa, and Abebe Shimeles. 2017. *Transforming Africa's Agriculture Through Agro-Industrialization.* Abidjan: AfDB.

World Bank. Various years. *World Development Indicators.* Washington, DC: World Bank.

Yongo-Bure, Benaiah. 2014. "Regional Development Poles and Self-Sustaining Development in Africa." In *Regional Economic Communities*, eds. Olanrewaju A. Olutayo and Adebusuyi I. Adeniran. Dakar: The Council for the Development of Social Science Research in Africa (CODESRIA): 23–36.

————. 2011. "A Two-Track Strategy for Viable Development in Africa." In *Rethinking Economic Development in the Context of Globalization and Sustainable Development in Africa*, eds. Bessie House-Soremekun and Toyin Falola. Rochester, NY: University of Rochester Press: 69–87.

2 Manufacturing and the transformation of African economies

Introduction

In the process of economic transformation, usually self-sustaining economic development has involved structural changes in output, exports, and employment. Economies have shifted from initially being predominantly agricultural to industrial (especially manufacturing), and eventually to services. But on critical examination, it is the growth of the manufacturing sector that enables the relative decline in the share of agriculture, as the increasingly smaller share of agriculture can still sustain the rest of the economy as manufacturing has enabled agriculture to become increasingly productive. The increasing share of the services sector is also facilitated by a nucleus of a manufacturing sector. The services sector grows to service the concentrated urban manufacturing economy and it depends on basic inputs from manufacturing. Even in the present services economy, the core of the information technology infrastructure, the fiber-optic cable, is dependent on manufactured inputs. Therefore, diversification and manufacturing are essential for integrated and self-sustaining economic development.

Among the manufacturing subsectors, capital goods manufacturing is the most dynamic. It has strong backward and forward linkages to the rest of the economy. It supplies inputs to various subsectors of industry as well as to the primary (predominantly agricultural) and the services sectors. Manufacturing has higher capacity to absorb labor and has higher and rising productivity. A major shortcoming of most African countries for self-transformation is their small size in terms of resources and domestic markets, which are necessary for the establishment of large capital goods industries.

At the beginning of decolonization, African leaders were aware of the small sizes of their countries and, hence, advocated African unity and/or regional integration as the appropriate solutions.[1] However, their legal and political conceptions of sovereignty have superseded their vision of economic necessity for larger political units. If African leaders persist with the view of narrow legal sovereignty, the continent will continue to be subservient in the increasingly globalizing international economy as the realization of the goals of regional and eventual continental integration will be hard to achieve. Consequently, poverty, inequality, unemployment, and instability will persist or even grow worse. Because the strategy of regional integration is slow, the regional development poles strategy should complement it.

The process of transformation of an economy involves growth with changes in the structure of the economy. It involves continuous shifting of the composition of output, a rise and subsequent decline of individual industries as technology modifies and consumer tastes change. Labor and capital are redistributed across industries and regions. Production methods change in the direction of more advanced mechanization. The input-output relations between raw materials and end products change as technology advances. There are also changes in the structure of exports and imports. The structure of employment changes between different industries and occupations. Overall, the structure of the economy and labor forces continuously becomes diversified. The relative share of agriculture declines; industry, especially manufacturing rises; and eventually the services sector becomes the dominant sector as manufacturing declines along with agriculture.

Structural changes in African economies

Structural transformation takes place during the transition from a low income, agrarian rural economy, to an industrial urban economy with substantially higher per capita income. Structural changes are important for continued growth. The principal changes in structure include increases in the rates of capital accumulation, shifts in the sectoral composition and changes in the location of economic activity (urbanization), and other concomitant aspects of industrialization such as demographic transition, income distribution, etc. The accumulation of capital and shifts in the composition of demand, trade, production, and employment are the economic core of transformation (Chenery 1979; Cornwall 1977; Chenery and Syrquin 1975).

Structural changes in African economies have varied depending on whether the country is oil or mineral producing or largely an agricultural economy.[2] But generally, the share of agriculture has declined during the two periods. They are comparable to those of low- or upper-middle-income countries.[3] The decline in the share of the agricultural sector does not reflect a general increase in productivity in agriculture, hence food imports fill substantial share of imports of many African countries (see Table 2.2). In addition to small farm holdings and inadequate use of modern technologies, there are widespread market failures due to lack of physical infrastructure such as roads, telecommunications, electricity, and absence of markets for credit and insurance. These are some of the fundamental problems that prevent efficient allocation of resources within the agricultural sector, as well as other sectors within rural spaces. As a result, not only has structural transformation of the agricultural sector not materialized, Africa is not producing enough food to feed its growing population.

The share of industry has either risen or remained stagnant depending again or whether the country is a mineral and/or oil producer. However, non–resource-dependent economies such as Ethiopia and Madagascar have also increased the share of industry. Manufacturing declined in most countries except in Mozambique, Nigeria, and Uganda. Except for Cameroon, DR Congo, Cote d'Ivoire, Kenya, Mozambique, Senegal, and South Africa, the share of manufacturing is below 10 percent. The share of manufacturing in the GDP of African countries is one of the lowest and has been decreasing over time. Although the total value added in manufacturing more than doubled during the periods, the share of manufacturing in GDP generally decreased. However, except for South Africa, which manufactures substantial amounts of capital goods, most of the African countries manufacture consumer goods and process primary products for export.

The share of services in all economies is high, ranging from about 50 percent to 69 percent. This is not consistent with the historical structural changes, where an increase in the share of services usually follows a rise in the share of manufacturing. Although some of the services in the African economies are in the modern sector, much of the increase in services is in the informal sector. Given the limited growth in the manufacturing sector, many of the rural migrants to the urban areas are self-employed in the low productivity informal sector, leading to rising underemployment, persistent poverty, and inequalities.

The services sector is one of the most important sectors in Africa. It employs over 60 percent of the workforce in some African countries. Combined with the informal sector, the sector is an important source of incomes and jobs for millions of Africans. In addition to trade, restaurants, and hotels, services such as telecommunications, financial services, and tourism are playing an important role in the growth of the services sector. However, the bulk of the services sector activities are in the non-tradable subsectors serving the domestic market, in wholesale trade, retail, restaurants, hotels, transport, storage, and communications.

The structure and direction of African trade has greatly changed since independence in the 1960s. From specializing in a few primary exports to their colonial powers, many African countries now export to many countries. This pattern of trade greatly changed with the rise of the newly industrializing countries such as China and India. However, the exports remain primary products such as food crops, petroleum, and minerals.

Except for South Africa, whose exports of manufactures are over 50 percent, manufactured exports in most African countries have remained low. Exports of manufactures have risen in Tanzania and Uganda in recent years. Cote d'Ivoire and Kenya have usually exported substantial manufactures to their neighbors. There is diversity in the nature of exports of various African countries. Although most African countries depend on the export of food products, a few depend on exports of petroleum and minerals. Angola, Cameroon, and Nigeria depend on exports of petroleum, while Zambia considerably depends on mineral exports. Madagascar, Mozambique, and South Africa export substantial percentages of minerals. Countries with a relatively more diversified export pattern include Cameroon, Madagascar, Mozambique, Senegal, and South Africa.

Table 2.1 Structural changes in large African economies

Country	Agriculture		Industry		(Manufacturing)		Services	
	1990–2016	1990–2000	1990–2000	2000–2016	1990–2000	2000–2016	1990–2000	2000–2016
Angola	...	...	...	...	...	...	...	...
Cameroon	21	23	32	28	19	14	47	49
Congo, DR	22	21	33	33	20	18	45	46
Cote d'Ivoire	...	21	...	33	...	15	...	45
Ethiopia	45	37	13	21	5	4	42	41
Ghana	41	20	27	28	9	6	32	52
Kenya	27	36	19	19	12	10	54	45
Madagascar	28	24	16	19	14	...	56	56
Mozambique	26	25	21	22	15	10	54	54
Nigeria	33	21	44	18	3	9	24	60
Senegal	17	18	24	24	15	13	60	58
South Africa	3	2	30	29	18	13	67	69
Tanzania	30	31	21	27	8	6	49	42
Uganda	27	24	25	20	7	9	48	56
Zambia	16	5	30	35	11	8	54	59
Low Income	33	30	21	22	11	8	46	48
Lower Middle Income	19	17	35	30	19	16	47	53
Upper Middle Income	8	7	40	34	24	...	51	59
High Income	2	1	27	24	16	15	72	74

Manufacturing is a subsector on Industry.

Source: World Bank. World Development Indicators.

Table 2.2 Structural changes in exports of large African economies

Country	Food 2005	Food 2016	Agricultural Raw Materials 2005	Agricultural Raw Materials 2016	Fuels 2005	Fuels 2016	Ores and Metals 2005	Ores and Metals 2016	Manufactures 2005	Manufactures 2016
Angola	0.1	0.1	0.0	0.0	95.7	95.0	2.7	3.3	1.5	1.5
Cameroon	14.7	26.0	19.3	16.9	56.9	44.6	4.7	3.6	2.8	8.9
Congo, DR	...	...	...	...	...	...	...	...	...	...
Cote d'Ivoire	38.3	68.8	8.3	8.7	27.8	13.8	0.2	0.3	18.7	8.1
Ethiopia	78.7	71.7	15.3	18.9	0.0	0.0	1.0	0.2	4.6	7.3
Ghana	51.7	...	7.2	...	3.4	...	5.0	...	32.5	...
Kenya	37.7	...	10.0	...	0.0	...	1.9	...	31.96	...
Madagascar	32.0	38.9	6.9	2.1	1.1	1.8	3.9	25.8	47.1	30.5
Mozambique	14.0	20.0	5.1	2.7	14.9	30.4	59.4	38.5	6.5	8.4
Nigeria	0.1	1.9	0.4	0.4	98.2	90.9	0.0	0.4	1.3	6.4
Senegal	28.8	36.8	2.1	2.2	21.1	12.2	2.8	7.8	43.4	36.5
South Africa	8.5	11.9	2.0	2.3	10.3	10.0	22.4	23.6	56.7	51.2
Tanzania	57.7	53.7	15.9	4.7	0.2	2.9	11.9	12.9	14.0	26.1
Uganda	70.6	67.7	13.3	4.9	1.9	1.1	2.7	0.5	11.5	24.6
Zambia	13.2	8.9	5.6	1.3	0.7	1.8	71.7	77.8	8.8	10.1
Low Income	...	...	...	...	...	...	...	...	...	...
Lower Middle Income	13.5	18.4	2.7	2.4	18.5	18.2	6.3	5.7	58.0	54.9
Upper Middle Income	72	9.4	1.4	1.3	20.3	16.0	4.1	1.4	65.6	68.4
High Income	6.2	9.6	1.5	1.6	10.5	6.1	3.2	4.5	74.2	73.1
World	6.9	9.5	1.6	1.5	13.4	8.3	3.7	4.3	71.1	72.3

Source: World Bank. World Development Indicators.

Although exports have grown, imports have been rising at a higher pace, increasing the deficit in the balance of trade. Reflecting the limited manufacturing subsector in virtually all African economies, most African imports are manufactures. Most of African capital and intermediate goods are imported. African countries also import substantial manufactured consumer goods.

Imports of manufactures by African countries range from about 50 percent to over 60 percent. For example, in 2016, imports of manufactures in African economies were: Angola (78%), Ethiopia (79%), Mozambique (67%), Nigeria (64%), South Africa (67%), Tanzania (69%), Uganda (66%), and Zambia (65%).

The imports of ores and metals have been very low, reflecting the insignificant presence of capital and intermediate inputs being manufactured in African economies. The imports of ores and metals are mainly used as inputs in the capital and intermediate goods manufacturing industries. Fuel imports are substantial in non-petroleum producing countries. But even in petroleum producing countries fuel imports reflect the importation of refined products as some of petroleum producing countries have limited domestic refining capacities. African countries spend substantial foreign exchange on food imports, except for South Africa, which produces much of its own food and is a net exporter.

The manufacturing subsector as the engine of growth

The emphasis on the size of the manufacturing sector in the preceding analysis is based on the historical findings that the manufacturing subsector is the engine of growth. By manufacturing being the engine of growth, it is meant that the manufacturing subsector is the key sector to the overall growth and the transformation of an economy. The growth of the manufacturing subsector not only stimulates productivity growth in manufacturing itself but also stimulates growth in the non-manufacturing sectors. *Productivity levels are higher in the manufacturing subsector than in any other sector of the economy.* Normally, overall economic growth rates are high only when the rates of growth of manufacturing output exceeds that of non-manufacturing output, and the more by which growth in manufacturing exceeds the non-manufacturing sectors, the greater is the overall growth of the economy (Cornwall 1977).

Two arguments to support the stress on the importance of the manufacturing subsector in explaining the overall growth performance of an economy are:

1 The rate of growth of productivity in manufacturing is dependent upon the rate of growth of manufacturing output; and
2 The rate of growth of manufacturing output is an important factor in determining the rate of growth of productivity in several non-manufacturing sectors as well as in manufacturing.

Cornwall distinguishes between static and dynamic economies of scale in manufacturing. A static economy of scale refers to the reduction of unit costs and an increase in productivity as output for a given period increases. The traditional

Table 2.3 Structural changes in imports of large African economies

Country	Food		Agricultural Raw Materials		Fuels		Ores and Metals		Manufactures	
	2005	2016	2005	2016	2005	2016	2005	2016	2005	2016
Angola	16.0	15.7	0.7	0.8	1.3	1.5	0.6	0.6	81.3	67.5
Cameroon	17.3	19.9	0.3	1.5	30.9	20.2	1.0	0.9	50.5	57.4
Congo, DR	..	..	..	..	..	..	..	..	..	..
Cote d'Ivoire	14.4	19.8	0.5	0.6	28.0	22.3	1.0	1.1	46.9	55.7
Ethiopia	10.6	8.4	0.9	0.4	15.1	10.9	1.2	1.3	72.0	78.8
Ghana	13.9	..	1.1	..	13.6	..	1.7	..	69.3	..
Kenya	9.5	..	1.7	..	22.9	..	1.5	..	64.3	..
Madagascar	15.4	15.4	0.4	3.4	15.9	16.2	0.4	3.1	65.3	60.9
Mozambique	15.0	11.9	1.0	1.3	6.6	13.0	0.5	6.5	50.7	67.4
Nigeria	18.0	17.0	0.7	0.7	2.9	16.3	2.8	1.9	71.9	64.1
Senegal	28.1	23.4	1.6	1.8	22.9	19.8	2.2	1.7	45.1	53.0
South Africa	4.4	8.4	1.1	1.0	14.3	13.6	1.8	2.2	69.6	66.6
Tanzania	9.6	10.9	1.1	1.3	22.3	18.1	0.9	1.1	66.0	68.7
Uganda	15.9	12.1	1.6	1.7	19.5	18.6	1.1	1.6	60.9	66.0
Zambia	6.2	5.6	1.3	0.5	10.5	18.6	2.6	9.9	78.1	65.2
Low Income	..	15.2	..	..	..	20.4	..	1.9	..	57.0
Lower Middle Income	8.4	10.5	2.5	2.1	25.1	21.8	3.6	4.4	59.1	59.5
Upper Middle Income	6.0	7.8	2.5	2.3	10.6	9.2	5.3	5.9	73.7	70.9
High Income	6.7	8.4	1.5	1.2	13.7	9.3	3.3	3.0	71.9	75.6
World	**6.7**	**8.4**	**1.8**	**1.5**	**13.8**	**9.9**	**3.8**	**3.8**	**71.4**	**73.7**

Source: World Bank. World Development Indicators.

source of static economies of scale has been an increase in plant, firm, or industry size. Dynamic economies of scale refer to a more or less continuous reduction in unit costs and continuous increase in productivity, owing to continuous increases in the output of a firm, industry, or economy over time. These economies are described as learning economies in that they are a function of cumulative output increases or cumulative gross investment and thus are partly a function of time. With time, the refinement of a product or a production process reduces costs and increases productivity. As production costs decline, quantity increases more than proportionately, and product prices decline.

Verdoorn's law has been used to test for the existence of economies of scale:

$$\rho = a_0 + a_1 Q_m$$

ρ and Q_m represent the rates of growth of labor productivity and output in manufacturing, respectively.

The rate of growth of manufacturing output determines the overall rate of growth of productivity. Hence, as manufacturing output grows, general productivity in the economy grows. But this is not the case for all manufactured goods. It is mainly associated with the manufacture of capital goods, and to some extent with the manufacture of intermediate goods.

Statistically significant results have been found by a number of investigators, whether cross-section or time series data have been used. A few examples include:

$$\rho_m = 0.67 + 0.64 Q_m \qquad R^2 = 0.90 \qquad (UN)$$

$$\rho_m = 1.035 + 0.484 Q_m \qquad R^2 = 0.826 \qquad (Kaldor)$$

$$\rho_m = 1.10 + 0.545 Q_m \qquad R^2 = 0.710 \qquad (Cornwall)$$

$$\rho_m = 1.12 + 0.532 Q_m \qquad R^2 + 0.804 \qquad (Cornwall)$$

Since the increase in the rate of growth of manufacturing output increases the rate of growth of productivity in manufacturing, it will also increase the rate of growth of the overall productivity and output as a result.

As a result of discoveries and innovations changes in technology and production, through their impacts on costs and prices, strongly affect the rate of growth of output. Sectoral shifts in the distribution of capital and labor also have a pronounced impact on growth rates because of differences in sector levels and rates of growth of factor productivities. But in addition, the rate of growth of the economy affects the nature and speed of the transformation since rising incomes generate shifts in the distribution of final demand and output; demands for intermediate goods, labor, and capital; and influence the rate and incidence of technological progress itself.

Table 2.4 shows the growth of GDP and of its sectoral components for the periods 1990–2000 and for 2000–2016. Generally, growth was higher in

Table 2.4 Average annual sectoral growth of output of large African economies

Country	GDP		Agriculture		Industry		(Manufacturing)		Services	
	1990–2000	2000–2016	1990–2000	2000–2016	1990–2000	2000–2016	1990–2000	2000–2016	1990–2000	2000–2016
Angola	1.8	8.7	...	4.0	...	1.2	...	2.1	...	4.8
Cameroon	1.8	3.7	5.3	2.6	-0.6	6.1	1.9	5.7	0.0	7.5
Congo, DR	-4.9	6.0	1.4	5.3	-8.3	5.5	-8.7	2.3	-4.7	3.5
Cote d'Ivoire	3.1	2.9	...	7.0	...	12.6	...	10.2	...	3.5
Ethiopia	3.8	9.7	2.6	4.0	4.2	10.4	3.7	3.6	5.6	12.1
Ghana	4.3	6.8	...	2.8	...	5.1	...	3.6	...	7.9
Kenya	2.2	4.9	1.9	1.4	1.2	4.4	1.3	...	3.2	5.4
Madagascar	2.0	2.8	1.8	5.7	2.4	7.3	...	4.2	...	1.3
Mozambique	8.6	7.5	5.7	7.2	10.6	3.2	10.2	10.3	5.1	8.4
Nigeria	1.9	7.5	3.4	3.2	0.9	4.0	-1.4	2.5	2.8	10.4
Senegal	3.0	4.0	2.4	2.2	3.8	1.6	3.1	2.0	4.5	4.6
South Africa	2.1	3.0	1.0	4.1	0.8	8.5	1.6	7.8	3.0	1.8
Tanzania	3.0	6.7	3.2	2.2	3.1	8.1	2.8	5.8	2.6	7.2
Uganda	7.0	6.9	3.4	-1.0	12.3	8.4	14.2	5.2	8.2	6.2
Zambia	1.6	7.1	1.6	3.4	-2.2	5.8	1.0	4.1	3.0	0.2
Low Income	2.3	5.3	3.1	3.8	0.5	5.5	-0.7	6.2	2.7	6.4
Lower Middle Income	3.4	6.1	2.8	3.4	3.4	6.3	4.5	...	3.8	7.4
Upper Middle Income	3.2	5.8	2.2	0.8	3.1	1.1	...	...	3.1	6.1
High Income	2.8	1.6	...	...	...	...	...	1.5	...	1.7
World	**2.9**	**2.8**	**2.2**	**2.8**	**2.9**	**2.9**	**...**	**2.1**	**3.4**	**2.8**

Source: World Bank. *World Development Indicators.*

the second period, but the sectoral performances were not markedly different. Where manufacturing grew at about 10 percent, services also grew by about the same rate in the second period.

In the early 2000s, most economies were making up for the depressing growth rates in the 1980s and 1990s. For most countries in the 2000s, GDP growth rates were over 5 percent. They were correlated to the growth rates in middle-income countries than to the rates in the high-income countries that were anemic throughout the two periods. This is consistent with the shifts in the direction of trade of most African countries during the second period. Growth rates were particularly high during the second period for Angola, DR Congo, Ethiopia, Ghana, Mozambique, Nigeria, Tanzania, Uganda, and Zambia. These countries included both mineral and petroleum exporters as well as non-mineral and non-petroleum exporters such as Ethiopia and Uganda.

The manufacturing sectors of the high growth economies also experienced high growth rates, especially for Ethiopia and Nigeria. In fact, all sectors of all countries that grew at high rates attained high growth rates. Changes in growth rates during the two periods also reflected the conflicts in some of these countries such as the DR Congo and Cote d'Ivoire.

The rate of growth of factor supplies, especially capital, in certain key sectors is key to understanding differences in rates of growth and transformation. Given the specificity and immobility of capital goods and labor, the development of new goods, new techniques, new industries and firms, and new locations of economic activities required new kinds of capital goods and a redistribution of the labor force. Growth of factor supplies in key industries became a critical feature in determining the speed and scope of the growth and transformation process. Therefore there is need for continuous technological flexibility as well as updating of skills and training.

Capital goods are more responsive to the need for changes in technology. For export dependent economies, continuous reliance on imported capital goods may be frustrated by shortages of foreign exchange. With domestic manufacturing of capital goods, domestic saving can more easily be translated to capital goods that are readily available in the domestic market. Hence, the necessity for locating capital goods industries in Africa accompanied with the development of intra-Africa transportation networks. This will minimize the need for foreign exchange for overseas importation of essential development inputs. Research and development (R&D) facilitates the economy's flexibility in adjusting to the industries of the future as the economy and per capita income grow and demand patterns change.

Flexibility abounds with capital goods rather than in consumer goods or assembling industries. Supplies of capital goods from domestic sources can be adjusted to changes in the structure of production. With domestic manufacture of capital goods, various consumer goods can be produced as consumer demand patterns change. Qualitative change is an integral component of the process of growth with transformation. This involves innovation in the form of new production function designed to produce new goods or to produce existing products better.

Labor productivity

With structural transformation, labor should be relocating to higher productive sectors, especially into modern manufacturing. However, with minimal sectoral transformation, much change in African labor productivity cannot be expected. Most Africans continued to be employed in the subsistence agricultural sector. Many of the migrants to the urban areas have been absorbed in the informal manufacturing and services sectors. The informal sectors, manufacturing or services have lower productivity than the modern manufacturing sector but have slightly higher productivities than the traditional agricultural sector.

Studies on labor productivity in African economies for the periods 1960–1975, 1990–1999, and 2000–2005 (McMillan, Rodrik and Verduzco-Gallo 2014; de Vries, Timmer, and de Vries 2015) show that labor productivity was higher in the first period than in the recent periods, and was particularly worse during the 1990s. The 1960s and early 1970s were the years African countries were pursuing the import substitution industrialization strategy. The 1980s and 1990s were the years when African countries were implementing the IMF structural adjustment programs. The IMF programs included privatization of public corporations that were implementing the import substitutions industries. They also included liberalization of foreign trade that exposed the infant import substitution industries to competition from the mature industrial economies.

From the beginning of the 2000s, African economies began to grow again after the lost decades of the 1980s and 1990s. This growth was based on the high demand for commodities in the world market. Growth in African natural resources, minerals, fuel, and agricultural products increased, leading to growth in African GDP and exports. The fuel and mining industries are capital intensive and hence would reflect high labor productivity. But they do not absorb much labor.

The late 1990s and the 2000s have been the period of the fruition of the computer technology. This period has witnessed the growth of high productivity ITC services in Africa. These technological developments have contributed to marginal increases in labor productivity in African economies in recent years. However, the majority of African labor is still engaged in the low productivity sectors of subsistence agriculture and urban informality.

The important question about raising labor productivity in most African economies should be: what are the development strategies that can bring about economic transformation of African economies? The strategies of commodity-based industrialization and the regional development poles are some of the policy frameworks aimed at encouraging the growth of manufacturing, and hence massive growth of labor productivity in Africa. Investigating for major rises in African labor productivity when the economies have not been markedly transformed is a mere exercise in demonstrating capabilities in current methodologies of econometric analysis.

Domestic investment and the growth of manufacturing output

Rising aggregate demand is important because, in addition to the ordinary capacity effect of investment and its influence on capacity in new industries and areas, investment plays the traditional and critical multiplier effect of determining the level of aggregate demand. Without a level of investment high enough to strain the productive capacity of the economy, growth and transformation would be slowed down. This stems from such factors as the stimulating effects of high and rising aggregate demand on the rate of innovation, technological progress, and productivity and the greater adaptability of labor, as well as on management's greater willingness to innovate when unemployment is low and capital utilization high. The role of demand is critical in the sense that the rate of growth and transformation is not independent of the level of demand.

Rising per capita income of most of the population is important to enhance the domestic market as well as to promote labor and general stability in the country. Therefore, there is the necessity of promoting domestic employment and equitable development and income. This will broaden the domestic market and the capacity to absorb the increasingly large and diversified domestic output. Without a substantial capital goods manufacturing capacity such domestic demand will be transmitted abroad through the demand for imports of essential developmental inputs as well as intermediate and consumer goods imports.

A large stock of technology, borrowed from industrial countries, is an important contributor to the growth of manufacturing output in newly industrializing countries. However, as much as capital goods and technology can be borrowed, domestic investment and major efforts to internalize technological development are essential. The rate of investment is the best measure of effort different countries made to avail themselves of borrowed technology. Technologies require substantial investment outlays if they are to be implemented. The borrowing country must invest to modify and adopt the technology to fit its national needs. Continuous borrowing of technology without transforming it to the local needs does not promote self-sustaining development. Domestic innovation of the borrowed technology is necessary for self-sustaining national development. Internalization of technological development, instead of continuously depending on importing technology, is possible with substantial domestic capital goods manufacturing capacity and human capital. In addition to investment, entrepreneurship, private and/or public, and a large range of skills are important for a continuous and sustained growth of the capital goods sector. But even if the entrepreneurship is in the private sector, the role of the state is crucial in encouraging and assisting the entrepreneurship or creating a conducive environment for the private sector to operate. This was the case for all the industrialized economies, especially for the Asian countries such as Japan, South Korea, and China.

The rate at which manufacturing output grows is best seen as the outcome of the extent to which an entrepreneurial class and/or a developmental state searches for new and better ways to expand markets. For most countries, borrowing new technologies is coordinated in the domestic arena. In the process, a deliberate, sustained effort is made to find and organize the capital and labor resources necessary for the task. The necessity of domestic capacity in research and development (R&D) is to be emphasized.

Capital accumulation is important for structural transformation. In the 1950s, capital accumulation was almost invariably referred to physical capital in commodity production and infrastructure. The question was how much to allocate capital between sectors producing consumption and production goods, and how much investment to be allocated for producing machines. The fact that domestic saving in underdeveloped countries cannot be directly translated into capital goods that were mainly imported was initially not recognized. As it became evident that, even if domestic savings were available, they could not be converted to investment without adequate foreign exchange for importing the capital goods, the dual-gap model of economic growth was introduced. It was soon realized that in addition to domestic savings, foreign exchange was needed to be able to convert the domestic savings into investible resources.

Another constraint to effective investment was absorptive capacity. This can be overcome with the development of human capital. These forms of capital are necessary requirements for long-run growth and transformation. Therefore, there was the call for foreign capital in the form of foreign investment and foreign aid. African countries can overcome this deficiency by investing in diversified human capital, particularly at the tertiary level of education.

For most countries on Table 2.5, household consumption and government consumption were consistent with levels in low-income and middle-income countries. However, they fluctuated substantially in many countries, except for Nigeria and South Africa. While the changes in Senegalese and South African macroeconomic variables were fairly stable, Nigerian capital formation, exports, imports, and saving were not as stable as its household and government consumption.

Capital formation was above 20 percent for seven countries and between 15 and 20 percent for five other countries. Capital formation shares were particularly high for Cameroon (26%), Ethiopia (40%), Ghana (23%), Mozambique (43%), Senegal (26%), Uganda (24%), and Zambia (43%).

The shares of gross savings were generally low, especially in Angola, Cameroon, the DR Congo, Madagascar, and Mozambique. They declined for all countries, except for Cote d'Ivoire, Mozambique, and Tanzania. As savings were generally below the ratios of capital formation in GDP, the gap was filled by foreign resources. This shortfall in domestic resources to finance national capital formation is repeated on the foreign exchange side. Import shares are higher than those of export earnings. But while the shares of export earnings

Table 2.5 Changes in demand structure of large African economies (percent of GDP)

Country	Household Consumption		Government Consumption		Gross Capital Formation		Exports of Goods and Services		Imports of Goods and Services		Gross Savings	
	2005	2016	2005	2016	2005	2016	2005	2016	2005	2016	2005	2016
Angola	39	74	20	15	9	10	86	33	54	33	27	1
Cameroon	72	65	10	15	19	26	20	23	21	29	17	10
Congo, DR	84	77	7	12	12	15	20	25	24	29	11	8
Cote d'Ivoire	66	56	14	11	14	21	50	32	44	20	13	28
Ethiopia	..	70	..	10	0	40	..	8	..	28	..	..
Ghana	81	67	15	18	29	23	36	41	62	48	19	17
Kenya	72	78	17	14	18	17	29	15	36	23	17	12
Madagascar	86	77	9	10	22	15	28	33	46	36	6	11
Mozambique	79	72	18	28	19	43	30	35	46	77	4	10
Nigeria	75	78	7	6	5	15	32	11	19	10	20	18
Senegal	78	75	13	16	24	26	27	29	42	45	16	16
South Africa	62	60	19	21	18	19	26	30	27	30	15	16
Tanzania	67	82	17	13	21	7	17	18	22	19	17	23
Uganda	74	80	14	6	22	24	14	18	25	28	20	16
Zambia	..	52	..	15	..	43	31	37	32	47	..	32
Low Income	81	80	13	13	17	24	22	20	36	36	..	15
Lower Middle Income	63	65	11	12	28	27	30	23	32	27	31	27
Upper Middle Income	50	50	15	16	30	32	33	24	28	23	34	33
High Income	59	60	18	18	23	21	27	31	27	30	23	23

Source: World Bank. *World Development Indicators.*

generally corresponded to those of low income and middle-income countries, the shares of imports were higher than those of low-income and middle-income countries.

The commodity-based industrialization strategy

The industrialization strategies pursued by African countries immediately after each country attained independence were reviewed in Chapter 1. These included the strategies of *import substitution, export of manufactures, and regional integration*. In the 2010s, the United Nations Economic Commission for Africa (UNECA) and the African Union Commission (AUC) developed the *commodity-based industrialization strategy*.

The *commodity-based industrialization strategy* involves adding value to African raw materials to reduce exposure to the risk of commodity price fluctuations, and at the same time move to higher value and more diversified product and end markets, where prices are more dependent on market fundamentals than speculation in commodity markets. It would strengthen industrial linkages to the commodity sector through building backward and forward linkages for commodity production. Furthermore, it would serve as a launching pad for long-term diversification and competitiveness in new and non-commodity sectors in Africa's commodity-rich countries (UNECA and AUC 2013a, 8–9).

The *commodity-based industrialization strategy* has been embarked on because of the lack of improvement in living standards of most Africans even though most African economies experienced high growth rates since the beginning of the twenty-first century. That growth was not translated into improvement in the living conditions of the poor. Unemployment, poverty, and inequality remained high. This was explained by the high growth rates realized without the transformation of the African economies. Hence, the *commodity-led industrialization strategy* was devised as a means to transform the African economies. This strategy is appropriate for all the African countries as most of the activities do not require large-scale plants as in the case of capital goods industries.

Unemployment, poverty, and inequality are widespread. Population growth and urbanization are high. Although education, especially at the primary level, has expanded, more still needs to be done at the basic level and especially at higher levels. Health services are still poor and inadequate. Hence, the need for socio-economic transformation is urgent.

Since 2000, African countries have shown strong economic growth. Even if most of that growth was due to a boom in prices of commodity exports, some of the African countries that recorded the fastest growth rates included countries that had no oil or mineral wealth such as Ethiopia.

However, that growth was not translated into improvement in the living conditions of the poor. Unemployment, poverty, and inequality remained high. The same pattern of growth during the colonial period and the early years of independence depended on the rise of prices of commodity exports to the colonial metropolis. Hence, the sources of African growth have changed very little over the years, with agriculture and mineral resources being the main drivers, and growth has been largely jobless. With growing population and fast urbanization, Africa cannot afford to continue to have jobless growth.

The *commodity-led manufacturing strategy* is not opposed to the *capital goods manufacturing strategy of regional growth poles* in Africa. In fact, it aids the manufacture of capital goods because abundant availability of food and other basic consumer goods facilitates the establishment of capital goods industries. Widespread establishment of commodity manufactures will raise incomes, increase skills and experience, supply raw material, and create a larger market for capital and intermediate manufactured goods. The various facilities for commodity manufacturing will need to be supplied with capital and intermediate goods. Every country will participate in commodity manufacturing unlike in the manufacture of large capital goods, which at the initial stages will be limited to relatively large economies. Not all countries have the capacity to participate during the early periods of capital goods manufacturing. Commodity manufacturing will widen and deepen intra-African trade since most of this trade is in manufactured goods.

A developmental state and industrial policy

The industrialization process has to be planned and coordinated. Throughout modern history, planning or/and coordination have been necessary at *the early stages of industrialization*. The market mechanism cannot be the *initial major driver* of such a fundamental transformational activity. The government has a very important leading role to play in paving the way for various types of firms: public, private, cooperative, and joint venture. Therefore African states seriously wanting to transform their economies have to put in place what has been referred to in the literature as the *developmental state* (UNECA and AUC 2011a).

According to the United Nations Economic Commission for Africa and the African Union Commission, an effective developmental state in Africa is:

one that has the political will and the necessary capacity to articulate and implement policies to expand human capabilities, enhance equity, and promote economic and social transformation. These policies must be derived from ... widespread consultative process and organized public deliberations that are not manipulated by technocratic and socio-political elites.

(UNECA and AUCa: 18–19)

For them, the basic components of a developmental state in the African case include: (i) a government that has the political will and legitimate mandate to perform specific, required functions in the context of a nationally owned development framework; (ii) a competent, professional, and neutral bureaucracy that ensures the effective and efficient implementation of strategies and policies in accordance with established national development goals; (iii) an interactive and institutionalized process in the context of which the political leadership and bureaucracy actively engage other societal actors in development policy design, implementation, and monitoring and evaluation; (iv) a comprehensive development framework in the context of which national development goals are established and the complementariness among social and economic policies are explicitly embedded; and (v) a governance system that ensures that the focus, context, contents, and implementation modalities of the national development program are fully deliberated upon and agreed by the full range of stakeholders and societal actors (UNECA and AUC: 18–19).

Therefore, constructing and operationalizing the developmental state approach in Africa involves several capacity-building and institutional reform challenges as well as new areas of cooperation and collaboration among key elements of the public and private sector and civil society. In addition, given the various historical, cultural, and political differences among African ruling elites in different countries, it is unlikely that one size of the developmental state concept will fit all countries.

From historical experiences, countries that have undergone economic transformation have not largely relied on market fundamentalism. *The market usually gained prominence after the process of structural transformation had advanced.* This is true of the old industrial countries of the west as well as of the recently industrialized Asian countries. The government has to play a major role in *the early stages* of diversification and structural transformation.

The developmental state is to focus on rebuilding and strengthening state capacity with a view to raising its ability to expand human capacity and promote equitable and efficient allocation of resources. State capacity comprises effective political, economic, and social institutions and the recruitment and retention of competent public servants as well as a framework that ensures wider stakeholder participation in policy making and implementation. The developmental state generates appropriate incentives such as to transform much of the informal businesses to enter the formal sector and become more productive, paying living wages. It should also build or rebuild and strengthen economic and socio-political institutions and coordinate them effectively.

The developmental state must strike a judicious balance between the roles of the state and the market. *Elites and powerful interest groups should not capture the state. Weak integrity and professionalism in the bureaucracy may lead to rent seeking, breeding waste and inefficiency.* This necessitates the establishment of a democratic state at all levels, from the central down to the local level. *However, democracy must not be interpreted merely as regular elections. The masses must have a say in the major decisions that affect their lives.* Resources must be allocated in a transparent manner and accountability made for all expenditures of public resources. Hence, the developmental state must have a committed political leadership, an autonomous and professional bureaucracy and academics, and key stakeholders including civil society, trade unions, and the media. The state should be ready to turn to the market where its role is necessary. There should be periodic national, regional, local, and sectoral conferences to assess the state of the nation in all aspects: political, economic, social, administrative; and the overall direction of the country. Therefore, constructing and operationalizing the developmental state involves several capacity-building and institutional reform challenges as well as new areas of cooperation and collaboration among key elements of public, private, and civil society.

East Asian countries have often been cited as more successful developmental states. Page and Tarp (2017) provide case studies of successful and unsuccessful attempts to implement industrial policy by different countries. While there is no single model of success, the case studies show that the relationship between the state and business has been a crucial element of success or failure in accelerating structural transformation. Success needs a committed political leadership to develop the institutions of public-private coordination. Observing studies of diverse East Asian countries, including China, Japan, Malaysia, South Korea, and Vietnam, Page and Tarp concluded that the objectives and instruments of industrial policy and the nature of the coordination process between government and business have varied across countries and over time within the same country. However, four key factors stand out as being common to all. These are *commitment, focus, experimentation, and feedback* (Page and Tarp 2017, 8–11).

A high level of commitment of senior government officials to the coordination agenda has been characteristic of the Asian economies. Senior members of the political and government elite were publicly committed to and accountable for industrial development outcomes. The public officials charged with coordination programs were sufficiently senior to make the decisions needed for implementation, and in most cases reported directly to the highest political authorities such as the president or prime minister. In China, party and government officials at all levels, ranging from the national to the municipal, are actively engaged in the industrial development agenda and they are judged on results achieved. Provincial governments are likely to be promoted or terminated based on the economic performance of their provinces.

Focus was on specific constraints to firm performance. Agreement was made with the private sector on a specific objective and the proposed course of action to remove the constraints and externalities that would facilitate success of firms in achieving the agreed objectives. A timetable for resolution of the problem was announced and progress in implementation was monitored and reported to the coordinating body.

Focus was also achieved by creating a localized enabling environment and extending the improvements across regions and sectors gradually in line with the government's available resources and implementation capacity. For example, in Malaysia and Vietnam, export-oriented industrialization was promoted through the opening of free trade zones (FTZs) that operated independently from the domestic policy environment. In China, various policy approaches have been adopted, at the provincial and municipal level, depending on the local context and stage of development. In decentralized systems, local governments have become more active in improving business environment by moving the focus of business-government dialogue closer to the provision of local public inputs.

East Asian industrial policymakers have been willing to experiment with examples generated by observing successful examples from elsewhere. Public actions were identified, developed, and implemented. When a chosen course of action failed to accomplish the desired outcome, it was either modified or abandoned. Successful policies were replicated in other settings. Such an approach to policy making of observing, experimenting, and implementing was heavily dependent on a strong two-way flow of information between the firms and government.

South Korea shifted the focus and instruments of industrial policy in response to changing circumstances. By the 1980s, many of its firms, especially the *chaebol* (large firms), had become too big to continue to depend on the state for resources. Hence, Korean policy shifted to building a symbiotic relationship with the big business and promoting competition among domestic firms. China's industrial policy of "backing winners" evolved by experimental design and was adapted to local circumstances.

Feedback was an essential element of East Asian industrial policy. This was partly done by measurement of observable outcomes such as the rates of growth of exports, jobs, or output or it depended on information gleaned from the private sector. Meetings are held with the business community to identify obstacles to their operation and development of business and to build trust. Local governments are directly connected to industrial clusters. By focusing on individual clusters and communicating frequently with local entrepreneurs, local governments devise policies clearly targeting specific industries.

Just as in East Asia, African experiences have been diverse. But three common features are observable in all case studies. These are what Page and Tarp refer to as *uneasy partners, right hand-left hand, and rewards without referees* (Page and Tarp 2017, 11–14). There is an uneasy partnership between the state and the business community, characterized by shifting perceptions, mistrust, and lack of mutual understanding. Many governments exclude the private sector from policy- and decision-making processes. Governments often accused business of corruption, ignoring corruption in the public sector. Even where tripartite bodies were set up between the state, labor, and business, uncertain commitment to implementation of decisions may lead to undermine the effectiveness of the coordination. Government bias towards some businesses may discourage others from participating, which may lead to a fracture in relations as some firms may accuse the government of lack of even-handedness to the whole industrial sector. In China, local authorities sought feedback from private firms located in nearby industrial clusters. Exchanges of observations between business, labor unions, and government is also important.

The government may lack effective internal coordination. Different bodies of the government connected to the industrial sector may not know what each unit is doing. All the relevant units of the industrial sector should be involved in the coordination. This is particularly true with the ministries of industry, finance, office of the president, and any development agency dealing with industry.

The coordination process may not be smooth regardless of whatever good intensions both sides have. Hence, there must be agreed rules, referees, and rewards used to address any disagreements. Benchmarks for compromises should be set. Undue use of pressure may lead to the collapse of the dialogue. Carrots and sticks may work, but not always. Collusion of key government and business in the coordination may render the process crippled.

To strengthen government-business coordination, which is both complex and country specific, Page and Tarp suggest that *leaders must lead, go local, clarify the rules, and limit the rewards* (Page and Tarp 2017, 14–18). High-level political commitment is crucial for successful coordination as it identifies the person who has the job of explaining the policy agenda and who can be held politically responsible for things going right or wrong. When the president or prime minister is responsible, it raises both the visibility of the coordination process and the level of accountability for its implementation. The leadership by the head of government also gives coherence within government in follow-up and the implementation of the decisions reached; hence facilitating coordination across various government ministries and agencies.

The public-private mechanisms must result from local efforts to shape institutions and set policy objectives. They must not originate from outside, such as from donors. Where donors have initiated such coordination efforts, the impacts are minimal as the exercise is conducted to fulfil donor pressures for reform. This was the case since 2001 when the World Bank and the International Monetary Fund (IMF) promoted reform of investment climate in Africa. Countries that set up public-private coordination bodies concentrated on issues with the World Bank *Doing Business Report*. Where local initiatives have occurred in Africa, they have been most successful when business has taken a leading role. It has led to increased dialogue and engagement between the state and business community.

Furthermore, successful coordination also requires that both government and the private sector are clear about objectives and how success will be measured. Clarity and transparency are also important tools for fostering accountability. Requests made by firms or business associations for government assistance should be public information. Publication of the activities and decisions of coordinating bodies and periodic accounting of the expenditures made to implement their recommendations can increase public scrutiny. The government-business dialogue should remain open to new entrants to reduce the perception that the process is being monopolized by incumbents. Broader representation can provide a check against conflicts of interest. It should not be limited to large firms only, but small and medium firms should also be included so that the business community sees the process as legitimate.

The financial incentives to business should be commensurate with their social returns. Governments often seem to be over-optimistic about the returns of new industrial activities to the economy. The role of the government is to remove constraints to industrial development and not to bribe firms to invest in the country. Efforts should be geared to identifying and removing specific constraints to the growth of industry. The government should principally focus on institutional and regulatory reforms as well as investment in infrastructure and human capital.

Coordination with the private sector should be used to identify which public investments in infrastructure or skills receive priority. Proposed investments should be subjected to vigorous cost-benefit analysis. Performance criteria should be demonstrated. Targets such as growth rates of output, exports, and employment can be used as measures of national benefits. Periodic reviews of industrial performance are important to justify renewal or extension of incentives.

Concluding remarks

Structural economic transformation is a prerequisite for the promotion of rapid, sustained, and inclusive economic growth and development in Africa. This is usually brought about through industrialization. Within industrialization, manufacturing is the most dynamic subsector that raises the general productivity of the economy, creating more good-paying jobs, thus raising incomes and reducing inequalities. For flexibility in the economy to be able to adjust to changing demand and meet emerging new supplies, a substantial capacity of capital goods manufacturing is essential.

Capital goods manufacturing has strong backward and forward linkages to the domestic economy. They also enhance technological dynamism of the national economy. Perpetual reliance on imports of most capital goods exposes an economy to the vagaries of the international economy as export markets fluctuate or shrink. It also limits the capacity for domestic technological progress, which is usually embodied in capital goods.

However, the manufacture of basic consumer goods and agricultural development are necessary in order to raise the general standard of living in the country because both activities are necessary for human decency and raise the productivity and purchasing power of the population. Human capital in the forms of general and tertiary education, training, and health development also plays a crucial role in the transformation process as it enhances the quality of the human resources and the skills necessary to operate the economy at various levels of sophistication.

But while resource accumulation and raising productivity are the basic ingredients of the transformation process, the underlying institutional factors must not be ignored. Among these, the government has a very important leading role to play in the process. There is need for a developmental state that can guide the various actors in the economy by providing a conducive environment for attaining the goal. This has been the historical path for those who have successfully transformed their economies. The process involves innovation and industrial processes; improvements in various types of infrastructure and institutional arrangements, which necessitate a careful balance between public policy and the market mechanism.

A developmental state should judiciously guide the various actors in the economy without coercion. Various groups in society should be willingly involved in decision making at their relevant different levels: national, regional, local; or state, private, and civil society. Democracy should not just be limited to mere regular elections but should extend to actual participation in decision making.

Given the limited resources of the state, the private sector, domestic and foreign, can supplement the investible resources. The state can learn from the experiences of others in coordinating industrial policy without sacrificing much national resources. The top political leadership should have a clear vision on where to guide the country and realize that an economy that works for all is key in reaching the national destination envisioned.

Note

1 A large geographical area contains many and diverse resources and can support the production of a large range of products. Large populations and high national incomes constitute large markets that can absorb large quantities and range of national products due to economies of scale.
2 A number of factors were taken into consideration in selecting the fifteen African countries being used as samples in this analysis. They must be contiguous (or easily linked) to most other African countries so that growth in them can more readily diffuse to the other countries. Countries in the Sahara and Sahel were excluded given the relative difficulty of linking them to one another and to the other countries as well as the frequent climatic hazards that often occur there. While the size of land area and resource endowments, population size, GDP (PPP), and per capita income were considered, relatively large middle-income countries were also included in the sample.
3 For uniformity or ease of comparison purposes, all the data used in this chapter were obtained from the World Bank, *World Development Indicators*.

Bibliography

Chenery, Hollis. 1979. *Structural Change and Development Policy*. New York, NY: Oxford University Press.
Chenery, Hollis and Moshe Syrquin. 1975. *Patterns of Development 1950–1970*. Oxford: Oxford University Press.
Cornwall, John. 1977. *Modern Capitalism: Its Growth and Transformation*. London: Martin Robertson.
Cypher, James M. and James L. Dietz. 2009. *The Process of Economic Development*. New York, NY: Routledge; Taylor & Francis Group.
de Vries, Gaaitzen J., Marcel P. Timmer, and Klass de Vries. 2014. "Structural Transformation in Africa: Static Gains, Dynamic Losses." *Journal of Development Studies* 51, no. 6: 674–88.

Hirschman, Albert A. 1958. *Strategy of Economic Development*. New Haven, CT: Yale University Press.

Lewis, Arthur W. 1955. *The Theory of Economic Growth*. London: Allen and Unwin.

———. 1954. "Economic Development with Unlimited Supplies of Labor." *Manchester School of Economics and Social Studies* 22: 139–91.

McMillan, Margaret S., Dani Rodrik, and Inigo Verduzco-Gallo. 2014. "Globalization, Structural Change, and Productivity Growth, With Update on Africa." *World Development* 63: 11–32.

Page, John and Finn Tarp. 2017. *The Practice of Industrial Policy: Government-Business Coordination in Africa and East Asia*. Oxford: Oxford University Press.

Syrquin, Moshe. 1989. "Patterns of Structural Change." In *Handbook of Development Economics, Vol. 2*, eds. Hollis Chenery and T. N. Srinivasan. Amsterdam: North Holland Publishers: 203–73.

Timmer, Peter C. 1989. "The Agricultural Transformation." In *Handbook of Development Economics, Vol. I*, eds. Hollis Chenery and T. N. Srinivasan. Amsterdam: North Holland Publishers: 276–331.

Todaro, Michael P. and Stephen C. Smith. 2015. *Economic Development*. New York, NY: Pearson Addison Wesley.

United Nations Economic Commission for Africa (UNECA). 2015a. *Economic Report of Africa Industrializing Through Trade*. Addis Ababa: UNECA.

———. 2015b. *Minerals and Africa's Development: The International Study Group Report on Africa's Mineral Regimes*. Addis Ababa: UNECA.

United Nations Economic Commission for Africa (UNECA) and African Union Commission (AUC). 2013a. *Making the Most of Africa's Commodities: Industrializing for Growth, Jobs and Economic Transformation*. Addis Ababa: UNECA.

———. 2013b. *Policy Brief No 3: Urbanization and Development Transformation in Africa*. Addis Ababa: UNECA.

———. 2011a. *Economic Report on Africa 2011: Governing Development in Africa-The Role of the State in Economic Transformation*. Addis Ababa: UNECA.

———. 2011b. *Africa Youth Report 2011: Addressing the Youth Education and Employment Nexus in the New Global Economy*. Addis Ababa: UNECA.

———. 2011c. *Policy Brief No 6: Unleashing Africa's Potential as a Pole of Global Growth*. Addis Ababa: UNECA.

Weil, N. David. 2009. *Economic Growth*. New York, NY: Pearson Addison Wesley.

Woldemichael, Andinet, Adeleke Salami, Adamon Mukasa, Anthony Simpasa, and Abebe Shambles. 2017. *Transforming Africa's Agriculture Through Agro-Industrialization*. Abidjan: AfDB.

World Bank. Various years. *World Development Indicators*. Washington, DC: World Bank.

3 Theoretical perspectives

An overview of development theories and policies

A review of some relevant development theories is necessary to put the emphasis on capital goods manufacturing in perspective. Development theories for explaining the development issues of underdeveloped countries came to existence after the Second World War. However, after mushrooming in the 1950s and 1960s, they almost dried up from the late 1970s. Market fundamentalism became the norm with the coming to prominence of the Washington Consensus, a policy framework promoted by the International Monetary Fund (IMF), the World Bank Group, and western bilateral aid agencies. The Washington Consensus essentially emphasizes privatization of the economy. Consequently, the western governments, the IMF, and the World Bank tied their aid to underdeveloped countries to market fundamentalism.

After two decades of developing development theories, focusing on economic growth, it was observed that the living conditions of the bulk of the population in most of the underdeveloped countries did not improve or even deteriorated. Rural-urban migration increased, leading to increase in open unemployment in the urban areas. Inequalities between the elite and the masses increased, and poverty grew worse, especially in the slums and for the landless. Hence, from the beginning of the 1970s, development policy was pursued without necessarily being based on explicit theoretical exposition. Policy first focused on the reduction or elimination of unemployment, poverty, and inequality.

It was argued that unemployment, poverty, and inequality could not be taken care of by the implicit assumption that the benefits of high growth rates would trickle down to the masses. If, during the growth process, poverty, unemployment, and inequalities have declined, then beyond doubt it has been a period of development for the country concerned. If one or two of these central problems have been growing worse, especially if all three have, it would be strange to call the result *"development"* even if per capita income doubled (Wilber 1973, 266–72).

With the worsening of the *energy crisis* and *stagflation in* the 1970s, the economies of most African countries deteriorated. Poverty worsened and development policy shifted to emphasize the production of basic needs of the poor. It was advanced that the problem of development should be redefined as a selective attack on the worst forms of poverty. Development goals should be expressed in terms of progressive reduction and eventual elimination of malnutrition, disease, illiteracy, squalor, unemployment, and inequalities. Social indicators must be developed, and progress must be measured in terms of specific and quantitative goals in these fields, and not in terms of average per capita income. In 1976, the basic human needs approach to development was formally launched (ILO 1972).

The basic needs were defined to include food, water, shelter, clothing, and health care. Development priorities were to be reoriented so that substantial investment would be made in these sectors. Education and health are required in addition to machines, land and credit to increase productivity. Many poor people, such as the landless or urban poor, have no physical assets. The only assets they possess are their labor and their willingness to work. Investment in education and health can greatly improve their chances of success in life. Production of wage goods and the expansion and redistribution of public services can improve the chances of meeting the basic needs of the majority of the population. Subsidizing the absolute poor in public works can enable them to transition into more productive activities that can meet their basic needs and even can progress beyond. The population should be involved in the definition and development of the basic needs programs and activities.

However, in spite of the redefinition of development and re-orientation of development policy, economic problems intensified as the international economic environment deteriorated further in the 1970s. In the early 1980s, the debt crisis of the underdeveloped countries surfaced. For the poor countries to acquire aid and debt relief from the west and the international financial institutions, the International Monetary Fund (IMF) imposed its conditions of *Structural Adjustment* as prerequisites for qualifying for foreign aid and debt relief. The basic components of the IMF structural adjustment policy package included devaluation of the national currency; abolition or liberalization of foreign exchange and import controls; limitations on bank credit; higher interest rates and reserve requirements; reduction in government expenditure and increases in taxes; abolition of consumer subsidies; dismantling of price controls; control of wage increases; and privatization of public enterprises and hospitality to foreign investment (World Bank 1981; 1984).

The arguments advanced by the IMF and other aid donors, both bilateral and multilateral, were that development programming should be discontinued and economies should rely on the market mechanism. However, most underdeveloped economies deteriorated further, and both poverty and debt grew worse. This led to further redefinition of development. In 1990, the United Nations Development Program (UNDP 1990) came up with the concept of *human development*.

The concept of human development looks at development as being much more than the rise or fall of national incomes. Although economic growth is important, it should be only a means of enlarging people's choices. Economic development should create an environment in which people can develop their full potentials and lead productive and creative lives in accord with their needs and interests (UNDP 1990). The most basic capabilities for human development are to lead long and healthy lives, to be knowledgeable, to have access to the resources needed for a decent standard of living and to be able to participate in the life of the community. Without these, many choices are simply not available, and many opportunities in life remain inaccessible.

Hence, since 1990, the measurement of the concept of human development has undergone some refinements. It was initially measured by the estimation of human development index (HDI). Human development index measures the overall achievements in a country in three basic dimensions of human development. These are longevity, knowledge, and a decent standard of living. It is measured by life expectancy, educational attainment (adult literacy and combined primary, secondary, and tertiary enrolment) and adjusted income per capita in purchasing power parity in American dollars.[1] Later in the decade, the HDI was refined to include other aspects of human progress such as human poverty index (HPI), gender development index (GDI), and gender empowerment measure (GEM).

The human poverty index (HPI) focuses on deprivation in three dimensions: longevity, as measured by the probability at birth of not surviving to age 40; knowledge, as measured by the adult illiteracy rate; and overall economic provisioning, public and private, as measured by the percentage of people not using improved water sources and the percentage of children under five who are underweight. The gender development index (GDI) is the HDI adjusted for gender inequality. It captures inequalities between men and women. The greater the gender disparity in basic human development, the lower is a country's GDI compared to its HDI. The gender empowerment measure (GEM) reveals whether women can take active part in economic and political life. It focuses on participation, measuring gender inequality in key areas of economic and political participation and decision making. It tracks the percentages of women in parliament, among legislators, senior officials, and managers and among professional and technical workers, as well as the gender disparity in earned income, reflecting economic independence. Difference between GDI and GEM shows inequality in opportunities in selected areas.

As the 1990s were coming to an end, while poverty was still raging, the World Bank and the IMF came up with the *Poverty Reduction Strategy Papers* in 1999. They mandated that all low-income countries receiving debt relief under the *Heavily Indebted Poor Country (HIPC)* initiative or concessional lending from the World Bank, through the International Development Association (IDA) or the IMF, through the Poverty Reduction and Growth Facility, should develop country-owned Poverty Reduction Strategy Papers (PRSPs). The World Bank Group and the IMF, together with the European Union, USAID, and other multilateral and bilateral aid agencies were committed to supporting these papers (Klugman 2002).

These strategies were to be country-driven and -owned, predicated on broad-based participatory processes for formulation, implementation, and outcome-based progress monitoring; result-oriented, focusing on outcomes that would benefit the poor; comprehensive in scope, recognizing the multidimensional nature of the cause of poverty and measures to attack it; partnership-oriented, providing a basis for the active and coordinated participation of development partners in supporting country strategies; and based on a medium- and long-term perspective for poverty reduction, recognizing that sustained poverty reduction cannot be achieved overnight.

In 2000, the United Nations declared the *Millennium Development Goals* as a commitment of the world community to overcome the problem of poverty and development in a holistic manner (*undp.org*). The Millennium Development Goals were to be attained by 2015. They consisted of: (i) eradication of extreme poverty and hunger; (ii) achievement of universal primary education; (iii) promotion of gender equality and empowerment of women; (iv) reduction of child mortality; (v) improvement of maternal health; (vi) combat of HIV/ AIDS, malaria, and other diseases; (vii) ensuring of environmental sustainability; and (viii) development of a global partnership for development. The United Nations has extended the global development goals to 2030 through the *Sustainable Development Goals (un.org)*.

The Sustainable Development Goals are aimed to attain:

1 No Poverty;
2 Zero Hunger;
3 Good Health and Well-being;
4 Quality Education;
5 Gender Equality;
6 Clean Water and Sanitation;
7 Affordable and Clean Energy;
8 Decent Work and Economic Growth;
9 Industry, Innovation, and Infrastructure;
10 Reducing Inequalities;
11 Sustainable Cities and Communities;
12 Responsible Consumption and Production;
13 Climate Action;
14 Life below Water;
15 Life on Land;
16 Peace, Justice, and Strong Institutions; and
17 Partnership for Goals.

However, in spite of the decline in the explicit propounding of development theories since about the mid-1970s, the earlier theories have continued to implicitly guide development policy. Development theories give policymakers a vision of where they are heading. It is impossible to go forward without visualizing where one is going.

Furthermore, in whatever way development is defined, it still needs instruments to attain it. The basic tools of production include capital goods. Without the availability of the instruments of development, any form of development is impossible to pursue.

While the economies of underdeveloped countries, including those of Africa, have evolved since development theories were de-emphasized, some of these theories, in a modified form, can still give an insight into the issues of development of underdeveloped countries. The development theories deemed most relevant for the strategy of capital goods manufacturing include: *the big push, the balanced and unbalanced growth strategies, the low-level equilibrium trap, the minimum critical effort, and the theory of circular and cumulative causation.*[1]

The big push and balanced growth strategies

Rosenstein-Rodan (1943) developed his model of *big push* to explain the problem of industrialization in Eastern and South-Eastern European countries, which were then underdeveloped. He suggested that a massive investment effort was required for the industrialization process to succeed in these countries because the process of industrialization, and development in general, is not smooth and uninterrupted. It involves a series of discontinuities and humps. A gradual process will not bring about industrialization. A big push is needed to undo the initial inertia of the stagnant economy. Unless a big initial momentum is imparted to the economy, it would fail to achieve a self-sustaining and cumulative growth. This was because of the problems of complementarity, indivisibility, market imperfections, infrastructure, and savings. A big thrust of a certain minimum size is needed in order to overcome the various discontinuities and indivisibilities in the economy and offset the diseconomies of scale that may arise once industrialization and development begin.

Individual firms or industries need suppliers and customers. Hence, to be profitable their activities are complementary. A few firms might not find enough market to purchase their output because an individual firm's own workers cannot buy all of its output. However, simultaneous investment in many industries will create sufficient demand for each other's products. He gave the example of a shoe factory whose workers cannot buy all its output unless there are employees in other industries who will complement the demand of the shoe workers for their own products.

External economies would encourage firms to start investment knowing that they can depend on each other's trained and experienced workers should their own workers quit their employment. This would increase productivity for all firms, consequently, generally lowering costs in the economy for every firm. Hence, private investors who may fear taking risks on their own would be more willing to undertake investment in the presence of large investment efforts by many firms, especially with government support such as creating infrastructure.

Many large industrial undertakings such as steel mills require large capital. Therefore there is need for a large-scale investment program for them to be viable. In such cases, there is need for heavy initial public sector investment in infrastructure and basic industries to encourage small investments to take advantage of the created capacity and reduced costs as the initial high fixed costs have been reduced considerably for the private sector. The long gestation period of infrastructure projects and heavy industries would have discouraged smaller firms from investing without initial government action.

Market imperfections and supply rigidities abound during the early period of economic development. By investing in infrastructure, government can encourage the private sector to undertake directly productive activities. Public sector investment has many positive externalities. This was recognized even by the early industrial economies. Hence, they invested in canals, railways, roads, bridges, electricity, and even in education and training.

In order to finance large investments, large amounts of savings have to be mobilized. These would be difficult to obtain from small voluntary individual savings. Public policy has been involved in mobilizing investible resources in the countries that have industrialized. Even in the earliest industrial countries, public policies were involved in creating institutions such as limited liability companies and stock exchanges. Such institutions have played a large role in mobilizing large capital for undertaking large-scale enterprises.

For Rosenstein-Rodan, proceeding bit by bit will not achieve the big results needed to initiate industrialization. A basic minimum level of investment is necessary for a country to create the conditions necessary for industrialization.

The concept of *balanced growth* is associated more with Nurkse (1953). For Nurkse, the major obstacle to the development of underdeveloped countries is a *vicious circle of poverty*. This vicious circle of poverty operates on both the demand and supply sides. The underdeveloped countries are poor because of their low incomes. Low income leads to low buying power; that is, limited market. Because of limited size of the market, investment is low. The low capital formation leads to low productivity as labor has little capital to work with; this sustains the low income.

On the supply side, due to the low income, savings are low and consequently, investment is also low, leading to low productivity and low income. This assumes that savings depend on income only and investment depends on savings.

For Nurkse, the underdeveloped countries can escape the vicious circle of poverty only by increasing the rate of investment, which will lead to rise in productivity, income, savings, investment, productivity, and income. In order for this *virtuous circle* of economic development to be initiated and sustained, a balanced investment is necessary to increase both demand and supply. This investment has to be undertaken in many industries and sectors so that they act as each other's market and suppliers. The initial capital may have to be mobilized from external sources. Nurkse uses the same example of a shoe industry as Rosenstein-Rodan did to illustrate the need to invest in many activities.

When investment is made in several industries or sectors simultaneously, the incomes of many people will increase. Hence, with the increased supply will also be appropriate increase in demand. The complementarity of the various activities in the economy will lead to balanced growth. This will lead to self-sustaining economic growth.

The breaking of the vicious circle of poverty will need public policy to bring it about as such a synchronized undertaking cannot be initiated simultaneously by private entrepreneurs. Government can induce the private sector to participate in many of the directly productive activities. Unlike the big push, the balanced growth was not limited to industrialization only.

Nurkse was also disillusioned with the operation of international trade in bringing about development in underdeveloped countries. Unlike in the nineteenth century when the demand for primary products was high in the developed countries, this was no longer the case for the primary exports of underdeveloped countries for the same reasons advanced by Prebisch and Singer as discussed in Chapter 1.[2] Hence, he argued that an underdeveloped economy must expand its domestic market through balanced growth since the world market was not always available for its products.

The unbalanced growth strategy

For Hirschman (1958), it is more feasible to pursue *unbalanced growth* than *balanced growth* given the resource limitations of underdeveloped countries, particularly their *decision-making and coordination capabilities*. The unbalanced growth strategy advocates focusing on leading sectors in the economy, which have *strong linkages* to other sectors and therefore will induce investors to complementary activities. For Hirschman, the initial investments should be chosen in such a way that investors would have an incentive to establish new firms and industries in order to take advantage of what had been put in place earlier. The concept of linkages is vital to the unbalanced growth strategy.

Hirschman distinguishes between *backward* and *forward linkages*. A *backward linkage* is the proportion of an industry's input that is purchased from other industries. For example, iron ore purchased from the mining industry; steel from iron; and tools from steel and other metal products. Or shoes require leather; leather requires skins and hides; and hides and skins need the development of animal resources.

A *forward linkage* is the proportion of an industry's output that is purchased by other industries, rather than the final user. Aluminum is purchased by makers of various utensils, textile machinery requires textile producers, and flour is needed by bakeries.

Linkages have huge multiplier effects on the rest of the economy, hence increasing income by more than just the activities of one firm. Capital goods industries have more profound multiplier effects than other subsectors of manufacturing or other sectors of the economy. Policymakers should analyze the set of possible industries for those whose activities are most likely to create the desired linkages.

With linkages, the strategy of unbalanced growth suggests two alternative directions of development. Initial investment could create *excess capacity*;

for example by *creating social overhead capital (or infrastructure)*, opening up the opportunities for private firms to take advantage of the available capacity. This would create *forward linkages*. In this case, government may not predict the precise linkages that would occur as it cannot know what entrepreneurs will find attractive to invest in. However, government could also provide *incentives* for particular activities to be undertaken by the private sector.

Alternatively, initial investments could create *shortages*, thereby providing the incentives for firms to meet needs for *backward linkages*. The firms may put pressure on the government to provide infrastructure such as roads, power, or training institutions.

Hirschman illustrates the strategy with the model in Figure 3.1. Since a country may not have enough resources to develop a balanced pattern of infrastructure (social overhead capital) and directly productive activities (DPA)

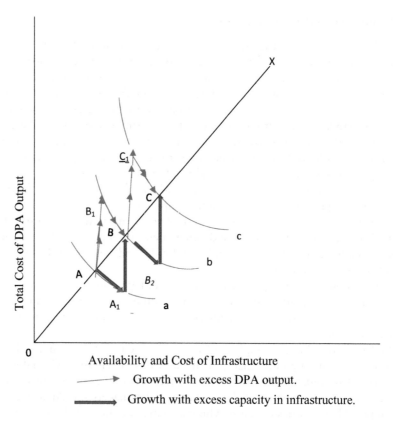

0   Availability and Cost of Infrastructure

⟶ Growth with excess DPA output.

⟶ Growth with excess capacity in infrastructure.

Figure 3.1 Unbalanced growth-induced decision making

Source: Hirschman, Albert O. 1958. *The Strategy of Economic Development*. New Haven, CT: Yale University Press: 87.

simultaneously, it could promote one and activities in the other sectors would respond to the pressures created by the differential growth in the sectors, depending on the strengths of the linkage effects. He referred to the case in which infrastructure proceeds the DPA as *development via excess capacity*; and in the case where the DPA precedes infrastructure (SOC) as *development via shortages*.

0X would represent the balanced growth path between infrastructure and DPA. But given the shortage of investible resources, expansion may have to be along path AA_1BB_2C (development via excess capacity) or AB_1BC_1C (development via shortages). Then balance will be brought about in a discontinuous way as investment in either sector responds to backward and forward linkages.

Public policy should give preference to the sequence that maximizes induced decision making. If infrastructure is expanded first, existing DPA becomes less costly, encouraging entrepreneurs to undertake more DPA. Alternatively, if DPA is expanded first, costs to the entrepreneurs will rise. The private sector will put pressure on the public authorities to expand infrastructure. For Hirschman, the choice of the sequence should depend on the relative strength of entrepreneurial motivations or the response to public pressure of the authorities responsible for investing in infrastructure.

The critical minimum effort and the low-level equilibrium trap

Both the *critical minimum effort thesis* and the *low-level equilibrium trap theory* accept the concept of a vicious circle of poverty and aim at how to pull the economy out of such a subsistence level of living. For both Leibenstein and Nelson, there is a direct relationship between the high rate of population growth and the low rate of growth of per capita income.[3] For both, population growth is related to growth of per capita income at various stages of development. At the subsistence equilibrium level of income, fertility and mortality rates are the maximum consistent with survival rates of population. As per capita income is raised above the subsistence equilibrium level, the mortality rate falls without any drop in the fertility rate. This results in an increase in the population growth rate. But this is only up to a biological maximum between three and four percent. Beyond that the increase in per capita income lowers the fertility rate. Hence, as development gains momentum, the rate of population growth remains fairly constant and then declines.

Leibenstein and Nelson believed that an underdeveloped economy can escape from the vicious circle of poverty by undertaking a level of investment that pulls it out of the low-income stability. *A level of investment large enough to break the stabilizing forces will drive the economy to high growth rates that are self-sustaining.* This is because with increase in per capita income, the desire to have more children declines as it becomes difficult and costly to support a large family. Hence, growth rate of population becomes constant and then gradually starts declining as the economy advances towards a self-sustaining path.

The critical minimum effort

For Leibenstein (1957), the critical minimum effort is the solution to achieve steady economic growth to raise the per capita income of overpopulated underdeveloped countries trapped in a vicious circle of poverty. *The critical minimum effort is a sufficiently large minimum level of investment necessary that can pull the economy to the minimum level of income that can unleash the economy to self-sustaining growth.*

Leibenstein identified two types of forces: *shocks that are income-depressing* forces and *stimulants that are income-increasing forces.* The shocks dampen and depress the forces of development through reducing output, income, employment, and investment. The stimulants raise output, income, employment, and investment. They generate the growth of income. As long as the magnitude of the stimulants are quite small, long-run economic development will not take place. Hence, to break the vicious circle of poverty, underdeveloped countries must mobilize levels of investment sufficient in magnitude to move the economy on the path to self-sustaining development. Such an effort can be mobilized through the importation of foreign capital, technological breakthrough, and/or emigration to reduce the overpopulation (Figure 3.2).

X_tX_t = Income-increasing forces; Z_tZ_t = Income-depressing forces

E is the subsistence equilibrium level of income. Intersections of X_tX_t and Z_tZ_t indicate the equality between the growth rates of population and income. Raising income from **oe** to **om** will not attain the minimum critical effort as the economy will fall back to the low-level equilibrium at **E** as shown by the arrows **abcd**. The income-depressing forces **bf** are stronger than the income-increasing forces **af**.

The minimum critical effort should raise per capita income above *ok*. Beyond point **G**, economic growth becomes self-sustaining. Hence, the critical minimum investment should raise per capita income to the level of at least **kG.**

The low-level equilibrium trap

Nelson (1956) uses three relations to analyze how an overpopulated underdeveloped economy can break out of the vicious circle of poverty in which it is trapped.

(1) Given the socio-political environment and the existing technology, *income depends on capital and labor:*

$$Y = Af(K, P);$$

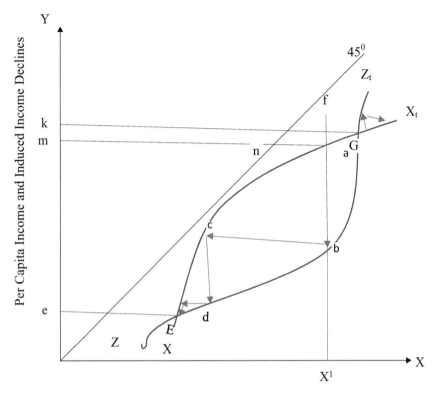

Per Capita Income and Induced Income Growth

Figure 3.2 Critical minimum effort

Source: Leibenstein, Harvey. 1957. *Economic Backwardness and Economic Growth*. New York, NY: John Wiley & Sons: 98.

where: Y= income; K = capital stock; P = Population; A = an index of productivity which changes with change in technology. Capital consists of *produced goods* and *arable land*.

K = K'+ L;

where: K = capital; K' = investment from saving; L = land under cultivation. Labor is assumed to be a constant proportion of the population. Land and produced capital are perfectly substitutable in production.

Improved use of existing resources, either by fuller utilization of available inputs or by use of better alternative techniques can lead to higher productivity and income. That is, innovation can lead to increased output.

(1) **Net capital formation:** Nelson identifies two sources of capital formation: (a) capital created from current income through savings and investment,
and (b) capital created from unused arable land by bringing this land under
cultivation.

dK = dK'+ dL

dK'/K'= f(Y/P)

Savings depend on per capita income. Investment depends on savings. Hence,
capital formation depends on per capita income.

The rate at which additional land is brought under cultivation is positively
related to the increase in population, but negatively related to the proportion of
total arable land already under cultivation.

$$dL = \frac{g(L*-L)dp}{L*}$$

L = Land under cultivation; L* = total arable land; P = Population.

As land under cultivation increases, the difficulty of bringing into cultivation
additional land of equal productivity increases.

(2) **Population growth:** The rate of population growth is the birth rate
minus the death rate plus the rate of net immigration. Short-run changes in
the rate of population growth depend on changes in the death rate. Changes
in death rate are caused by changes in the level of per capita income (Nelson's
assumption). Once per capita income reaches a level well above subsistence
requirements, further increases in per capita income have negligible effect on
the death rate.

dP/P = (dY/Y) – S = (dP/P)★

dY/Y = dP/P = 0 at the subsistence per capita income level.

S = Subsistence level of per capita income; (dP/P)★ = maximum rate of
population growth. This is the low-level equilibrium trap per capita income
(S= $(Y/P)_0$) (Figure 3.3).

S = $(Y/P)_0$ is the subsistence level of per capita income at which level,
dK/K = dY/Y = dP/P = 0.

At the low-level equilibrium trap per capita income, S = $(Y/P)_0$, there is no
saving and hence no investment. Consequently, per capita income growth as
well as population growth rates are zero. As per capita income grows beyond
$(Y/P)_0$, savings and investment rise. But between $(Y/P)_{0}$ and $(Y/P)★$, the rate of
population growth is higher than that of per capita income growth. This pushes
per capita income back to low-level equilibrium trap, that is, to the subsistence
level of income.

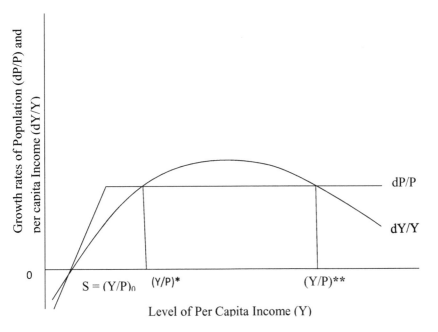

Figure 3.3 Low-level equilibrium trap

Source: Nelson, Richard R. 1956. "A Theory of the Low-Level Equilibrium Trap in Underdeveloped Economies." *American Economic Review* 46, no. 1 (December): 894–908.

To escape from the trap, the rate of growth of per capita income must exceed the rate of growth of population such as between (Y/P)* and (Y/P)**. Beyond the level of per capita income (Y/P)**, action is needed to raise the growth rate of per capita income above the population growth rate, otherwise per capita income will stop rising.

Hence, growth may be continuous or discontinuous beyond the low-level equilibrium trap, depending on the gap between the growth rates of income and population. It can be rapid and continuous, if the per capita income growth rate remains above the population growth rate. Alternatively, economic growth may be slow and discontinuous, if the gap between the growth rates of per capita income and population narrows or closes as at (Y/P)**. Government policy and technological innovations may shift the growth rate of per capita income upwards or a decline in the birth rate occurs for the growth of per capita income to continue.

The process of circular and cumulative causation

Myrdal's model explains the persistent and increasing inequalities between developed and underdeveloped regions and countries.[4] For Myrdal (1957), economic development results in a circular causation process which leads to enhanced development of the developed countries while the underdeveloped countries tend to remain poor. These differences cumulatively increase, particularly left to market forces, which tend to reinforce the initial inequalities through migration of capital, labor, and entrepreneurship from the poorer countries to the richer ones. Migration from the poor countries to the rich countries is selective. The more educated and skilled labor is the one that migrates from the poor to the rich countries. Thus, the little accumulated human capital in the underdeveloped countries is drained to the developed countries. With respect to capital movement, because the risks associated with investment tends to be higher in underdeveloped countries, the tendency for the poorer countries is to be net exporters of capital. Capital, labor, and entrepreneurship will tend to migrate together.[5]

Myrdal identified international trade as the main mechanism that causes market forces to increase inequalities between developed and underdeveloped countries (Meier 1964, 344–48). Through trade, the rules are set by the rich countries, forcing most of the small poor countries to depend on primary exports with inelastic demand with respect to price and income. This has led to persistent balance of payments and shortage of foreign exchange for most small, underdeveloped countries. As discussed in Chapter 1 under the *export of manufactures strategy*, generally tariffs on manufactured exports from underdeveloped countries face higher tariff rates in developed countries.

Myrdal uses the concepts of *backwash effects* and *spread effects* to sustain the inequalities through the process of cumulative causation. The *backwash effects* are forces emanating from the prosperous regions or countries that discourage growth in the lagging countries. Examples of these forces include migration, capital movements, and trade. Through the cumulative process, they tend to reinforce the advantages of the rich countries and disadvantage the poor countries. Migration is selective. It is the young, strong, educated, and skilled who move from the poor countries to the rich countries. Capital and entrepreneurship together are attracted to the prosperous countries from the poor countries. Diseconomies of the rich countries tend to be offset by other economic and socio-psychological benefits.

The *spread effect* refers to expansionary momentum emanating from the centers of economic development to the poor regions or countries. They have a positive impact on the development of the other regions or countries. Examples include increased demand for imports and the extension of advanced technology. Also diseconomies of scale in the prosperous regions will lead to the dispersal of activities to the poorer regions or countries. In the marginal case the spread effects may balance out the backwash effects, but in most cases the backwash effects are stronger than the spread effects.

For Myrdal, the backwash effects can only be overcome by a major force that reinforces the spread effects so as to reverse the situation in favor of the disadvantaged. This needs an integrated development plan, which allows the implementation of investments, which are beneficial for the whole society directly and indirectly through their external economies.

An appraisal of the theories

In the early post-war period, savings were mainly conceived as primarily derived from rising per capita income. However, many African countries have earned huge surpluses from rises in commodity (oil and mineral) prices. The problems of such countries have been the way the African elites have allocated those surpluses. Corruption and conspicuous consumption have drained most of these surpluses.

Skills and entrepreneurship are not as scanty today in most African countries as was the case at independence. How effectively are these African skills being utilized? In what sectors are the African entrepreneurs investing? What policies and incentives are being devised to encourage the various talents to be deployed in the relevant productive activities?

Population growth rates in Africa are stabilizing and will stabilize further with development, especially the development of education. Education of both sexes, up to tertiary level, is vital for African development and stabilization of population growth. As youth pursue education, they postpone childbearing until their twenties. After graduation, university-educated women will focus on building their careers; this will limit the number of children per woman. Hence, population growth can no longer be blamed for the shortages of savings and capital formation. In fact, since the beginning of the twenty-first century, many African countries have been experiencing income growth rates faster than population growth rates, except during periods of depressed commodity prices in the world market.

Conspicuous consumption and corruption have drained huge surpluses that could have made major differences in African economic growth. The resource surpluses earned during years of international commodity booms, channeled to productive investment such as infrastructure, education, and training, could have pulled many countries out of poverty. Moreover, the shortages of capital, entrepreneurship, and decision makers can be more easily overcome today than at the time of independence in the 1960s because some institutions and structures have been established since then and substantial achievements have been made in general education. There is an urgent need to focus higher education to promote and develop the appropriate values, attitudes, and skills for economic development.

The concepts of big push and *balanced growth* are still relevant although not in the context they were originally conceived. Some of the diseconomies resulting from infrastructure bottlenecks and complementariness are not as perverse as at independence because some infrastructure and industries have been established, although there are still many structural rigidities and major supply bottlenecks. *The big push* strategy of today needs to be understood in terms of large-scale investment in strategic sectors such as capital goods manufacturing. The *balanced growth* would mean investment in such a way that major structural imbalances are not allowed to develop to create inflationary pressures that may cause macroeconomic imbalances. Such macroeconomic imbalances, if allowed to develop, may frustrate the whole development effort.

Furthermore, the development of capital goods industries must not be the sole emphasis as the development of consumer goods industries and agriculture are prerequisites for the viability of capital goods manufacturing. Hence, both strategies still make sense in the context of the importance of large-scale investment programs and the expansion of complementary activities.

The critical minimum effort needed to pull out the economy from the low-level equilibrium trap cannot be garnered without a massive investment program. A major investment effort on capital goods production will have profound impact on the growth and structure of African economies. But most African countries are too small to initiate an investment of sufficient magnitude to move them to the path of self-sustaining development. However, there are a few large African countries that can undertake such programs on their own to a considerable level.

Unbalance is inevitable during the development process, especially in underdeveloped economies with low elasticities. As Streeten pointed out (Meier 1964, 259–63), all investment creates unbalances because of rigidities, indivisibilities, and sluggishness of response to both supply and demand. There are plenty of difficulties in meeting many urgent requirements, whether of workers, technicians, managers, machines, and transport facilities; and in finding markets permitting full utilization of equipment. Public policy should be focused on removing these bottlenecks in the development process.

Hirschman's theory of unbalanced growth can be geared to unbalance within the manufacturing sector. Manufacturing activities generally have greater backward and forward linkages to the domestic economy. But capital goods manufacturing has the strongest backward and forward linkages to all sectors of the economy. Capital goods have very high forward linkages to all directly productive activities, including the construction industry. They also have very high backward linkages to the mining and drilling subsectors. Consequently, the bias towards unbalanced growth in the large African countries should be towards capital goods manufacturing. Incentives should be given to the private sector to fill the imbalances in most of the manufacturing of intermediate and consumer goods. The latter subsectors of manufacturing are commercially profitable and will be appealing to the private sector, especially if the capital goods are available in the local economy or in the neighborhood.

The contribution of Myrdal's theory of cumulative causation to understanding perpetual underdevelopment is its emphasis on economic and social development as a cumulative phenomenon. Its challenge to static equilibrium theory that countries that gain an initial advantage may maintain that advantage to the development in the poor countries *unless major actions are undertaken to reverse the initial setting*. The emphasis on the forces of backwash effects and the spread effects is also important, particularly the emphasis that the backwash effects are stronger than the spread effects. Hence, a major effort has to be exerted to overcome the backwash effects. The backwash effects will still work within Africa, but they will not be as strong as from outside the continent given the availability of capital goods in the neighborhood. Moreover, these capital goods can be acquired much more easily and cheaply given their proximity and ease of purchase with the currency of the regional development poles, which are closer to their clients.

Myrdal's emphasis on international trade as the main vehicle for the back-wash effects on underdeveloped countries still holds true today (Carbaugh 2015, 3–6, 185–98; and Salvatore 2013, 354–55). The rounds of international trade negotiations under auspices of the *General Agreement on Tariffs and Trade (GATT)*, since 1947, have focused on the reduction of tariffs on industrial goods and not on primary products, which have been the main exports of underdeveloped countries. Dissatisfaction of the underdeveloped countries with the operation of GATT led to the establishment of the *United Nations Conference on Trade and Development (UNCTAD)* in 1964, to focus solely on trade issues of underdeveloped countries. Even the world trade negotiations under the reformed GATT, *World Trade Organization (WTO)*, have not helped the resolution of the problems of farm subsidies in the industrial countries in relation to agricultural exports from underdeveloped countries. An example is the collapse of the *Doha Round*, which was dubbed as *Development Round*, meant to address many of the underdeveloped countries' issues that were postponed during the *Uruguay Round*. The underdeveloped countries' call for a *New International Economic Order*, from the 1970s, did not achieve much, if anything.

Concluding remarks

A wide range of development theories have been advanced to illuminate the problem of development of underdeveloped countries in general. A few of these theories have been selected in this chapter because they continue to be relevant in understanding the main issues of African development. However, the degree of their relevance has changed as African economies have evolved since the 1960s. Hence, there is need to modify their assumptions and the emphasis on various variables that affect the development of the continent.

The development problems seem to be perpetuated by the African political leaders. Out of either ignorance on the issues of development or greed, many political leaders believe that they can further the welfare of their families only without caring about the rest of society. As they blindly pursue such short-sighted objectives, they invite resentment, opposition, and eventually rebellion; thus, rendering the country, including themselves, feeling insecure.

However, even if the assumption of theories such as the big push, balanced growth, unbalanced growth, critical minimum effort, and low-level equilibrium trap need to be modified, the concepts by themselves give an accurate description of the development situation in the continent and what needs to be done to set the continent on the path to self-sustaining development.

Myrdal replaces the assumptions of stable equilibrium with the hypothesis of circular and cumulative causation. This is why international differences in development persist and even widen over time. This also demonstrates the inappropriateness of underdeveloped countries to mainly rely on market fundamentalism. The backwash forces can only be reversed through major policy interventions. Capital goods manufacturing is one such major intervention in the African case. This will have to be complemented with the urgency of regional and continental integration in Africa. Even if the *regional development poles strategy* will create polarization in some locations within Africa, its *spread effects will be stronger than those from outside the continent* as can be seen from how the countries of the European Union benefit from trading with Germany; the countries of East and South-East Asia benefit from intra-industry trade among themselves; and Brazil's neighbors benefit from trading with a major industrial neighbor.

The manufacturing of capital goods in Africa coupled with the development of intra-Africa infrastructure networks will reduce the cost of key development inputs, hence lowering the costs of investment and production. Manufacturing of capital goods within Africa will promote the development of appropriate technology. This will lead to increased productivity, which may push per capita income growth above the low-level equilibrium trap, thus breaking the vicious circle of poverty and lifting the countries beyond the minimum critical level to self-sustaining development.

Notes

1 Other early theories of growth and development least relevant to this work have been excluded from the analysis.
2 Nurse's arguments are reproduced in Meier 1964, 358–63.
3 Nelson indicates that while he was working on his theory, Libenstein's book on "The theory of critical minimum effort," was published. Footnote 1, *American Economic Review.* 1956: 894.
4 Although Myrdal's theory of *cumulative causation* has been used to explain the persistence of differential geographical development within regions of a country and between countries, we will limit it here, as much as possible, to explain the international aspect of dualism only.
5 The Website of the United Nations Economic Commission for Africa discusses many of the issues concerning capital outflow from Africa as well as brain drain. See uneca.org. Also see Ibi Ajayi and Leonce Ndikumana 2015.

Bibliography

Ajayi, Ibi and Leonce Ndikumana, eds. 2015. *Capital Flights from Africa: Causes, Effects and Policy Issues.* Oxford: Oxford University Press.
Carbaugh, Robert J. 2015. *International Economics.* Boston, MA: Cengage Learning.
Chenery, Hollis and T. N. Srinivasan, eds. 1988. *Handbook of Development Economics, Vol. 1 & 2.* Amsterdam; New York, NY: North-Holland.
Hirschman, Albert O. 1958. *Strategy of Economic Development.* New Haven, CT: Yale University Press.
International Labor Organization (ILO). 1972. *Employment, Income and Equity: A Strategy for Increasing Productive Employment in Kenya.* Geneva: ILO.

Klugman, Jeni. 2002. *A Sourcebook for Poverty Reduction Strategy Vol. 1: Core Techniques and Cross-Cutting Issues.* Washington, DC: World Bank.

Leibenstein, Harvey. 1957. *Economic Backwardness and Economic Growth.* New York, NY: John Wiley & Sons: 98.

Meier, Gerald M., ed. 1964. *Leading Issues in Development Economics.* New York, NY: Oxford University Press.

Meier, Gerald M. and Joseph E. Stiglitz, eds. 2001. *Frontiers of Development Economics: The Future in Perspective.* New York, NY: World Bank; Oxford University Press.

Myrdal, Gunnar. 1957. *Economic Theory and Underdeveloped Regions.* London: Duckworth.

Nelson, Richard R. 1956. "A Theory of the Low-Level Equilibrium Trap in Underdeveloped Economies." *American Economic Review* 46, no. 1 (December): 894–908.

Nurkse, Ragnar. 1953. *Problems of Capital Formation in Underdeveloped Countries.* New York, NY: Oxford University Press.

Rosenstein-Rodan, Paul N. 1943. "Problems of Industrialization of Eastern and South-Eastern Europe." *Economic Journal* 53, no. 2 (June-September): 202–11.

Salvatore, Dominick. 2013. *International Economics.* New York, NY: John Wiley & Sons.

United Nations Development Program (UNDP). 1990. *Human Development Report.*

Wilber, Charles K., ed. 1973. *The Political Economy of Development and Underdevelopment.* New York, NY: Random House.

World Bank. 1984. *Toward Sustained Development: A Joint Program of Action for Sub-Saharan Africa.* Washington, DC: World Bank.

———. 1981. *Accelerated Development in Sub-Saharan Africa: An Agenda for Action.* Washington, DC: World Bank.

Websites

www.un.org/sustainabledevelopment/sustainable-development-goals/
www.undp.org/content/en/home/sdgoverview/mdg-goals.html

4 The Congolese economy

An overview

The Democratic Republic of Congo (DRC) covers an area of about 2,344,858 square kilometers. This land area is approximately equal to the combined territories of Austria, Belgium, France, Germany, Luxembourg, Netherlands, Norway, Spain, and Sweden (a total of about 2,346,417 square kilometers). A most frequently cited statement about the DRC is that its resources are valued at $24 trillion.[1] However, while the DRC is endowed with tremendous valuable mineral, agricultural, and water resources (fertile soils, ample rainfall, and many rivers), the country's development has been slow on account of years of plunder, maladministration, armed conflicts, and violence. With a domestic market estimated at about 80 million people, bordered by nine countries with a potential market of over 200 million consumers, and located in the center of Africa, economic transformation of the DRC would signal a period of general prosperity in large parts of Africa.[2]

The Congolese economy has been recovering and experiencing rapid growth since 2003, after the major regional Congo Wars, especially in the mineral-rich Katanga Province and around Kinshasa, the capital city.[3] Renewed activity in the mining and export sectors has accounted for most of the growth and improvement in government revenue. However, much of economic activity is still undertaken in the informal sector, especially in the interior of the country. This is not reflected in the GDP figures (UNEP 49–53).[4]

In 2007, China signed a massive deal with the DRC's state copper company in which resources were being exchanged for infrastructure development. The deal that was initially valued at $9 billion was later reduced to $6 billion due to International Monetary Fund (IMF 2010) opposition.[5] In 2009, the country signed a Poverty Reduction and Growth Facility with the IMF and received $12 billion in multilateral and bilateral debt relief in 2010, but in 2012, the IMF suspended the last three payments, totaling $240 million, because of concern about the lack of transparency in mining contracts. In 2012, the DRC updated its business laws by adhering to the Organization for the Harmonization of Business Law in Africa (OHADA) (IMF 2010).

Power supply has been inefficient and unreliable and no longer adequate to meet electricity demands within the country. Due to years of conflict and political instability, some of the established infrastructure has been destroyed and further infrastructure repair and development delayed.

The majority of the population is young and growing at around 3 percent a year. Despite the immense resource wealth, the majority of the population remains very poor, with an estimated GDP per capita of just $241 in 2013. The DRC was ranked low in the 2013 United Nations Human Development Index (HDI) with a development index score of 0.304 (IMF 2014). With regard to basic education, some developments have been made in primary-level enrolment; however, the quality and efficiency of the educational system have remained very low. In addition, despite some improvement in recent years, infant/child and maternal mortality rates remain among the highest in the world at 148 per 100,000 and 549 per 100,000, respectively. Malaria is a leading cause of morbidity. Armed conflicts have led to the internal displacement of millions of people. Increased food insecurity has been affecting around 75 percent of the population (UNEP 2011). In part due to the involvement of multinational operators with existing Corporate Social Responsibility (CSR) programs, the mining industry's contribution to communities in which miners operate is growing. The 2002 Mining Code made a miner liable for any damages it causes that may affect the rightful occupants of the land on which it mines. Mining companies were also required to support infrastructure projects, such as roads, schools, and hospitals (2002 Mining Code). If implemented, these measures can substantially improve the living conditions of the local population.[6]

Macroeconomic performance

After decades of war and contraction, DRC's economic growth revived after the peace agreement of 2002. GDP registered an average growth of 5.8 percent through 2012. In 2013, the nation's GDP grew by 8.5 percent while growth in 2014 was 9.5 percent (IMF 2015). In addition to the impressive growth figures, other macroeconomic indicators showed encouraging signs of progress. Inflation declined. The national currency, the Congolese franc, became stable. Prudent macroeconomic policies and structural reforms led to the DRC receiving debt relief under the Heavily Indebted Poor Countries (HIPC) debt relief initiative in 2010. Being the beneficiary of the largest amount distributed to any HIPC eligible country, the DRC's external debt burden was reduced from about 123.4 percent of GDP in 2009 to around 35.9 percent of GDP at the end of 2010 (IMF 2010).

Notwithstanding a dip in 2009, due to the worldwide Great Recession and renewed violence in the eastern and northern parts of the country, in which real GDP growth only reached 2.8 percent, economic growth remained strong until the political uncertainty brought about by President Kabila's dishonoring of the constitutionally mandated elections of December 2016. Before the political uncertainties, the economy was buoyed by strong trade and investment flows. This resulted in strong GDP growth as summarized in Table 4.1.

However, despite the positive outlook for many macroeconomic indicators, the country remains one of the least developed in the world. The mining

Table 4.1 Macroeconomic performance (percent in real terms)

Item	2001–05	2002–06	2003–07	2004–08	2005–09	2006–10	2007–11	2008–12	2009–13	2010–14	2011–15
GDP Growth	4.1	5.5	6.1	6.5	5.4	5.5	5.9	6.0	6.5	7.8	7.9
Per Capita GDP Growth	0.6	2.4	3.0	3.4	2.3	2.4	2.8	3.0	3.4	4.6	4.7
Consumer Prices (2000 = 100)	84.2	15.3	13.6	14.7	23.1	23.5	24.0	21.1	17.6	8.6	4.1
Gross Investment	10.6	12.3	14.1	16.1	16.5	16.2	16.0	14.9	13.5	13.6	14.3
Gross Domestic Savings	5.6	5.6	8.2	8.6	6.9	7.6	7.9	5.6	5.6	5.4	7.8
Fiscal Balance (Including Grants)	-3.5	-3.4	-3.6	-3.8	-2.2	-2.5	-2.4	0.2	1.6	1.6	1.5
Fiscal Balance (Excluding Grants)	-5.4	-7.0	-7.6	-8.2	-6.8	-6.2	-5.1	-4.1	-2.7	-2.0	-1.0
Government Revenue (Excluding Grants)	8.6	10.0	7.5	13.4	13.7	13.8	13.6	13.5	12.4	12.9	13.2
Government Expenditure	10.5	16.9	18.9	21.6	20.5	20.0	18.6	17.5	15.0	14.9	14.2

Source: IMF: Various years. Regional Economic Outlook: Sub-Saharan Africa. Five-year moving averages calculated from IMF annual data.

industry will continue to receive interest from foreign investors driven mainly by the abundance of natural resources in the country, while the lack of transparency and poor governance will ensure that large corporations and the politically connected are the main beneficiaries of its expansion. This condition was expected to improve with the government joining the Organization for the Harmonization of Business Law in Africa (OHADA) and the Extractive Industries Transparency Initiative (EITI). In July 2014, the Democratic Republic of Congo became a full member of the Extractive Industries Transparency Initiative (EITI), the global organization promoting good management of oil, gas, and mineral resources (Carter Center Report 2017).

The Government Action Plan (GAP) for 2012–2016 focused on aspects of modernizing the state and improving the population's quality of life. Significantly more revenue can be collected through the full implementation of value added tax (VAT), the elimination of various tax exemptions, a reduction in the number of taxes, and the improvement of natural resource management. Implementation of tax reforms has been slow, particularly with regards to the elimination of numerous taxes that enable tax evasion.

Since relative stability was restored in most parts of the country in the beginning of the twenty-first century, the various modern subsectors of the economy have recorded impressive growth (AfDB 2012; Bikalemesa 2014). Agriculture, hunting, forestry, and manufacturing grew by over 20 percent between 2003 and 2013. Wholesale and retail trade as well as transport, storage, and communications grew by over 10 percent over the same period, while mining, construction, finance, real estate, and business services grew by over 5 percent.

International trade

Exports rose substantially from the end of the war to about the end of the decade but declined slightly by the mid-2010s. Terms of trade were favorable, but slowed down towards the end of the decade. Imports rose along with the exports, as reconstruction and development depend on imports. Overall, merchandise trade was balanced. However, the imbalance on service account kept the current account in deficit throughout the period. Grants did not offset the current account deficit. The country's reserve position remained precarious throughout the fifteen years. Reserves hardly covered a month's value of imports of goods and services.

While there are no consistent records of DRC's trade figures since the end of the country's major wars, indications are that the international trade of the DRC has gained momentum.[7] Exports amounted to $5.8 billion in 2015. The highest value of these exports included copper at $2.9 billion (60.2%); other base metals: $792.1 million (16.3%); ores, slag, ash: $569.1 million (11.7%); gems, precious metals: $225.7 million (4.6%); oil: $111.2 million (2.29%); wood: $110.6 million (2.28%); coffee, tea, and spices: $16.3 million (0.34%); cocoa: $16.3 million (0.34%); inorganic chemicals: $14.3 million (0.3%); and machines, engines, and pumps: $10.6 million (0.22%). Cocoa was the fastest growing among the top ten export categories, up in value by 528.6 percent for the five-year period starting in 2011. In second place for improving export sales were other base metals, which was up 62.3 percent led by cobalt including cobalt waste and scrap. Congolese copper posted the third-fastest gain in value at 17.7 percent. The other seven top product categories posted declines, ranging from 3.1 percent for precious gems and metals to 92.7 percent for inorganic chemicals (USAID, IMF). Copper, cobalt, tin, and oil accounted for more than 85 percent of the country's exports, underscoring the dominance of the mining industry.

In light of the need of the large industrial and mining sectors, imports of capital goods are significant in the country's import bill (IMF 2015, 15). The country's top three imports by value are mining machinery, trucks, and electrical equipment. Light and heavy manufactured goods account for only 3 percent of export revenues, indicating that domestic factory output is overwhelmingly aimed at servicing the needs of the local market.

In 2015, Congo's total imports amounted to $6.2 billion. Foodstuffs and consumer goods constitute a large share of the country's imports. The other leading imports, most of which currently cannot be produced in the country, included packaged medicaments ($227 million), refined petroleum ($207 million), human and animal blood ($155 million), delivery trucks ($114 million), and excavation machinery ($113 million).

The DRC's direction of trade changed greatly within the ten years of 2005 to 2015. The ten leading export markets of the DRC in 2015 were: China (41.6%), Zambia (14.9%), South Korea (4.7%), Belgium (4.6%), France (2.5%), United States (2.4%), Turkey (2.0%), South Africa (1.7%), India (1.4%), and Italy (1.4%). The rest of the world took (22.5%) of DRC's exports. This was a major shift from ten years ago. In 2005, the DRC exported mainly to Europe (43.4%). The ten leading export markets were: Belgium (23.9%), United States (11.2%), China (7.3%), France (5.0%), Finland (4.8%), Zimbabwe (3.2%), Portugal (1.1%), Zambia (1.0%), Italy (0.89%), and Germany (0.89%), and the others took (40.9%). No single Asian country figured as a major market for DRC's exports in 2005. But in 2015, three Asian countries took 47.9 percent of DRC's exports; distributed as follows: China (41.7%), South Korea (4.7%), and India (1.6%) (IMF 2005–2016).

DRC's sources of import supplies also changed over the period 2005–2015 as follows. In 2005, the main sources of imports were Africa (29.2%) and Europe (26.6%), while in 2015, they were Africa (31.6%) and Asia (30.7%). The ten leading import sources of DRC in 2005 were: South Africa (12.9%), Belgium (11.1%), France (6.3%), Kenya (5.5%), Zambia (4.9%), Germany (3.2%), United Kingdom (3.1%), Cote d'Ivoire (3.0%), Uganda (2.9%), Netherlands (2.9%), and the rest of the world (44.2%). In 2015, the direction of imports changed as follows: China (25.0%), South Africa (18.2%), Zambia (9.3%), Belgium (8.4%), Zimbabwe (6.2%), India (5.7%), France (4.8%); Uganda (3.3%), Germany (2.9%), United States (2.4%), and others (13.6%) (IMF 2005–2016).

Table 4.2 The performance of the external sector (percent of GDP in real terms)

Item	2001–05	2002–06	2003–07	2004–08	2005–09	2006–10	2007–11	2008–12	2009–13	2010–14	2011–15
Export of Goods and Services	26.0	28.7	37.5	45.0	43.9	45.7	47.7	41.1	35.3	36.6	33.3
Imports of Goods and Services	31.1	35.3	43.8	53.0	53.9	55.2	56.7	50.4	42.7	43.7	40.6
Balance of Trade (Goods only)	0.5	–0.8	1.0	0.4	–1.2	0.3	1.8	0.1	1.0	1.2	–0.1
Current Account (Including Grants)	–3.9	–4.5	–4.1	–7.5	–8.6	–8.5	–8.1	–9.1	–7.7	–8.3	–8.4
Terms of Trade (Index: 2000 = 100)	132.4	137.4	279.0	643.0	496.2	613.3	712.8	666.9	635.4	637.9	571.1
Reserves (Months of Imports of Goods and Services)	1.4	1.2	0.8	0.4	0.6	0.7	0.8	1.1	1.4	1.4	1.4

Source: IMF, Regional Economic Outlook: Sub-Saharan Africa (various years). Five-year moving averages calculated from IMF annual data.

Minerals and the mining industry

The DRC is one of the world's most important mining countries, and the significance of the mining industry should greatly increase with political stability in the country. The mining sector of the DRC is divided into large-scale industrial mining and artisanal and small-scale mining (ASM). With the decline of state mining conglomerates during the conflict periods, ASM emerged as the most widespread form of mineral exploitation since the early 1990s, accounting for around 90 percent of production (De Koning 2009; Pact 2010). An estimate of about two million ASM workers is involved in mineral extraction, and as many as 12 million people are dependent directly or indirectly on artisanal mining. Environmental issues associated with large-scale mining include landscape degradation, water and air pollution, radioactive contamination, and deterioration of social welfare. The small-scale and artisanal mining sector brings with it additional concerns. There is widespread and dangerous use of mercury in artisanal gold processing. Land degradation with direct disturbance of water bodies, floodplains and riverbanks is also common. In addition, among the impacts of the ASM sector on forests, biodiversity, and protected areas are deforestation, illegal poaching, and park encroachment, related to the *ad hoc* establishment of settlement camps by the miners as well as the actual mining operations (UNEP 2011).

Mining has attracted foreign investors from all major countries, especially from the United States, Canada, South Africa, China, India, and Turkey, which in turn has fueled growth within supporting sectors such as banking, digital commerce, and mobile services. The DRC holds more than 70 percent of the world's coltan, used to make vital components of mobile phones; 30 percent of the world's diamond reserves and vast deposits of cobalt, copper, and bauxite. Additionally, the DRC contains huge quantities of gold, platinum, oil, tin, and uranium; indeed, of nearly every other precious mineral on the planet (US Geological Survey 2013).

The DRC is the largest producer of cobalt globally, accounting for about 55 percent of the global output in 2012 (US Geological Survey 2013). It was the second largest producer of industrial diamonds in 2012, contributing about 21 percent of global production behind only Botswana, which accounted for about 31 percent of global industrial diamond output. Furthermore, the country boasts some of the highest quality copper reserves globally, with some of the mines estimated to contain grades above 3 percent, significantly higher than the global average of 0.6–0.8 percent. In turn, with operating costs that are lower than traditional gold-producing countries like South Africa, DRC's gold mining sector is also witnessing renewed interest from mining companies.

The DRC has some of the largest deposits of non-ferrous metals in the world. It has about 3 percent of the global copper reserves and 45 percent of global cobalt reserves, about 25 percent of the global diamond reserves, and reserves of some precious metals such as gold and tantalum. In relative terms, the DRC is the largest cobalt producer globally; it boasts the tenth-highest gold reserves globally.

The DRC boasts around 3.4 million tons in cobalt reserves. Cobalt is the DRC's second-biggest export earning product, after being overtaken by copper in 2011. In 2011, mine production of copper in the DRC increased by an estimated 28 percent, reaching 520,000 tons. This is equivalent to around 3.2 percent of global copper output. Copper production has increased significantly in recent years due to large projects by international mining companies coming on stream. The DRC has around 20 million tons of copper reserves, about 2.8 percent of global known reserves. Copper accounts for over 30 percent of DRC's export receipts. According to the state-owned miner, Gecamines, copper miners in the DRC were forecast to produce 1.5 million tons of copper by 2015, up from about 600,000 tons in 2012 (kpmg.com). Prospects for the copper and cobalt industries in the DRC seem exceptionally bright, given that both metals are predominantly mined in the relatively war-free Katanga. However, the copper output target can only be reached if more investments are made in energy and transport infrastructure.

The discovery of Africa's largest high-grade copper deposit and the world's largest undeveloped high-grade copper deposit in the DRC has immensely increased FDI in the country. The current base-case involves a 5 million tons a year mine plan. However, the rates of up to 20 million tons a year were believed to be possible. This has great potential to attract FDI over the medium to long term, with benefits that should potentially spread to the rest of the economy. Furthermore, the planned upgrades by the company (Ivanplats) of the Mwadingusha and Koni hydroelectric plants would provide required infrastructure and supply clean energy to the power grid. In addition, about 60 percent of the bulk earthworks at copper producer Tiger Resources' Kipoi Stage-two solvent extraction and electro-winning plant development project have been completed. Construction of the $30 million facility was on schedule for first production of copper cathode in 2014.

Exportation of tin from North and South Kivu provinces has resumed after being validated as conflict-free under the Conflict-Free Tin Initiative (CFTI). North Kivu accounts for at least 80 percent of the DRC total tin exports. The DRC is also the world leading producer and exporter of tantalum. The major use for tantalum is in the production of electronic components, mainly capacitors and some high-power resistors. Tantalum is also used to produce a variety of alloys that have high melting points, are strong, and have good ductility.

The traditionally secretive diamond trade in the DRC has had a mixed effect on the country, amassing substantial wealth for few individuals, while causing insecurity and detriment to others. DRC legislation reserves the right to diamond trading inside the country to Congolese nationals, with two layers of middlemen involved. Some are based close to the mines and buy directly from artisanal diggers, while Kinshasa-based traders are closer to the foreign exporters. The diamond trade has gained some legitimacy in recent years, with diamonds becoming one of the country's largest exports. According to the Banque

Centrale du Congo (BCC), the central bank, total artisanal diamond production reached 20.1 million carats in 2012. This was an 8.3 percent increase from the 18.6 million carats produced in 2011. The figures for artisanal and small-scale production, however, could be a significant underestimate due to unregulated activity in the informal sector.[8] This has some significant consequences when diamond prices fall because many small-scale producers shut down and workers are forced to seek employment in other sectors.

Artisanal and small-scale miners produced gold in the Orientale, North, and South Kivu provinces. However, in October 2011, Canada-based Banro Corporation launched the first commercial gold mine in the country in fifty years. This could increase DRC's gold output from around 2.5 tons in 2012 to some 12.4 tons by 2017. Banro Corporation and Randgold Resources have been developing projects that are expected to provide a significant surge to the country's gold sector. Banro Corporation is developing the Twangiza and Namoya mines, which were expected to have a combined output of about 7,000 kg per annum by 2013. The Twangiza mine is the first new gold operation in the country since independence in 1960. Randgold Resources is expected to produce 15,000 kg per annum from its Kibali mine when at full capacity over the long term (kpmg.com).

The Kibali gold project is estimated to be the largest undeveloped gold mine in Africa with about 13–14 million ounces of gold reserves. However, the mining sector faces significant growth challenges due to political instability, and a severe lack of robust infrastructure and reliable electricity supply. Despite these challenges, the DRC's mining sector is expected to grow substantially on the back of the growing interest from mining companies from China, Australia, Canada, the UK, and the US, among others, due to the large untapped mineral reserves and perceived low mining costs. The country received about $8 billion in foreign investment during 2009–2012 with the majority being invested in the mining sector.

The considerable global interest in DRC's minerals is expected to result in further development of the transport network as well as other infrastructure, including electricity and water supply, hopefully supporting the overall development of the country. Inadequate electricity supply is a significant constraint on the development of the mining sector, with many large mines investing in mining-specific energy generation.

Artisanal mining and local employment

Like most African countries, the DRC faces a major employment crisis particularly for its youth. Furthermore, an increasing number of university graduates are annually joining the labor market. In the second Poverty Reduction Strategy Document (DSCRP 2), over 2012–2016, the country targeted the creation of 900,000 jobs annually for the young. However, considering the present economic conditions and youth employment scenario, such a high target appears difficult to achieve.

The artisanal and small-scale mining subsector (ASM) provides a lucrative but very risky source of employment. In 2010, an extensive study estimated that up to a million people could be active in artisanal mining in the entire DRC, but acknowledged that any estimates would necessarily be very rough (Pact 2010). Owing to the country's massive infrastructure deficit, industrial mining is only possible in a small number of places such as Katanga. The government recognizes the importance of artisanal mining in allowing the development of the sector, especially in areas where prospecting is still necessary or where local conditions make industrial operations impossible, and as such, issues artisanal licenses to promote this sector and defines certain areas as "artisanal operating zones."

With the collapse of the economy, during the war times, and corruption in the government, the enforcement of the mining code was negatively affected. The working conditions of mining workers in the country are poor. The miners are exposed to landslide hazards, especially during heavy rains, and to heavy metals through dust inhalation and water contamination. Child labor is prevalent in the informal sector. Artisanal mining presents some risks, notably in the areas of health and safety and of child labor. Artisanal miners are routinely victims of digging collapses, and generally work in very strenuous conditions. Artisanal gold miners still work with mercury, although this is illegal. Not only do the miners and their communities suffer from the effects of artisanal mining, but the government also loses considerable revenues from it. But both the state and private actors are complicit in the illegal patterns of production, trade, and revenue generation. Various parties move around the mining areas, demanding illegitimate taxes and fees or confiscating minerals from miners and traders (De Koning 2009).

Such a situation cannot be allowed to continue if the Congolese state is to gain credibility from its people and mobilize efforts for national development. The government should put in place a regulatory regime that mainly benefits the miners and their communities. Appropriate mining tools should be available in the mining areas. Supplies of essential products must be within easy reach of the miners. Agricultural development in areas surrounding the mining sites must be developed so that the mining communities can procure much of their food supplies locally. Likewise, schools and health facilities must be established within the mining communities. The miners can help the government finance such social services.

Extension services should be established for the ASM in areas such as microfinance, training, environmental and safety standards, and the preserving and taking care of other natural resources around the ASM sites. The local and provincial administrations should encourage dialogue between the ASM operators and the large mining companies since the latter depend on the former for substantial supplies of their raw material. ASM operators should pool their supplies through cooperatives and sell them to the large companies in bulk. The artisanal miners should organize annual conferences to share experiences and strategize. Civil societies should help the ASM operators to develop such activities as conferences, dialoguing, and the formation of cooperatives.

Public sector revenue from mining

Reforms in the mining sector include various types of taxes: profit-based tax, tax on the surface area of mining, annual area fee per square, and royalty. According to the 2002 Mining Code, mining companies are subjected to a professional tax of 30 percent instead of the 35 percent net profits tax. A research permit holder is required to pay tax on the surface area of mining at the rates of $0.02 per hectare for the first year, $0.03 for the second year, $0.035 for the third year, and $0.04 for each subsequent year, while an exploitation permit holder is taxed at the rates of $0.04 per hectare for the first year, $0.06 for the second year, $0.07 for the third year, and $0.08 for subsequent years.

Mining companies are subjected to an annual fee on the number of squares held, with one square being equal to 84.955 hectares. While a research permit holder is required to pay the annual fee of $2.55 per square for each of the first two years, $26.34 for each subsequent year, $43.33 for each year of the first renewal period, and $124.03 for each year of the second renewal period, an exploitation permit holder is required to pay $424.78 for an ordinary exploitation permit, $679.64 for a tailings exploitation permit, and $195.40 for a small-scale exploitation permit. Mining companies are required to pay a mining royalty from the date of commencement of effective exploitation, which is equivalent to the value of sales made, less transport costs, costs of assay, as well as insurance and marketing costs. The rate of the mining royalty is 0.5 percent for iron or ferrous metals, 2 percent for non-ferrous metals, 2.5 percent for precious metals, 4 percent for precious stones, 1 percent for industrial minerals, solid hydrocarbons, and other not-cited substances, and no royalty is to be paid for standard construction material (2002 Mining Code and kpmg.com). The Mining Code has been changed since 2002.

Diligently implemented, these reforms should bring in substantial revenue to the DRC government at various levels. These sources of revenue are important for socio-economic development, if used efficiently for the purposes for which they are designed. They must be legally and practically distributed to the various levels of government instead of being concentrated in the central treasury.

However, the central government does not transmit the legally due amounts of revenues to the subnational levels of government, while the companies do their best to not reveal their true rates of profits (Carter Center Report 2017). The various challenges that reduce the contribution of revenue from the mining sector to the welfare of the Congolese include the non-retrocession of the mining royalty by the Congolese government in accordance with the Mining Code, minimization of profit tax payments to the Congolese state by mining companies, non-publication by mining companies of their financial statements, undervaluation of mining assets sold by mining state-owned enterprises (SOEs) without a public tender, lack of transparency on the management of the revenues generated by the SOEs, and the incomplete publication of contracts, annexes, and amendments of mining projects by the Ministry of Mines. According to the Mining Code, 25 percent of the revenue from the mining royalty should be allocated to the province and 15 percent to the Decentralized Territorial Entity (ETD). Mining companies minimize paying profit tax to the Congolese state by manipulating transfer pricing. Mining companies do not publish their financial statements. The mining assets of the state and state-owned enterprises (SOEs) are often sold without a public tender or a good valuation, which may lead to loss of potential revenues. The publication of contracts, annexes, and amendments by the Ministry of Mines is neither complete nor up to date, which hinders the monitoring and follow-up on the obligations of mining companies.

Petroleum exploration and development

Oil production in the Democratic Republic of the Congo (DRC) began in the 1960s along its 37 km-long Atlantic Ocean coastline in Bas-Congo Province. In the mid-2010s, the DRC produced between 27,000 to 28,000 barrels per day (bpd), partly because its exclusive economic zone (EEZ) is very small. The country's sea access, as well as its territorial waters, is squeezed between Angola and Angola's Cabinda enclave. Angolan oil blocks surround Congolese territorial waters (ICG 2012).

Furthermore, the significance of petroleum in the DRC has been overshadowed by the mineral wealth and consequently, mainly ignored by successive governments. But, after the frenetic upsurge in exploration on the continent from the 1970s, DRC's increasingly prominent oil sector became the subject of renewed interest by international oil companies. Hence, there has been a revival in exploration in Bas-Congo since 2000 and in eastern DRC since 2006. In both regions, the oil reserves straddle borders with Angola and Uganda, respectively. Given the flawed Berlin 1884/85 demarcation of the African borders, these oil findings have led to tensions with both Angola and Uganda.[9]

Angola has increased oil production from deep-water operations in the disputed blocks since the beginning of the century. In the mid-2010s Angola produced about 1.7 million bpd, including 220,000 bpd in block 14 and 640,000 bpd in block 15, which are in DRC's claimed EEZ. Since June 2003, the DRC has officially claimed a proportion of the oil extracted from the deep-water Angolan production blocks. The two countries began negotiations and signed their first memorandum of understanding (MOU) in August 2003. This agreement established joint technical committees mandated to prepare proposals to resolve maritime border disputes. In 2004, the two countries created, in principle, the common interest zone (CIZ) as a new special exploration area. The CIZ arranged for the two neighbors to share oil revenues equally; once the arrangement was implemented, the DRC would receive the pro-rata reimbursement of revenues made by Angola from its investments in the CIZ and unitization agreements for the oil fields that straddle the border. However, the CIZ has not resolved the territorial dispute between Angola and the DRC. In 2009, 32,000 Congolese and 18,000 Angolans were respectively expelled from each other's country (ICG 2012).

Reciprocal financial claims are one of the root causes of this dispute. Angola estimated that the illegal production of diamonds by Congolese prospectors in its northern provinces cost the country between $350 million and $700 million in annual revenues, while the DRC claimed that Angola owed it $650 million in oil revenues. The two countries agreed to create a joint working group to demarcate their maritime borders.

The gas pipeline between the Cabinda enclave and the town of Soyo, in northern mainland Angola, was another bone of contention between Luanda and Kinshasa, but both governments eventually reached an agreement. This project, which is run by Chevron and its subsidiary Cabinda Gulf Oil, was to transport gas extracted from the Cabinda waters to the Angolan liquefied natural gas plant in Soyo through DRC's territorial waters.

The DRC's borders with its eastern neighbors pass through Lakes Albert, Edward, Kivu, and Tanganyika. The demarcation between Uganda and the DRC became a problem as soon as oil exploration started. In 2007, the imprecise delimitation of the border on Lake Albert led to brief military clashes between the DRC and Uganda. Despite attempts to reach agreement, mistrust remains a prominent feature of Uganda–DRC dialogue, which stumbles over several outstanding issues.[10]

In 2002, while Ituri District of the DRC was in the throes of violence and occupied by the Ugandan army, Heritage Oil, approached the DRC government about assessing the oil potential for the Ituri. Heritage Oil signed a Memorandum of Understanding with Kinshasa on June 2, 2002 to explore an area of 30,000 km^2 stretching from south of Lake Edward to the northern end of Lake Albert. Despite the agreement, no exploration took place on the Congolese side. However, it was carried out on the Ugandan side, reviving tensions between the two countries, particularly over the sovereignty of Rukwanzi Island in Lake Albert.

Exploration continued on the Ugandan side but the legacy of the war and Congolese resentment towards Kampala was exacerbated, notably by Kampala's refusal to pay war reparations. In frustration, many Congolese accused oil companies working in Uganda of a biased approach to drilling in the lake and of "stealing Congolese oil." On September 8, 2002, the two countries signed an agreement to improve cooperation, especially for cross-border oil exploration and production. They reaffirmed acceptance of the borders inherited from the colonial period and provided for the joint development of Lake Albert's oil reserves.[11]

Geologists believe that DRC has other promising geological basins such as Lakes Edward, Kivu, and Tanganyika, which are all "natural" borders. The Central Basin covering 800,000 km^2 at the heart of the DRC also contains oil. It stretches across the borders with Congo-Brazzaville and the Central African Republic, but the demarcation of these borders is also imprecise.

At Lake Edward, Dominion Petroleum obtained exploration rights for Uganda's block 4B while the Congolese government allocated block 5 to Soco International and Dominion Petroleum in 2010. Block 5 is located at the center of troubled areas in North Kivu with 52 percent of the block being within Virunga National Park, which poses a major environmental challenge.

Belgian experts identified significant quantities of methane gas in Lake Kivu in 1935, but the first attempt to extract it from the lake only took place in 1963. The gas was used until 2005 to supply a brewery in Rwanda. The unclear borders around the lake have not caused problems between the DRC and Rwanda. An agreement, signed in Bukavu in 1975, provided that operations to extract methane must be conducted jointly. This was reaffirmed at a bilateral summit meeting at Gisenyi, in March 2007, to which international experts were invited. Only Rwanda has begun to implement some projects. The most serious project started in 2009. After conducting research into the lake's potential, Contour Global signed an agreement with the Rwandan government in March 2009 for a 100 MW project. In August 2011, Contour Global launched the first stage of the project by installing a methane extraction barge with a production capacity of 25 MW.

Rwanda has been planning for the joint development of gas reserves with the DRC. Following a meeting in June 2009 between the Congo National Electricity Company (SNEL) and the Rwandan energy minister, an agreement was signed for the construction of a joint 200 MW project to extract methane gas from Lake Kivu hydrocarbons. Meanwhile, the Rwandan government has reportedly been negotiating with a company that was to begin oil exploration research in Lake Kivu in 2012.

Lake Tanganyika is a new oil exploration area shared by four countries: Burundi, DRC, Tanzania, and Zambia. Tanzania allocated its southern block to the Australian company Beach Energy and its Tanzanian subsidiary Beach Petroleum Tanzania in 2008, and the northern block to Total in 2011. Burundi has granted Surestream a license for blocks D and B, A-Z Petroleum for block A and Minergy Ree for block C.

In 2008, the Congolese hydrocarbons ministry divided the country's share of the lake into ten blocks. However, this division is not yet official. The lake is not currently a focus of major problems, but the Ruzizi River delta was disputed in the 1980s. In May 2008, the DRC and Tanzania signed an agreement for joint exploration of the lake, which DRC senators strongly criticized.

The Central Basin (Cuvette centrale) stretches from the edge of Kinshasa Province through the provinces of Equateur, Bandundu, Kasai Oriental, Kasai Occidental, and Maniema to the north of Orientale Province, with some geological continuity in Congo-Brazzaville and South Sudan. The absence of infrastructure and the dense equatorial forest represent a major logistical challenge and a consequent exponential growth in research costs (Delvaux and Fernandez-Alonso 2015).

In the 1970s, the American companies Esso and Amoco carried out seismic studies and drilled test wells, but the results were disappointing. Japan National Oil Corporation also conducted some geological studies in the Kisangani area, again without results. In the 1980s, the World Bank provided $6 million to studies conducted by Petrozaïre, particularly in Bandundu. However, the area was neither mapped nor divided into exploration blocks. At the end of 2005, DRC hydrocarbons ministry officials visited Tervuren Museum in Belgium to examine all the available geological data with a view to preparing a map.

On 30 January 2008, the DRC government contracted the Brazilian company, High Resolution Technology Petroleum (HRT), to review the available geological data and issue a call for tenders. Before withdrawing in 2009, HRT proposed dividing the Central Basin into 21 blocks, but a decree of 2 August 2007 had already opened the basin to exploration and some blocks had been allocated to Comico, Soco, and Divine Inspiration. However, no presidential decree allowing prospection was issued for these blocks.

More parties expressed interest in exploring the basin. The DRC and South Korea signed several investment agreements, notably in the energy sector. A contract was signed between the Korean National Oil Agency and Cohydro, after an initial agreement on 10 August 2010. On 24 June 2011, Cohydro and the Brazilian company Petrobras signed a technical and financial support agreement.

In order to anticipate possible problems on the border, the two Congos drafted a joint agreement to exploit hydrocarbon reserves. On 24 April 2011, the National Assembly of Congo-Brazzaville ratified the agreement, but Kinshasa did not do the same.

Infrastructure development

The DRC faces significant infrastructure challenges. The country is spatially and structurally disconnected, with vast hinterland areas geographically isolated into virtual "islands" that are cut-off both from the center and from each other. Physical isolation has curtailed large-scale commerce and economic life has become acutely localized. Furthermore, the high vulnerability of the DRC's mainly earth-road network to frequent equatorial torrential rainfall, coupled with limited maintenance capacity, means that they are at high risk of rapidly degrading into gullies.

Conflict and instability have had a major impact on infrastructure development, with decades of war not only destroying some of the established infrastructure, but due to the complete inattention to the issue, the post-war government was practically starting from scratch. The most serious impact of insecurity on infrastructure development has been felt in the east, where there has been little or no infrastructure development except in close proximity to the Rwandan and Ugandan borders, in areas where most trade is international. In Katanga, specifically around Lubumbashi, there has been some progress in the area of infrastructure development, and the same is true along the lower reaches of the Congo River on the border with the Congo Republic. In addition to security concerns, in much of the country geography and weather makes infrastructure development a real challenge. As a consequence, the freight tariffs in the DRC are high both on the road and the rail network, even in comparison to other countries in the region. The national power utility, Société Nationale d'Electricité (SNEL), serves less than a million customers, and almost half of the country's available electricity is consumed by just 20 large clients. The post-war Congolese government has set a highly aggressive target to provide 60 percent of the population with access to electricity by 2025 (IMF; World Bank; USAID).

In September 2007, a $9 billion deal was signed between two Chinese state construction companies and the DRC's state copper company in which resources would be exchanged for infrastructure. Not only is China set to invest heavily in the mining industry, but public-private projects were to be implemented as part of a joint agreement. China was to build or rehabilitate some 3,500 km of roads and 3,200 km of railroads, 32 hospitals, 145 health centers, and two universities in the country. Gecamines, the state-owned mining company, was then in turn to cede a potential 10.6 million tons of copper and 626,619 tons of cobalt to the joint venture. The period over which the loans were to be disbursed was extended, with the last disbursement expected in 2019 instead of 2014, while the amount of each disbursement is also smaller than initially projected (Davis 2008; Kabemba 2016).

In May 2013, the World Bank pledged $1 billion in funding for the African Great Lakes region to support infrastructure development and increase regional trade. The funding includes $150 million toward rehabilitating the Ruzizi I and II hydropower plants, as well as to finance Ruzizi III to supply electricity to Rwanda, Burundi, and the DRC. Furthermore, the DRC was to receive $165 million to build roads in the North and South Kivu and Orientale provinces, while $180 million was to be directed towards infrastructure improvement and border management along the Rwanda-DRC border (World Bank 2013).

Telecom and ICT

Estimates have mobile penetration rate slightly above 25 percent, but the coverage is spreading fast. News circulation is limited outside the main cities of Kinshasa and Lubumbashi. Internet penetration is limited outside Internet cafes. Mobile phones provide an opportunity for accessing a vastly growing consumer base, especially with a large number of Congolese outside its urban areas.

The government has focused on increasing mining and oil production in the country. Ramping up such efforts requires connecting the various parts of the country, especially to the capital city where most decisions are made. With a vast country such as the DRC, fast means of communications are vital. Orientale, North, and South Kivu provinces, with plenty of gold and other metals, are still fairly disconnected with Kinshasa. Oil potential in the regions is unknown but thought to be high. An improvement in the telecom industry is essential to these sectors. Accessing untapped resources also includes connecting one side of the country to the other.

A new Telecommunications Act has been passed to reform the telecom sector, and for the establishment and maintenance of regulatory independence.

There are efforts aimed at rehabilitation of the cable network, restoration of the telecom system, interconnections, spectrum management and planning, satellite and fiber-optic installations for international communications, rural telecommunications, capacity building, introduction of new technologies and applications, and postal services re-engineering.

Power and energy development

For the DRC, one of the immediate challenges on the infrastructure front is to increase the supply of power in a cost-efficient manner. The country has huge hydropower potential, the largest in Africa, estimated at over 100,000 megawatts (MW), of which about 44 percent (44,000 MW) is concentrated at the site of Inga, located at 150 km from the mouth of the Congo River (AfDB 2013). However, only a fraction of the total potential, estimated at 2,540 MW, has been developed, mainly consisting of hydro-based stations and thermal power plants. This represents only 2.2 percent of the country's hydropower capacity, with a majority of thermal power stations often not functioning due to lack of spare parts and recurrent shortages of gas oil (kpmg.com).

Société Nationale d'Electricité (SNEL), the public utility, owns an estimated thirty-nine power stations, comprising twenty-four thermal-powered stations (with a negligible electricity output) and fifteen hydro-powered stations, with the latter accounting for 98.5 percent of the total installed capacity. Guaranteed electricity capacity currently stands at approximately 1,245 MW (interconnected). The Inga I and Inga II hydropower stations account for approximately 78.5 percent of the current installed capacity (interconnected), with the remaining electricity production supplied by thermal plants scattered across the country (kpmg.com).

Another serious current constraint in the power sector is the inefficiency and unreliability of the power delivery network. The transmission and distribution systems have also suffered due to limited funding. As a result, they are no longer adequate to meet the current electricity requirements in the country. This is compounded by an overload of transmission installations, which has resulted in recurring drops in voltage and failures of transformers. The DRC's national power utility, SNEL, has been ridden with huge inefficiencies in the form of high distribution losses and non-payment of dues.

The DRC is currently operating with a national energy deficit, which needs to be urgently addressed to provide one of the key inputs for economic growth in the mining sector and other sectors of the economy. Consequently, many mining companies in the country have set up and operate their own local hydroelectric schemes, costing about 10 US cents per kWh. In comparison, the long-run marginal cost of grid supply is estimated at about 4 US cents per kWh. The country will require investments to the tune of $750 million a year over the next decade for setting up new generation and transmission capacity to realize its potential as a power exporter *(IMF 2015)*.

The South African energy minister and his Congolese counterpart have signed a treaty to develop the Inga III Hydro Plant in the DRC. The South African government agreed to buy over half of the power generated by the first phase of the Inga III project, amounting to around 2,500 MW. Construction of the 4,800 MW first phase was set to begin in October 2015, and could take five to six years before completion. The $80–$100 billion Grand Inga project will be built in six phases before reaching full capacity of about 44,000 MW. Sizeable investments are required to make use of the country's hydropower potential, which, if fully exploited, will enable it to not just meet its own energy demands but also turn the DRC into the continent's largest exporter of power. Furthermore, hydroelectricity generation is expected to be hugely cost efficient, with the long-run marginal cost estimated at 1.4 US cents per kWh (kpmg.com).

In May 2003, the DRC parliament enacted a bill to govern the electricity sector which was passed into act by Parliament in May 2013. This act ushers in numerous innovations that will result in changing various aspects of the DRC's electrical energy law. These include liberalizing the electrical energy sector and opening the electricity market to operators, establishing a regulation mechanism for settlement of disputes amongst operators as well as between operators and customers, creating servitudes inherent to power public utility activities, and establishing tax, customs, and financial regimes under common law or contracts. However, it is only compliance with and efficient implementation of the provisions of the law by the government, operators, and consumers that will determine the success in achieving the set energy objectives.

The Inga Power Complex is the hope of many economies experiencing major power constraints. As the DRC looks to capitalize on its economic momentum, the country's energy sector is attracting the attention of international investors especially as its large-scale mining and industrial sectors continue to see significant growth. Paramount to the energy future of the DRC and the African continent is the Inga Dam Project, which is one of the largest infrastructure projects ever undertaken on world scale. The centerpiece of the project, the Grand Inga Dam, will be the world's largest hydropower project and is an instrumental part of Africa's future energy strategy. The dam has the potential to generate 38,000 MW of energy at a cost of $80 billion. It will help power South Africa, Namibia, Botswana, and Angola, and is planned to be able to export power to Europe. In 2013 the United States formally expressed interest in joining the project and is currently engaged with foreign counterparties as studies are being conducted and has pledged financial aid to help develop the project.

Manufacturing

The periods of war have led to deep de-industrialization and de-mechanization of the DRC economy as informalization spread in the economy. With growing world demand for natural resources, the DRC manufacturing may become limited to exports of mere processed primary products. Hence, while manufacturing in the DRC reaches about 16 percent of GDP, it is largely accounted by the processing of minerals for the export market. However, if supported by strategic policies and investments, the DRC's low level of industrialization, combined with its rich natural resource base can be promoted into higher levels of manufacturing.

Manufacturing activity in the DRC has contributed little to overall economic growth due to the burden of poor power supply, outdated capital equipment affecting the quality of produce, and strong competition from imported goods. Breweries, cement makers, palm oil refineries, and flour mills have, however, delivered some success. Processing of domestic minerals constitutes a large part of the manufacturing sector. These mainly include copper, cobalt, gold, diamonds, coltan, zinc, tin, and tungsten. Processing of consumer goods, including textiles, plastics, footwear, and cigarettes, is also significant. There is also manufacturing of metal products, processed foods and beverages, timber, cement, and commercial ship repairs.

With increasing population and urbanization the country could considerably expand its establishment of building-material industries such as cement, ceramic, and glass factories. The pharmaceutical industries have scope for major expansion. Manufacturing and packaging industries include food products, tobacco products, leather, wood and paper, chemical manufacturing, oil, coal and their by-products, rubber, and plastics. Basic metallurgical industries include steel making, production and first processing of non-ferrous metals, manufacture of metallic items, appliances and electric supplies, and manufacture of automotive vehicles.

Agribusiness

In spite of the DRC's sizeable fertile land mass, the Congolese still endure a system that provides an insufficient number of crops. The main agricultural exports in terms of value include unmanufactured tobacco, green coffee, sugar, wheat, and dry rubber, which still have great potential, as commercial agriculture is limited. Most farmers are subsistence or small-scale. A lack of manufacturing and packaging infrastructure hinders the country's ability to move the value chain further on shore and capture greater profits and rewards for the farmers.

The livestock and fishery sectors have high potentials. Imported frozen chicken and fish are the norm in the DRC. The cost of chicken and eggs in Kinshasa is approximately twice the price paid in South Africa. The same situation applies to milk and cheese. Both poultry and dairy suffer from a lack of capital and outdated equipment. Boosting acreage, productivity, output, and lowering costs should be the solution. By using the nation's water, land, and energy resources, the DRC can develop an industry of commercial farms offering fishing, livestock, and vegetable production, connected to a coherent network of production, processing, and food distribution.

Developing the agricultural and forestry subsectors

Located on both sides of the equator and spanning two tropical zones (equatorial and savanna), the DRC has a climate that favors the cultivation of a wide range of tropical and even Mediterranean crops. It is considered that around half of the DRC's land is arable and suitable for farming, although the records show that an estimated 1 to 2 percent only of the country's farmable land has so far been put under cultivation. Coffee beans, potatoes, and leeks have a perfect environment in the high plains of the east and south for plantation. Cool temperatures and fertile soil in the region of Eastern Highlands favor the cultivation of tomatoes, sweet potatoes, yam, and pumpkins, and even Mediterranean vegetables such as artichokes and asparagus. There is a high agricultural yield; when the rainy season is very long, it is possible to replant immediately after harvest and get a second crop during the same season.

However, much of the DRC's population is dependent on slash-and-burn, rain-fed agriculture for its subsistence. Such farming practices are unsustainable and inefficient, and with little or no inputs, large areas of land are required as soil fertility is rapidly depleted. Disintegration of transport infrastructure and resulting geographical isolation has led to the collapse of the rural economy as farmers are unable to easily sell their produce, purchase inputs or receive support from agricultural extension services. Due to lack of facilities for refrigeration or for appropriate storage of food crops, post-harvest losses can reach up to 80 percent in some areas (UNEP 2011).

Food crops in tropical areas principally comprise of maize (corn), groundnuts, millet, cassava, and rice. The commercial crops such as coffee, cocoa, rubber, tea, palm oil, and sugar cane are mostly grown in plantations, with the production of tobacco and cotton largely in the hands of private small-hold farmers. Fishing has a huge potential. The lakes in eastern and southern regions of DRC are a massive reserve of a variety of freshwater species. The Congo River is another important source with major fishing ports in Kisangani and Mbandaka supplying the millions of people living in the Kinshasa region. Encouragement of private sector investment is a main government objective. It aims to foster the professionalization of agriculture through training and the importation of foreign skills. The land for food crop production will be made available to foreign farmers by the government, while the rehabilitation of cash crop production will be on a joint venture basis. Rehabilitation of livestock farming in the short term is also a priority. However, development of the indigenous capacity is essential and must be prioritized as such development is the surer way of raising the living conditions of the bulk of the population.

By using the country's water, land, and energy resources, the DRC can develop peasant and commercial farms offering crops, fishing, livestock, and vegetable production, connected to a coherent network of production and food distribution. Development of extension services for peasant farmers will help in the fight against hunger and malnutrition throughout the country. Commercial investments, both by the government and the private sector, will provide thousands of jobs, bring broad education to the masses, and enable a generation of Congolese to develop and become self-sufficient.

To support agriculture and encourage private-sector participation, the government developed and launched a nationwide program known as the National Agricultural Investment Plan (NIPA). NIPA's main objectives are ensuring food security and developing the agribusiness sector. Its first project will be the development of sixteen large agro-parks. These parks will serve as an important part of the country's rehabilitation and construction process by providing access to agricultural inputs and by combining laboratories, training facilities, storage centers, and health facilities. The agricultural sector is where there can be the most significant impact on raising the living standards of most of the population.

In the area of environmental regulations applicable to the mining industry, the Mining Code and the Mining Regulations as well as the preservation of the Congo Basin Forests must be enforced. In 2002, the DRC started working toward modernizing the legal framework of the forest, environment, and tourism sectors with the adoption of a new Forest Code mainstreaming sustainable development. Since then, while a large number of illegal forest concessions have been terminated, sustainable forest resource management remains a challenge. This is illustrated by a deforestation rate of 0.2 percent annually in the Congo Basin (UNEP 2011). The country is also developing a Reduction of Emissions from Deforestation and Forest Degradation (REDD+) national process aimed at establishing a national measurement, reporting, and verification system of carbon stocks and flows. The DRC has been selected as one of the eight pilot countries for the Forest Investment Program (FIP). It also benefits from the Congo Basin Forest Fund (CBFF). (Mining Code & Regulations, UNEP, REDD+).

Overall, the DRC's extensive forest resources are being lost and degraded at an increasing rate, particularly in critical areas such as gallery forests in the west and hilly landscapes in the east. While the overall national deforestation rate remains relatively low, at 0.2 percent, in some parts of the country, notably in the north and south savanna plateaus and gallery forests, deforestation rates are much higher.

The key drivers of forest degradation and deforestation include (i) slash and burn agriculture with reduced fallow periods; (ii) fuel-wood and charcoal collection which accounts for 95 percent of the population's energy needs; (iii) artisanal and small-scale logging which is estimated to represent 75 percent of total timber exports from the DRC; and (iv) road infrastructure opening previously pristine areas up to human activities. Non-Timber Forest Products (NTFPs), such as medicinal plants and foods, are of particular importance to a large majority of the Congolese population and the international community as a whole (UNEP 2011). Many causes of the degradation of the environment can be greatly reduced by considerably raising the living conditions of the bulk of the population so that they do not survive through eking out of the natural environment.

Concluding remarks and the way forward

The DRC is potentially one of the richest countries on Earth. But it is still a fragile post-conflict country with enormous needs for reconstruction and economic growth and development. The opportunities are huge given the country's vast natural, especially mineral, wealth. Since 2003, progress has been made in rebuilding the state and economy, including the holding of national elections in 2006 and 2011. Important improvements have been made in terms of macroeconomic management, raising primary education enrolment, reducing infant and maternal mortality, improving drinking water supply, and alleviating malnutrition. There has been rapid growth of new information and communication technologies.

DRC's successful completion of the Heavily Indebted Poor Countries Initiative (HIPC) in 2010 and increased revenue from rising commodity prices provided an important opportunity to increase national budget spending (World Bank 2013). However, President Joseph Kabila's dishonoring of the constitution plunged the country into crisis again, setting back the gains that have been made since 2003. The challenges for the DRC to overcome entrenched poverty and recover decades of lost development opportunities are immense. Establishing a pro-people governance system, building human capital at all levels of administration (national, provincial, and local governments), and developing physical infrastructure are critical. With the establishment of such capacities and rational utilization of the country's tremendous resources, the DRC can recover and build a self-sustaining economy with wide-ranging impacts on all of its people and in its neighborhood. Economic transformation that leads to creating many employment opportunities, considerably reducing absolute poverty and inequalities, will help bring about sustainable economic recovery and development, lasting stability, and peace.

The DRC's national development vision as set out in its Poverty Reduction and Growth Strategy Papers (PRGSP 1 and 2) is to stimulate economic recovery and alleviate poverty through a growth focused strategy. It emphasizes generating economic growth by attracting large-scale infrastructure investments and leasing industrial concessions to extract the country's vast natural capital. Specifically, over the period 2011–2015, the PRGSP2 aimed to accelerate growth in extractive industries and infrastructure investments to an average of between 8–9 percent. In fact, the key natural resource sectors – mining, forestry, oil and gas – have been experiencing rapid growth since the end of the major Congo wars.

The key question is how to promote and maximize broad-based benefits from the development of the DRC's natural assets given the state's limited institutional capacity for controlling fraud and corruption, and managing wealth redistribution and social service provision. Specifically, the Congolese elites should evolve a development model that ensures that the harnessing of its natural resources is socially inclusive, environmentally sustainable, and supports peace consolidation.

Such a model will involve the promotion of sustainable wealth creation, poverty alleviation, and long-term peace building. It should combine both national development and local development. It should not only focus on infrastructure investments and industrial concessions. The local and informal economy is an integral part of the Congolese reality involving a vibrant and growing group of actors that have emerged from the DRC's vast informal and artisanal sector. This sector generates employment and supports inclusive growth and peace building. Encouraging and transforming it will eventually raise incomes, skills, increase and widen the domestic market, consequently leading to the transformation of the Congolese economy.

These forms of social enterprises and collective action have the potential to become a major foundation for national economic development. Most of these activities are found across natural resource-based sectors of agriculture, mining, forestry, fisheries, and water. They were created by Congolese people who used their resources to deal pragmatically with their own development priorities as the state was collapsing. Such social enterprises must be supported at the level of public policies and improved access to resources including micro finance.

In view of the enormous size of the DRC, regional disparities, variable security conditions, internal geographic isolation, and limited government reach, practical action projects and programs should be designed and implemented using an area-based approach. The underlying premise of this strategy is that in determining the best course of action, the geographic area and its specific set of inter-related problems is generally a more appropriate entry point than a single issue or sector. The spatial scale for intervention can be set at the territorial-administrative level (province, district, urban area, and/or by physical or geographical region). The area-based approach can better inform national macro and sectoral policies and programs and can be appropriately integrated into the provincial and national programs. National, regional, and international integration and self-sustaining integrated development will eventually be achieved through the building of an integrated nationwide infrastructure. Through such zonal, sectoral, and grassroots development, the transformation of the Congolese economy will become possible and sustainable. This necessitates effective decentralization of authority and resources such that while the national government concentrates largely on the nationwide programs, the local and provincial governments have powers and substantial resources to focus on the basic needs of the population in their areas of jurisdiction.

Notes

1 The date for this valuation is not always given. The value of these resources should be rising over time as they appreciate or as the value of the dollar changes over time.
2 The neighbors of the DRC are Angola, Burundi, Central African Republic (CAR), Congo Republic, Rwanda, South Sudan, Tanzania, Uganda, and Zambia.
3 Ending the war in the DRC was accomplished through four incremental peace agreements: the Lusaka Ceasefire Agreement (1999), the Sun City Agreement (April 2002), the Pretoria Agreement (July 2002), and the Luanda Agreement (September 2002) that

ultimately contributed to the Global and Inclusive Agreement of December 2002 which finally ended the war. Even though these agreements did not effectively curb violence in many parts of the DRC, they served as instrumental pillars for the Global and Inclusive Agreement which led to the formation of a unified Transitional Government of the DRC in 2003. This agreement, however, did not succeed in ridding the DRC of violence, especially in the eastern parts of the country.

4 During the war periods, the informal economy which cuts across all sectors overtook the formal economy. An estimated 80–90 percent of the DRC's population was engaged in the informal sector. In economic value, this parallel economy was estimated to be three times the size of the DRC's formal GDP. In the conflict areas informal war economy took over with militarized natural resources exploitation and trade lying beyond the purview of state administrative institutions.

5 For details, see discussion in this chapter on infrastructure development.

6 In spite of increasing the positive impact of the mining industry on the local population, the mining companies and even the Congolese government are doing the opposite. The Congolese central government refuses or reduces the transfer of the amount of royalty revenues due to the provincial and local governments. The mining companies through transfer pricing and other corporate murky ways underestimate or hide their true profits from the tax authorities.

7 Data on DRC trade were not available at the same source as for Ethiopia, Nigeria, and South Africa. Hence, many sources were consulted to piece together the DRC trade data. They included: IMF (2005–2016); World Bank, *Development Indicators*; UNECA, African Statistical Yearbook, (2005–2016); https://atlas.media.mit.edu/en/profile/country/cod/ (Accessed February 22, 2017).

8 The central bank (BCC) does not provide figures for industrial diamond production as diamond production is dominated by artisanal and small-scale miners in the DRC, which are together classified as artisanal. Consequently, some diamond production will be considered as artisanal by the BCC, but classified as industrial by the USGS, albeit through numerous, small-scale "industrial" mines. This variation in category definitions explains the large industrial diamond production figures according to the USGS.

9 The existing borders of African countries were drawn up by European governments in their Berlin Conference of 1884/85 when they carved up Africa into their various spheres of influence and colonies.

10 The presence of oil in the region has been known for a long time. Shell explored the Ugandan side of Lake Albert in 1938 and the Congolese side between 1952 and 1954. Interest in the lake only revived with the signature of the first exploration contract in 1997 between the Ugandan Government and Heritage Oil and the arrival of the Tullow Oil Company in 2006 in the DRC.

11 However, they also recognized that the 3 February 1915 agreement between Belgium and the UK was insufficiently precise to determine the border on Lake Albert. Hence, the accords provided for the creation of a joint commission to determine the exact border on the lake, demilitarize the disputed area and establish a joint administration for Rukwanzi Island.

Bibliography

African Development Bank (AfDB). 2013. *Democratic Republic of Congo: 2013–2017 Country Strategy Paper (Translated from French)*. Abidjan: AfDB.

———. 2012. *Democratic Republic of Congo*. www.africaneconomicoutlook.org (Accessed October 8, 2016).

Bikalemesa, Muhaise. 2014. "Investment Opportunities in Democratic Republic of Congo." January 27. http://afkinsider.com/103587/drc-is-the-largest-market-in-sub-saharan-africa-for-south-african-products/#sthash.iIzsJg7J.dpuf (Accessed October 8, 2016).

The Carter Center. 2017. *Improving Governance of Revenues from the Mining Industry: Cross-Cutting Lessons from Fiscal and Para-Fiscal Analyses of Five Mining Projects in the D.R. Congo*. Kinshasa: Ministry of Planning, February.

Davis, J. Martyn. 2008. "China and the Democratic Republic of Congo: Partners in Development?" *The China Monitor*, no. 34 (October).

De Koning, Ruben. 2009. *Artisanal Mining and Post Conflict Reconstruction in the Democratic Republic of Congo*. Stockholm: International Peace Research Institute (SIPRI), October.

Delvaux, Damien and Max Fernandez-Alonso. 2015. "Petroleum Potential of the Congo Basin." In *Geology and Resource Potential of the Congo Basin*, eds. Maraten J. de Wit, Francois Guillocheau and Miciel C. J. de Wit. Brussels: Royal Museum for Central Africa: 371–91.

Democratic Republic of the Congo. 2016. *The Mining Law Review-Edition 5 Mining: Democratic Republic of the Congo*, December.

———. 2015. *REDD+ Investment Plan (2015–2020)*.

———. 2011a. *Growth and Poverty Reduction Strategy Document: Priority Action Plan*. Kinshasa: Ministry of Planning.

———. 2011b. *Growth and Poverty Reduction Strategy Paper [GPRSP 2]*. Kinshasa: Ministry of Planning, October.

———. 2011c. *Growth and Poverty Reduction Strategy Document*. Kinshasa: Ministry of Planning. www.imf.org/external/pubs/ft/scr/2013/cr13226.pdf (Accessed October 8, 2017).

———. 2003. *Law No. 007/2002 of July 11, 2002 Relating to the Mining Code Decree No 038 / 2003 of 26 March; Mining Regulation*.

European Forest Institute. 2015. *REDD+ Investment Plan (2015–2020)*. Barcelona, Joensuu, and Kuala Lumpur: EUREDD Facility.

Fall, Latsoucabe. 2010. "Harnessing the Hydropower Potential in Africa: What Should Be the Place and Role of Grand Inga Hydropower Project?" *XXIst World Congress*, Montreal, Canada, September 12–16.

Herdeschee, Johannes, Kai-Alexander Kaiser, and Daniel Mukoko Samba. 2012. *Resilience of an African Giant: Boosting Growth and Development in the Democratic Republic of Congo*. Washington, DC: World Bank.

International Crisis Group (ICG). 2012. "Black Gold in the Congo: Threat to Stability or Development Opportunity?" *Crisis Group Africa Report N°188 (Translation from French)*. Kinshasa; Nairobi; Brussels, July 11.

International Monetary Fund (IMF). 2015. "Democratic Republic of the Congo: Selected Issues." *IMF Country Report No. 15/281*, October.

———. 2014. "Financial Sector Stability Report, Democratic Republic of the Congo." *IMF Country Report No. 14/315*.

———. 2010. *Democratic Republic of the Congo: Enhanced Initiative for Heavily Indebted Poor Countries-Completion Point Document and Multilateral Debt Relief Initiative Paper*. Washington, DC: IMF.

———. 2007. *Democratic Republic of the Congo: Poverty Reduction and Growth Strategy Paper*. Washington, DC: International Monetary Fund. www.imf.org/external/pubs/ft/scr/2007/cr07330.pdf (Accessed October 9, 2017).

———. 2005–2016. *Direction of Trade Statistics Yearbook*. Washington, D.C.: IMF.

Kabemba, Claude. 2016. "China-Democratic Republic of Congo Relations: From a Beneficial to a Developmental Cooperation." *African Studies Quarterly* 16, nos. 3–4 (December). www.africa.ufl.edu/asq/v16/v16i3-4a6.pdf (Accessed April 8, 2018).

Pact. 2010. *Promise Study: Artisanal Mining in the Democratic Republic of Congo*, June.

Tegenfeld, Mark and Michael Trueblood. 2012. *The Democratic Republic of Congo: An Economic Growth Diagnostic Study*. Kinshasa: USAID.

United Nations Environment Program (UNEP). 2011. *The Democratic Republic of the Congo: Post-Conflict Environmental Assessment; Synthesis for Policy Maker*. Nairobi: UNEP.

United States Agency for International Development (USAID). 2014. *Country Development Cooperation Strategy: Democratic Republic of the Congo 2014–2019*. Washington, D.C.: USAID.

———. 2011. *Central Africa Regional Program for the Environment (CARPE): Regional Development Cooperation Strategy 2012–2020*. http://pdf.usaid.gov/pdf_docs/PDACT704.pdf (Accessed October 22, 2017).

US Geological Survey (USGS). 2013. *Mineral Commodity Summaries*. Washington, DC: U. S. Department of Interior.

World Bank. 2013. *Country Assistance Strategy for the Democratic Republic of Congo for the Period FY2013-FY 2016*. Washington, D. C.: World Bank.

World Wide Fund for Nature and World Bank Global Alliance. 2007. *Forests in Post-Conflict Democratic Republic of Congo: Analysis of a Priority Agenda*. Jakarta, Indonesia: Center for International Forest Research.

World Trade Organization (WTO). 2010. *Trade Policy Review: Democratic Republic of Congo*. October. Geneva: WTO.

5 The Ethiopian economy

Introduction

From the beginning of the 2000s, Ethiopia has been one of the fastest growing economies in the world with growth averaging 11 percent per annum. Despite the 2015/16 drought, the worst in fifty years, Ethiopia was able to maintain positive growth at 8 percent in 2015/16. This was impressive compared to previous drought years which often resulted in economic contraction. The newly completed high-speed railway, the Addis Ababa–Djibouti Standard Gauge Railway, has significantly eased the country's trade logistics-related constraints. The government's increased focus on industrial parks and the increasing capacity in power generation, along with the completion of electric transmission lines to neighboring countries (Djibouti, Kenya, and Sudan), should improve export performance and increase growth. However, the political leaders should address political dissatisfaction as this can have serious negative effects on the country's economic progress. On the other hand, the addressing of political grievances should not be done at the expense of sacrificing the economic gains of the recent past.

The performance of the export sector and the current account balance, however, has been weak. The chronic current account deficit (including official transfers) remained high in 2015/16 at 10.4 percent of GDP due to the large imbalance in import and export of goods and services. Low commodity prices led to a decline in the value of exports of goods and services by 4.1 percent in 2015/16. Export of goods contracted significantly over 2015 to 2016, owing to declining export prices and a supply shock from drought, which meant foregone agriculture output and exports.

According to the World Bank (2016), Ethiopia should (i) encourage firm creation and growth that creates jobs for non-graduates with a special focus on service and manufacturing sector growth; (ii) increase labor productivity in the low-skill segment by addressing constraints faced by firms in accessing capital (financial and physical) to ensure that the labor productivity increases and wages can rise; (iii) invest further in job and technical training programs to build the skills of those in the job market, both for low-skilled workers and at higher levels of education in order to increase their productivity; (iv) introduce targeted urban safety nets and labor market programs to invest in skills of low-skilled employees and the unemployed and provide financial support to enable their job search; and (v) enhance the use of ICT to provide information on job vacancies throughout Addis Ababa and reduce the cost of job search (World Bank 2016).[1]

Macroeconomic performance and economic structure

Ethiopia's overall development strategy is to bring about structural changes in the country's economy through industrial development by increasing the share of industry as percentage of GDP from the 2013 level of 13 percent to 27 percent by 2025. During the same period, the share of manufacturing in GDP is to be increased from 5 percent to 17 percent; agriculture is to decrease from 38 percent to 33 percent; and the share of services will decrease from 46 percent to 40 percent. The economy is to grow at about 10 percent throughout the period. Poverty (headcount) is targeted to decrease from 24.4 to 11.1 percent. The strategy also focuses on promoting rapid growth of employment and exports.[2]

The specific strategic objectives set for the manufacturing sector include further expansion and development of the existing manufacturing priority sectors; diversification of the manufacturing sector to new sectors; increase of public, private, and foreign investment; and development and establishment of industrial zones and cities. The key implementation strategies are to include ensuring a conducive business environment; availing competent human resource and quality industrial inputs; developing and diversifying local, regional, and global markets; enhancing technology transfer; and developing and providing institutional support.

Growth was concentrated in services and agriculture on the supply side and private consumption and investment on the demand side. While agriculture was the main economic sector at the beginning of the period, the services sector gradually took over and was complemented by a construction boom. Out of the average annual growth rate of 10.9 percent in 2004–2014, services contributed by 5.4 percent, agriculture 3.6 percent, and industry 1.7 percent. Private consumption contributed to most growth on the demand side with public investment becoming increasingly important.

While capital and labor accumulation were important for growth, Ethiopia stands out from other non–resource-rich fast-growing countries by its very high total factor productivity growth of 3.4 percent per year. Ethiopia's strong commitment to agricultural development is noteworthy as reflected by high government spending and the world's biggest contingent of agricultural extension workers.

Despite low domestic savings and taxes, Ethiopia was able to finance high public investment by keeping government consumption low to finance budgetary public infrastructure investment as well as tapping external concessional and non-concessional financing. Policy kept interest rates low and directed the bulk of credit towards public infrastructure. Monetary expansion, including direct Central Bank budget financing, earned the government substantial seigniorage revenues.

The government continued to intervene in most sectors of the economy. Indeed, apart from market-oriented reforms implemented during the 1990s, structural economic reforms have been absent from Ethiopia's growth strategy in part because of initial economic success. Although it applied the developmental state model, Ethiopia focused on agriculture instead of manufacturing as in the case of East Asia countries. This was appropriate to the domestic situation as it reduces poverty and raises the size of the national market as agriculture is the largest sector in terms of both GDP and employment, and hence income.

The strong contribution of infrastructure investment arises from a substantial physical infrastructure expansion. Ethiopia registered very rapid infrastructure development in the 2000s. Public investment was concentrated in providing basic infrastructure such as energy, roads, and telecommunications. In 2016, a modern and fast railway was opened linking Ethiopia to the Port of Djibouti. Public infrastructure investment, facilitated partly by restrained government consumption, was the key structural driver of growth. The government deliberately emphasized capital spending over consumption within its budget. This shift was facilitated by declining military spending following the 1998–2000 war with Eritrea giving rise to a "peace dividend." "*Getting infrastructure right*" at the early stage of development has gone a long way in supporting broad growth in Ethiopia.

Ethiopia's growth acceleration was also supported by positive demographic effects. The rapid economic growth coincided with a marked increase in the share of the working-age population, giving a positive boost to labor supply. But for the country to fully reap these benefits it must equip workers with marketable skills to be attractive to prospective employers. Expansion of secondary education and increased openness to international trade also supported growth.

As a result of the sustained growth of GDP and per capita income, poverty declined substantially from 55.3 percent in 2000 to 33.5 percent in 2011. The country achieved most of the Millennium Development Goals.

The remarkable economic performance of Ethiopia in the 2000s is a cumulative consequence of four public development programs that started in 2002/03 with the launching of Ethiopia's Sustainable Development and Poverty Reduction Program (SDPRP, 2002/03–2004/05). The Sustainable Development and Poverty Reduction Program (SDPRP) was Ethiopia's first explicit development program to prioritize poverty reduction. The targeted high rate of growth of 11 percent was a means to poverty reduction. However, due to drought, a negative growth rate of 3.3 percent was experienced in the first year of the plan. This was followed by positive performance of 11.9 percent and 10.6 percent during the subsequent two years, 2003/04 and 2004/05, respectively. Consequently, the growth rate during the whole three-year plan period averaged 6.4 percent. The agricultural sector grew by 17.3 percent in 2003/04 and 13 percent in 2004/05, after declining by 11.4 percent in 2002/03. The high growth rate of

Table 5.1 Macroeconomic performance (percent in real terms)

Item	2001–05	2002–06	2003–07	2004–08	2005–09	2006–10	2007–11	2008–12	2009–13	2010–14	2011–15
GDP Growth	5.8	6.1	8.1	11.8	10.4	10.5	11.0	10.4	10.1	10.2	10.1
Per Capita GDP Growth	2.9	3.2	5.3	9.2	7.9	8.2	9.0	8.5	8.4	8.4	8.4
Consumer Prices (2000 = 100)	3.6	5.1	10.0	18.0	15.9	16.1	22.3	23.7	16.4	16.2	16.6
Gross Investment	20.3	20.7	20.8	22.7	21.1	21.9	24.2	26.2	29.1	31.8	35.5
Gross Domestic Savings	3.4	3.9	8.1	21.2	13.2	17.6	23.2	24.7	26.8	29.5	29.2
Fiscal Balance (Including Grants)	–6.1	–5.7	–4.6	–3.5	–3.3	–2.6	–2.1	–7.9	–1.4	–1.7	–2.0
Fiscal Balance (Excluding Grants)	–11.1	–10.7	–4.1	–7.7	–7.6	–6.7	–5.9	–5.8	–4.2	–3.9	–3.6
Government Revenue (Excluding Grants)	17.6	17.2	15.7	14.2	13.9	13.5	12.8	13.0	13.5	13.9	14.1
Government Expenditure	28.6	27.9	25.3	21.9	21.5	20.2	18.7	17.9	17.6	17.8	17.7

Source: IMF:Various years. Regional Economic Outlook: Sub-Saharan Africa. Five-year moving averages calculated from IMF annual data.

agriculture was attributed to both good weather and the provision of adequate supply of agricultural inputs. During 2003/04 to 2004/05, the industrial sector registered 10.0 percent and 8.1 percent growth rate, and distribution and service sectors registered 7.3 percent and 8.4 percent.

Policy measures undertaken included income tax streamlining and closing of loopholes, improving the incentive system, strengthening tax administration, overhauling the income tax law and regulations, introducing a broad-based Value Added Tax (VAT), and rationalizing tariff rates. As a result, tax revenue increased to 13.7 percent of GDP in 2004/05 from nearly 12 percent in 2002/03. External resource flows increased from $693.6 million in 2002/03 to $937.5 million and $1,055.9 million in the fiscal years 2003/04 and 2004/05, respectively.

Utilization of resources, mainly on infrastructure and human resources development, greatly contributed to the achievement of growth and macro-economic stability. Government expenditure during the plan years registered substantial increase. The main reason being the increased expenditure allocated for capital expenditure and pro-poor sectors (agriculture and food security, education, health, HIV/AIDS, and provision of clean water supply) as well as on infrastructure development, particularly in road construction. Total government spending on poverty-oriented sectors increased to 56.5 percent in 2004/05 from 43.0 percent in 2001/02.

Exports increased substantially owing to both increase in volume and the prices of major exports. In 2003/04 and 2004/05, the total value of exports grew by 25.0 percent and 41.6 percent, respectively. Imports also surged in 2004/05, reflecting a general rise in private sector investment and consumption demand, and government spending on capacity building and poverty-reduction projects, in addition to escalating prices of basic imports such as fuel and construction materials. The unparalleled increase in imports of goods led to widening of the trade deficit. The external current account deficit widened to 15.3 percent of GDP in 2004/05 from 11.3 percent in 2003/04. However, the increase in inflows of long-term official loans served as a cushion, protecting the country's reserves from declining. At the end of 2004/05, foreign exchange reserves stood at 4.5 months of import coverage.

The *Agricultural Development-Led Industrialization (ADLI) Strategy* was among the pillars of the SDPRP. At the end of 2004/05, a total of 23,378 Development Agents (DAs) were trained through the agricultural Technical Vocational Education and Training (TVET) initiative, which was designed to train DAs and farmers in leadership skills. A total of 5,493 Farmers Training Centers (FTCs) were constructed. Assisted by DAs, several peasant farmers were trained and encouraged to shift to small-scale modern farming practices. Improved extension package services were implemented. The National Food Security Program was launched, aimed at attaining food security for five million chronically food insecure people and another ten million who were badly affected by food shortages in drought years. A public works program to employ the poor in building roads and other infrastructure during difficult times was implemented as well as free distributions of food to orphans, the elderly, the disabled, and others who could not work. The size of irrigated land and the number of farmers using irrigation increased significantly. Support to Micro-finance Institutions (MFIs) as well as efforts to intensify and improve financial services in rural areas were launched. Development of livestock through improved breeds, forage development, and veterinary service were expanded. Other programs carried out included the implementation of the national environmental program that initiated the establishment of regional environmental agencies and institutions by developing the necessary guidelines and laws that promote proper land use and soil conservation, water resource management, and forest resource management as well as wildlife and biodiversity utilization and conservation.

As for industrial development, which is the driving force for the overall development of the economy, some progress was achieved. The Industrial Development Strategy was also launched in 2002. A conducive environment was created to encourage private and foreign investment by streamlining bureaucratic procedures such as customs clearance within hours and removing institutional bottlenecks, increasing the supply of affordable land, strengthening finance and banking services, quality management, and improving the market for businesses. Consequently, there was significant growth in services, trade, industry, and construction during the SDPRP. For instance, there was the investment of 2.6 billion Birr (over $300 million) in new horticulture businesses that supplied the European market. This created many new jobs for the rural poor, especially for women, as well as generating new export earnings valued at over $8 million during 2004/05. The annual growth of value added for private medium and large-scale manufacturing industries averaged about 21 percent, while that of the public sector averaged 7 percent. The share of the private sector in the value added of medium and large-scale manufacturing increased from 27.4 percent in 2002/03 to 29.9 percent in 2003/04.

Consequently, the Plan for Accelerated and Sustained Development to End Poverty (PASDEP), (2005/06–2009/10), was to focus on strengthening the small-scale manufacturing enterprises, as they are the foundation for the establishment and intensification of medium and large-scale industries, in addition to opening the opportunity for employment generation in the non-agricultural sector. These industries would also serve as alternative or additional income source for those involved in agriculture. Achievements in the areas of textile and garment, metal and woodwork, food processing, construction work, and municipality services were cited as best examples.

The main objective of the PASDEP was to lay out the directions for accelerated, sustained, and people-centered economic development as well as, at the minimum, pave the groundwork for the attainment of the Millennium Development Goals (MDGs) by 2015. The PASDEP represented the second phase of the Poverty Reduction Strategy Program (PRSP) process, which was begun under the SDPRP program period. The PASDEP carried forward important strategic directions pursued under the SDPRP in infrastructure, human development, rural development, food security, and capacity building. But new directions were also embodied in the PASDEP; foremost among which included emphasis on greater commercialization of agriculture and enhancing private sector development, industry, urban development, and a scaling up of efforts to achieve the Millennium Development Goals (MDGs). The pillars of the plan included a massive push to accelerate growth; creating a balance between economic development and population growth; unleashing the potentials of Ethiopia's women; strengthening the infrastructure backbone of the country; strengthening human resources development; managing risk and volatility; and creating employment opportunities.

The government established two alternative growth scenarios under PAS-DEP. The first scenario (*the base case*) was established in line with the requirements of MDGs, while the second scenario (*the high case*) which is equivalent to the "*MDGs Plus*" scenario was based on the requirements of the country's vision. In the base case scenario, 7 percent annual average real GDP growth was targeted while the target in the higher case scenario was set at an average real GDP growth of 10 percent. The performance achieved in the five years of PAS-DEP implementation was 11 percent of GDP growth. The base case for agricultural growth was 6.0 percent, while the high case target was 6.4 percent. The achieved rate for the sector was 8.0 percent. The corresponding growth rates for industry were 11.0 percent, 18.0 percent, and 10.0 percent, respectively. Services were to grow by 7.0 percent and 10.3 percent, but actually grew at 14.6 percent.

The high growth rates were achieved due to a combination of emphasis on diversification and commercialization of small-scale agriculture, expansion of non-agricultural production in services and industry, capacity building and good governance, off-farm employment especially through small enterprises, and massive investment in infrastructure. The major challenges encountered during the implementation of the PASDEP included high inflationary pressure; inadequate capacity for domestic revenue collection; and low level of domestic savings to support the huge demand of the country's investment for accelerating growth and development in the process to eradicate poverty. Delayed rains in parts of the country led to a serious look into expansion of small-, medium-, and large-scale irrigation programs.

The first Growth and Transformation Plan (GTPI), (2010/11–2014/15), was articulated through four overarching objectives: (i) maintaining at least an average real GDP growth rate of 11 percent per annum and attaining the Millennium Development Goals (MDGs) by 2014/15; (ii) expanding access and ensuring the qualities of education and health services and achieve MDGs in the social sectors; (iii) establishing conditions for sustainable nation building through the creation of stable democratic and developmental state; and (iv) ensuring the sustainability of growth through maintaining macroeconomic stability. The share of gross domestic saving (GDS) in GDP was to be increased to 15 percent and that of export to 22.5 percent.

Real GDP growth averaged 10.1 percent per annum during the period of GTPI implementation, a one percentage point shortfall from the base case scenario of an 11 percent target. Remarkable achievements were also made in infrastructure development, social development, and capacity building. However, even though significant improvements were made in domestic saving and investment, the gap between domestic saving and investment widened as investment grew faster than savings. Similarly, the trade deficit widened during the GTPI implementation period. The share of merchandise imports bill financed by merchandize export earnings declined over the period. Notwithstanding the encouraging achievements registered in the manufacturing subsector, performance fell short of the targets set in the plan.

The major objective of the GTP II (2015/16–2019/20) is to serve as a springboard towards realizing Ethiopia's national vision of becoming a lower middle-income country by 2025, through sustaining rapid, broad-based and inclusive economic growth. This will accelerate economic transformation through enhancing productivity of agriculture and manufacturing, significant shift in export development, improving quality of production, and stimulating competition in the economy. The focus of the expansion of industrial development will be on light manufacturing.

The following are the specific objectives of GTPII: (i) achieve an annual average real GDP growth rate of 11 percent within a stable macroeconomic environment, while pursuing comprehensive measures towards narrowing the saving-investment gap and bridging the widening trade deficit; (ii) develop the domestic engineering and fabrication capacity and improve productivity, quality, and competitiveness of agriculture and manufacturing to speed up structural transformation; (iii) further solidify the ongoing public mobilization and organized participation to ensure the public become both owners and beneficiaries from development outcomes; and (iv) deepen the hegemony of developmental political economy by strengthening a stable democratic developmental state.

The following measures were to be pursued to realize the objectives of GTPII. Agriculture will remain the main driver of the rapid and inclusive economic growth and development. Besides promoting the productivity and quality of staple food crops production, special attention will also be given to high-value crops, industrial inputs, and export commodities. Irrigation-based agriculture, horticulture, fruits and vegetables, livestock and fisheries development is being promoted. Schemes have been devised to provide support to smallholder farmers such as peasants and pastoralists. Joint participation of educated young farmers and private investors in the sector is being facilitated. Hence, addressing constraints entrenched in the agricultural development and marketing systems will be given utmost emphasis and priority.

A new vision has been set to render the country a global leader in light manufacturing. Special emphasis is being given to the development of an export-oriented manufacturing industry. Clear targets are set to increase efficiency, and particular attention is given to the quality, productivity, and competitiveness of the agricultural, manufacturing, and modern tradable service sectors. For this, the implementation of *kaizen* and benchmarking tools, which started during GTP I will be strengthened and scaled up.[3]

The two imbalances of investment-saving and export-imports are to be seriously addressed. Thus, clear targets have been set to mobilize domestic resources and aggressively pursue the efforts of domestic resource mobilization, and rigorous efforts are being made to promote export through increased investment in expanding productive capacity, increased productivity gains, quality, and better competition in the external markets.

Strategic policy framework has been formulated which aims to properly manage and administer the construction industry and development projects with enhanced project planning and management capacity in the sector. Particular attention is to be given to proper management of the construction and development of mega public projects, such as dams, roads, irrigation developments, etc. to ensure their completion within the specified time, standard, and allocated resources during GTP II.

Due emphasis will be given to the promotion of domestic private sector development in the manufacturing industry. This initiative will be enhanced and supported through engaging the private sector in continuous dialogue with the government, providing incentive packages such as guidance and provision of institutional and regulatory support, access to credit, etc. Existing domestic small manufacturing enterprises will be encouraged to grow and transition to medium- and large-scale manufacturing enterprises by providing all-round support and nurturing their entrepreneurship and business management capabilities; supporting and enhancing the capacity and capability of local construction industry enterprises to encourage them in producing construction inputs and using locally produced inputs; and value addition to support import substitution to ensure the transformation of the domestic private sector. In addition, investors involved in the service sector (wholesale trade and other business) will be encouraged and provided with incentive packages (provision of land, logistics, credit, etc.) to invest in manufacturing. Furthermore, particular attention will be given to create the linkages between local and foreign enterprises to facilitate knowledge and technology transfer.

Due emphasis will also be given to human capital capacity development supported by technology and innovation to sustain rapid economic growth. Particular emphasis will be given to ascertaining quality and access to social services such as education and health thereby creating an educated, healthy, competent, motivated, and innovative work force.

Emphasis is given to building a climate-resilient green economy in the context of sustainable development. Accordingly, enhanced efforts will be made in improving crop and livestock productivity to ensure food security through reducing emissions; protecting forests and re-afforestation including carbon stocks; expanding electricity generation from renewable sources; and leapfrogging to energy efficient technologies in transport, industry, and construction.

The existing dominant rent seeking political economy will be transformed to ensure the hegemony of developmental political economy is a top priority. Hence, developmental attitudes are to be strengthened while draining the root sources of rent seeking, controlling corruption, and lack of good governance. An enabling environment will be created to ensure society's involvement with a sense of ownership, in activities that concern strengthening a developmental mindset.

International trade

The growth acceleration was also supported by a relatively favorable external environment. Exports quadrupled in nominal terms, while volumes doubled, reflecting a substantial positive commodity price effect and significant increases in agricultural output.

Imports by far exceeded exports. The country experienced trade deficit throughout the whole period. The terms of trade deteriorated until 2009 when they slightly improved. The reserve position of the country declined over time from over four to two months of imports. Drought also affects the export and import position of the country as most of the exports are farm products. In 2015, Ethiopia's total exports amounted to $5.0 billion, while imports amounted to $25.8 billion, resulting in a huge trade deficit of $20.8 billion. Foreign aid filled most of the gap. The ten top exports were coffee and spices (20.9%), vegetables (17.95%), live plants (14.8%), oil and mineral fuels (13.8%), oil seeds (10.6%), live animals (6.6%), precious stones and metals (3.5%), meat (2.1%), hides and leather (2.0%), knit apparel (1.0%), and others (7.2%).

The ten leading imports in 2015 were industrial machinery (13.3%), electrical machinery (12.9%), oil and mineral fuels (9.9%), motor vehicles and parts (9.6%), plastics (5.4%), iron and steel articles (4.8%), fats and oils (4.4%), iron and steel (4.2%), cereals (3.0%), pharmaceuticals (2.7%), and others (29.9%).[4]

The ten top destinations of Ethiopian exports in 2015 took about 73.4 percent of the country's total exports. Somalia was Ethiopia's leading export market in 2015, taking about 13.4 percent of the country's exports. This was followed by Kuwait (12.8%), the Netherlands (10.7%), China (7.5%), Saudi Arabia (7.1%), Germany (6.4%), the United States (5.5%), Djibouti (4.3%), Switzerland (3.2%), the United Arab Emirates (2.5%), and others (26.6%).

The ten leading sources of imports for Ethiopia in 2015 were China (36.0%), Kuwait (7.4%), India (6.8%), the United States (5.3%), Japan (4.6%), Sweden (3.6%), Italy (3.2%), Turkey (3.1%), Saudi Arabia (3.0%), Indonesia (2.4%), and the rest of the world (24.7%).

The manufacturing sector

Marked growth in the Ethiopian manufacturing subsector began in the early 2000s as a result of conscious industrialization policy. The ADLI was launched in 1994. Between 2007 and 2011, the Ethiopian manufacturing sector grew strongly at the average rate of 12.9 percent. The government has been promoting foreign investment, supplying inputs, improving customs services, and foreign trade. However, the sector is still dominated by light manufacturing and

Table 5.2 The performance of the external sector (percent of GDP in real terms)

Item	2001–05	2002–06	2003–07	2004–08	2005–09	2006–10	2007–11	2008–12	2009–13	2010–14	2011–15
Export of Goods and Services	14.9	15.1	15.0	13.7	13.4	13.3	13.8	14.0	14.1	14.4	13.2
Imports of Goods and Services	31.7	34.1	35.0	33.1	34.4	33.3	32.3	32.3	31.8	32.2	31.9
Balance of Trade (Goods only)	–19.2	–21.2	–9.5	–20.9	2.5	15.4	6.7	–5.1	–16.6	–17.3	–18.4
Current Account (Including Grants)	–4.1	–5.5	–8.6	–5.4	–12.9	–11.8	–10.2	–7.5	–4.6	–4.9	–7.2
Terms of Trade (Index: 2000 = 100)	80.0	79.9	71.7	45.8	65.9	72.4	82.6	97.3	107.7	115.6	107.1
Reserves (months of Imports of Goods and Services)	4.7	4.2	3.6	2.2	2.1	1.8	1.9	1.9	2.1	2.0	2.0

Source: IMF, Regional Economic Outlook: Sub-Saharan Africa (various years). Five-year moving averages calculated from IMF annual data.

agro-processing with products mainly consisting of leather and leather products, textiles and garments, chemical and pharmaceutical products, and processed agricultural products. The government planned the country to export more than $1 billion worth of apparel by 2016.

Furthermore, the government offered tax breaks and competitive interest rates to the manufacturing subsector. As a result, some large foreign firms have started sourcing clothes from Ethiopia (for example, clothing megabrand H &M, Tesco, and Walmart). With rising cost of labor in the industrializing Asian countries, low labor costs in Ethiopia make it competitive with Asian manufacturers. Ethiopia's climate is favorable for growing cotton and the closer Suez Canal to Europe makes the country's accessibility to large market easier. Through the Africa Growth Opportunity Act (AGOA), Ethiopian exports have easy access to the huge United States market. Ethiopia's recent massive investment in hydroelectric power provides abundant and cheaper energy for industry. The country's recent expansion of higher education and vocational and technical education should soon be able to supply large numbers of managerial and technical workers.

Ethiopia already has an industrialization strategy in place. The country is endowed with a large number of natural resources that can provide valuable inputs for light manufacturing industries that serve both domestic and export markets. Among its abundant resources are a large cattle population and other livestock, whose hides and skins can be processed into leather and leather products; forests whose wood can be used in the furniture industry; cotton that can be used in the garments industry; and agricultural land and lakes that can provide inputs for agro-processing industries. The country also has abundant labor whose low costs offer it a comparative advantage in less-skilled labor-intensive sectors such as light manufacturing. Hence, Ethiopia has the potential to become globally competitive in large segments of light manufacturing such as apparel, leather products, and agribusiness that could create millions of productive jobs given its low wages that can be enhanced with high labor productivity. Even if input prices have been high, they can be reduced through development of agriculture, forestry, and the livestock sectors. Other important constraints are poor trade logistics and poor access to industrial land, finance, and skills, which particularly affect smaller firms. Policies to remove these constraints would include removing import tariffs on additional light manufacturing inputs, developing plug-and-play industrial parks, improving customs procedures, reducing transport costs, developing collateral markets, and deploying targeted technical training programs. These measures are already being undertaken.

SMEs and MLEs development

Particular emphasis is being given to the promotion of *small and micro enterprises (SMEs)* as well as supporting the development of *medium and large-scale enterprises (MLEs) industries.* The role of SMEs is important to stimulate economic growth, create employment opportunities, and reduce poverty. These enterprises have been booming in different towns and expected to produce industrial products that are competitive in local and international markets. They are also expected to play a crucial role in technology transfer. These industries helped to reduce the unemployment rate.

In the GTP1, the government allotted 1,015 million Birr in order to strengthen the capacity of SMEs and to solve their financial constraints. In addition, training has been offered for SMEs members in different thematic areas such as business management, entrepreneurship, technical, and vocational training. Moreover, 5,000 hectares of production area, 1,757 shades, and 46 buildings were constructed and offered for SMEs. In the last two years of the GTP1, the government strived to enable the medium and large-scale manufacturing industrial sector to play its role in assuring rapid and sustainable technological development so as to make the economy to be competent, resolve the shortage of foreign currency, and to support the progress of SMEs, and the agricultural sector.

With regard to enterprise capacity utilization, many firms claim that the first major reason for their low capacity utilization is inadequate and poor quality of raw materials. Because of this and many other factors, the contribution of the sector to GDP has remained at less than 5 percent for the last twenty years. The average cost of the ratio of imported to total consumed raw materials was 70 percent for chemical industries, 92 percent for rubber and plastics, 80 percent for basic iron and steel, 85 percent for fabricated metals, and 60 percent for paper. These challenges resulted in low local investment, low productivity, weak international competitiveness, weak technology transfer, low capacity utilization, high investment and production cost, and slow progress in the country's industrialization.

Industrial zones development

The Great Transformation Plan (GTP) also emphasizes the establishment of industrial zones in different parts of the country. Accordingly, the industrial zone development plan was designed and is being implemented. Infrastructure networks are being built in order to create market linkages for these zones. Supports are provided to establish industrial zones in different parts of the country. However, investors are not engaged as it was expected. The Ministry of Industry (MOI) has also signed part of a 1.2 billion Birr civil works agreement with 13 local contractors for the construction of Bole Lemi Industrial Park that has been inaugurated. In a similar manner, medium industrial zones have been established by a few regional states in the past few years, but their performance has not been according to the plan. The Ministry of Industry has also received 3,537 hectares of land at Addis Ababa, and other cities in different parts of the country.

In realizing Vision 2025, the Ethiopian Industrial Parks Development Corporation (IPDC) Board plans the development of a "world-class, specialized, sustainable, vertically integrated, export-driven and competitive industrial parks" (Tekle 2017). The Hawassa Industrial Park (HIP) exemplifies the strategy. Phase one of the massive Chinese-constructed Hawassa Industrial Park (HIP) was inaugurated in 2016. The park, featuring state-of-the-art, environmentally friendly technology was built by the Chinese Civil Engineering Construction Corporation (CCECC) at a cost of about $322 million. It covers an area of 1.3 million square meters, of which 300,000-meter square is factory shed build-up area. By early 2017, the park had attracted eighteen leading textile and garment companies from across the world including from the United States, China, and India. Also, eight domestic investors were selected, and necessary preparations finalized to facilitate their investment inside the park (IPDC 2018).

In 2016, there were about 10,000 employees in the Hawassa Park, but at full capacity, the park is planned to have around 60,000 employees. Some companies in the park have already started to export and when the park starts production at full capacity, Ethiopia will earn around one billion dollars every year from Hawassa Park alone. In 2017, Ethiopia was building a total of fifteen industrial parks across the country as part of its goal to emerge as Africa's manufacturing hub. The Industrial Zones and Cities are allocated countrywide with each region having at least one. Four of these parks, Mekelle, Kombelcha, Adama, and Dire Dawa parks, were to be inaugurated in September 2017 (www.ipdc. gov.et/index.php/en/).

The Ethiopian industrial classification divides the Ethiopian manufacturing sector into eleven main groups. Accordingly, 32 percent of them fall under the category of food products and beverages, 20 percent of them under engineering industries, and 19 percent of these industries are categorized under non-metallic products. According to the 2010/11 Central Statistics Agency (CSA) report, there were 2,170 medium and large-scale industries established in Ethiopia out of which more than 40 percent were located in Addis Ababa. The other regional states had the following share: 23 percent in Oromia, 11 percent in Amhara, 11 percent in SNNP, 9 percent in Tigray, 3.23 percent in Dire Dawa, 1.01 percent in Harari, 0.6 percent in Somali, 0.37 percent in Afar, 0.09 percent in Benshangul, and 0.05 percent in Gambella.[5]

Metal industry subsector performance

The metal products industry is a basic component of the capital goods industries. In Ethiopia, according to the CSA (2012), the total number of medium and large establishment in the sector was 194. Manufacturer of fabricated metal products, except machinery and equipment, contributed a share of 72.7 percent from total number of establishments in the metal sector whereas manufacture of basic iron and steel, manufacture of motor vehicles, trailers and semi-trailers and manufacture of machinery and equipment contributed 20.1, 4.1, and 3.1 percent respectively.

Ethiopia exported $41 million of steel products in 2009, while importing more than $350 million, an imbalance that points to the possibility that domestic products can at least partially replace imports in metal products, a sector with a fast-growing domestic market. Ethiopia's competitiveness in metal products is constrained by poor skills and high input costs because the steel is imported and subject to import tariffs. Informal micro firms dominate the metal products industry in Ethiopia. Reducing the cost of steel and providing technical training can speed up the development of this subsector

Ethiopia could develop a competitive domestic industry in metal products. Wages are low and productivity can be high. Many metal products are heavy and bulky, with a low value-to-weight ratio, making imports relatively expensive even with improved trade logistics. Iron ore deposits together with competitive sources of hydro-energy create the possibility that Ethiopia could launch a competitive domestic steel industry.

High import tariffs, compounded by poor trade logistics, are the main driver of the high price of imported steel. Small and medium enterprises cannot expand because of restrictions in acquiring formal finance and land. Investors see the potential for growth, but access to finance is a constraint on efforts to upgrade the industry. Lack of entrepreneurial and worker skills are other main constraints. Measures to improve the competitiveness of the metal industry would include reducing import tariff on steel, improving trade logistics, and the promotion of the exploration and development of domestic iron ore deposits.

Chemical and pharmaceutical subsector performance

These industries include basic chemicals, pharmaceuticals and medical equipment, paint and varnish, plastic and rubber, paper, pulp and printing, soap and detergent, cosmetics, glass, cement, and non-metal construction materials. According to the 2010/2011 CSA data, the total number of medium and large establishments in the sector was 712. In terms of regional distribution, Addis Ababa City Administration contributed 42.2 percent of the total number of establishments whereas Oromia and Tigray regions contributed 21.0 and 11.9 percent respectively.

Textile subsector performance

The textile subsector is one of the major sectors of the manufacturing industry in Ethiopia.

Textile manufacturing industry consists of both medium and large enterprises. The sector comprises of a small number of State-Owned Enterprises (SOEs) and a growing number of private sector participants at all levels. The main activities of these industries include spinning, fabric formulation, dyeing, finishing, and sewing. Ethiopia also has a cotton-based traditional handloom industry with a large number of traditional weavers.

The contribution of this sector in the country's foreign currency earning has significantly improved from year to year mainly due to market access to major industrial countries. The export performance has also increased from $11.1 million in 2005/06 to $84.6 million in 2011/12 (Dinh et al.). In the domestic market, the value generated by the sector has also showed an increasing trend.

Ethiopia has indigenous raw cotton and the potential to produce other natural fibers such as hemp, ramie, flax, linen, silk, and bamboo. In addition, there is a potential in silk production, though the current production is very low. On the other hand, the country entirely depends on imports for other textile raw materials such as synthetic fiber/yarn, wool, dyestuffs, chemicals and related accessories.

Ethiopia has an integrated textile supply chain that includes spinning, weaving, knitting, dyeing and finishing although they need modernization and expansion to attain better achievements in the future. The industry largely caters to the domestic market although it exports a small proportion of output to USA, European, and other African markets.

In terms of the domestic market, competition has become very tense due to the penetration of low-priced imported textile and clothing. In addition, the country's domestic trade environment is facing a number of challenges which include: low productivity of the industries; competition from illegal imports of textile and apparel; limited product mix, and low quality of products; expansion of used cloth trade throughout the country; and low purchasing power of majority of the population. All these challenges limit local demand.

The technology used in most textile and garment units in Ethiopia is at a basic or medium level. However, in the newly established clothing factories, equipment, and machineries are modern.

There are some spare parts and hand tool manufacturers who supply to the textile industry, and each factory has its own workshops that can produce some parts for its own use. Machineries used in the textile sector come mainly from suppliers in China, Italy, Germany, Japan, and South Korea.

Leather subsector performance

The leather subsector has three major industrial components. These are tanneries, footwear manufacturers, and leather products manufacturers. There are large- and medium-size plants in the formal sector and micro enterprises operating in the informal sector of the economy, particularly in footwear manufacturing. According to the CSA report of 2010/2011, among the total of 141 large and medium establishments, most of them (87) were found in Addis Ababa City Administration. During 2010/2011, the subsector created employment opportunity for 14,019 persons.

Following the adaption of *the agriculture-led and export-oriented industrial development strategy*, the government has focused on promoting value addition and encouraging the tanning industry to move towards producing finished leather goods. After January 2009, 150 percent tax had been levied on export of pickle and "wet blue" products in order to fulfil the value addition strategy of the subsector. The banning of pickle and wet blue products was helpful in shifting the finishing capacity of tanneries from these first stages of the material to crust and finished leather. Similarly, 150 percent tax had been levied on export of crust starting from December 2011. As a result of the value addition strategy, more factories managed to attain leather finishing capabilities resorting from crust leather to finished leather. The major import competition in this subsector is dominated by footwear products.

The main challenges of the leather industry include low off-take rates of live animals, and weak meat industry, weak linkage between the leather industry and agriculture, lack of chemicals, accessories and spare parts, low capabilities in product development, R&D, fashion, and design. Other constraints include scarcity of working capital, less productivity and capacity utilization; environmental challenges, infrastructural problems, transport and logistics constraints; and limited marketing capacity at factory levels.

Developing a competitive leather supply chain would position Ethiopia to become one of the leading global centers for producing quality leather goods as it has a huge livestock population. Due to good climatic and soil conditions, Ethiopian cattle produce some of the world's best leather. Ethiopia is Africa's leading cattle-producing country. The combination of ample supplies of high quality leather and competitive hydro-energy should enable the development of a world-class leather industry.

As with apparel, Ethiopian leather products have duty-free access to the EU and US markets. The most binding constraint is the shortage of quality processed leather. With development of the domestic leather industry, Ethiopia can be globally competitive.

The shortage of quality domestic processed leather results from a number of causes. As a result of poor disease control and weak veterinary services, only small pieces of skin are free of blemishes. This is largely the result of failure to control for a disease that causes skin blemishes and the domination of the livestock industry by farmers who own only a few animals and sell skins as a side business at best. Supply of quality processing of raw hides and skins should be improved.

The Leather Institute of Ethiopia has been established to improve product quality through enhancing entrepreneurial, managerial, and technical skills. Difficulties on the part of smaller firms accessing land, finance, and skills keep smaller firms in a low-productivity, low-quality trap, unable to upgrade technology or expand production. The government should pursue efforts to control cattle disease. When successful, these efforts will also benefit the dairy and meat-processing industries.

Providing technical assistance to improve entrepreneurial skills in product design and factory floor operations have helped to improve labor efficiency as well as the quality and price of exportable shoes. Developing plug-and-play industrial parks near to Djibouti and Addis Ababa can help to address the missing middle linkage and further improve trade logistics. The completion of the construction of the fast-electric standard-gauge railway between Djibouti and Ethiopia will tremendously benefit the development of the Ethiopian economy, including manufacturing.

Wood products manufacture

Ethiopia is reported to have the biggest bamboo endowment in Africa (Dinh, et al.). Fueled by strong domestic demand for wood construction materials and furniture, Ethiopia's wood products industry currently employs more than 40,000 workers, mostly in small, low-productivity informal firms producing low-quality products for the domestic market. The country could become competitive in wood products by providing technical training to entrepreneurs and workers, making access to industrial land and finance easier, and by facilitating the development of sustainable wood plantations to take advantage of the country's unique bamboo resources. However, the immediate opportunity in the wood product industry still lies in the fast-growing domestic market for domestic fuel, construction materials, and furniture. In the initial phase of manufacturing growth, this subsector's potential seems to lie in import replacement rather than in exports.

Labor productivity in the wood manufactures is very low, even in the larger firms. This is mainly due to the small scale of operations and low skills of managers and workers. The main constraints are lack of organized supplies of domestic Ethiopian wood; lack of entrepreneurial and worker skills; and difficulties in access to land and finance.

Competitiveness can be increased by facilitating access to land and financing for sustainable private wood plantations of fast-growing species on degraded land close to the main urban centers. This would improve the quality of wood and reduce its cost via economies of scale and lower transportation costs. Developing of plug-and-play industrial parks would help the better small and medium enterprises to access utilities, land, finance, and skills, with technical assistance programs for both owner-managers and workers. Improved trade logistics would reduce the cost of other inputs that may not be competitively produced in Ethiopia such as adhesives, varnish, and finishing oils.

Agro-processing sector performance

In 2011/12, within the manufacturing sector the share of agro-processing was around 20.2 percent, next to the leather and textile subsectors which had 44.1 percent and 33.0 percent shares respectively (GTPII). Two years after the GTP1, the export of agro-processing shifted to non-sugar products such as processed oilseeds, food, spices, honey, beverages, and other processed export products. Moreover, the export performance of meat and meat products increased from $26 million in 2009/10 to $78 million in 2011/12.

According to the 2010/11 CSA data, out of 686 food-processing companies about 482 were operating under capacity and 251 of them were facing shortage of raw materials. The level of capacity utilization in different agro-processing subsectors was grouped as: industry group with better capacity utilization (brewery and winery 101 percent, sugar 99.7 percent, malt and liquor 85 percent); industry group with moderate capacity utilization (edible oil and fats 53 percent, macaroni and spaghetti 42 percent, flour mills 40.4 percent); and industry group with least capacity utilization (meat, fruit, and vegetable 19 percent).

According to the CSA 2010/11 data, the agro-processing sector likely employed about 60,110 people both SMEs and large factories under government and private owned companies. The sector shows an increasing employment trend particularly in selected subsectors like food, bakery, grain milling, and malt sectors.

Agriculture and agribusiness

To unleash the potential of agribusiness, the government is transforming agriculture and reforming agricultural input and output markets. The Agricultural Transformation Agenda (ATA) aims are transforming the agricultural sector as the basis of *commodity-based industrialization*. This process will enhance the growth of the capital goods manufacturing subsector as domestic demand expands for various kinds of products as economic transformation considerably progresses.

As shown by the success of the Ethiopian coffee and cut-flower industries, the country's agribusiness potential is great for both the domestic and export markets. The country has great agricultural potential. Low wages combined with good labor productivity result in competitive wheat-milling processing costs. Exceptional and varied climatic and soil conditions for growing a variety of crops, including cotton, wheat, coffee, and fruits that are suitable for export, industrial processing, or both. It has the largest livestock population in Africa. It has large tracts of unused arable land and low yields on cultivated land. Proximity to large importers of food products, in the Gulf countries, provides a ready competitive market. The main constraints to competitiveness are high cost and low quality of agricultural inputs. The quality of milk is low due to undeveloped animal husbandry and transport conditions.

Various distortions are evident in the agricultural input and output markets. Shortages of high-yielding seeds due to inefficiencies in the seed production and distribution systems as well as delays in the certification of imported seeds result in unnecessarily low crop yields and therefore high unit costs, which diminishes the prospects for potentially viable development of downstream processing operations.

To unleash Ethiopia's potential for *commodity-based industrialization*, the policy interventions should aim to create incentives to improve productivity and ensure that farmers have access to technical assistance, land, and finance to make improvement. Promoting crossbreed cows and enabling the use of cattle as collateral would increase the incentives and financial means for farmers to access veterinary services. The establishment of plug-and-play industrial parks would help leading agribusiness enterprises to enter the industry and better-managed small and medium enterprises to access utilities, land, finance, and skills. But the greatest benefit to the subsector would come from the overall development of the agricultural sector.

Transforming Ethiopian agriculture

Ethiopia's agricultural sector has recorded remarkable rapid growth and was the major driver of poverty reduction. The sector is the biggest employer in Ethiopia, accounts for most merchandise exports, and is the second largest in terms of output, next to the service sector. The sector also contributed to most of the employment growth over the period of analysis. Although some labor has shifted out of agriculture, substantial shifts are likely to take a long time.

Agricultural output increases were driven by strong yields growth and increases in area cultivated. Yield growth averaged about 7 percent per year while area cultivated increased by 2.7 percent annually (EATA).[6] Increased adoptions of improved seeds and fertilizer played a major role in sustaining higher yields. While starting from a low base, these inputs more than doubled during the 2000s. Factor productivity growth averaged 2.3 percent per year.

The factors associated with agricultural production growth include extension services and farmer's education. Farmers that received extension visits, less remote households, and more educated farmers were more likely to adopt improved agricultural technologies. Recent agricultural growth is largely explained by high government spending on extension services, roads, and education as well as favorable price incentives.

Ethiopia has built up a large agricultural extension system, with one of the highest extension agent-to-farmer ratios in the world. Furthermore, there has been a significant improvement in access to markets. Improved access to education led to a significant decrease in illiteracy in rural areas. High international prices of export products as well as improving modern input-output ratios for local crops have led to better incentives. Other factors that played a role include good weather, better access to microfinance institutions in rural areas, and improved land tenure security. However, poor rains in Ethiopia such as during 2014 and 2015 continue to pose a major challenge to the country and the impact of climate change stresses the importance of continued investment in irrigation to reduce reliance on rain-fed production.

The significant performance of the Ethiopian agricultural sector, over the last two decades, has been largely a result of the government policy of ADLI Strategy. This strategy puts agriculture at the forefront of the country's development process. It provides an overarching plan for economic development on the basis of agricultural transformation for increased productivity, output, and product quality. This has led to increased employment, incomes, and investable surplus for the development of other sectors of the economy. As a consequence, Ethiopia has consistently met both of the African Union's Comprehensive Africa Agricultural Development Program (CAADP) targets of (i) increasing public investment in agriculture by ten percent by year 2008; and (ii) boosting agricultural production by an average annual growth rate of at least 6 percent by 2015 (NEPAD).[7] Ethiopia has been investing an average of 14.7 percent of government spending on the agriculture sector since 2003. There have also been considerable gains in increasing agricultural productivity since 2006/07.

As a result, overall agricultural production of cereals has increased by 45 percent, while average production levels per hectare have grown by 22 percent in the same period (EATA 2013/14).

Despite the dominance of traditional smallholder farmers in agriculture, a new type of dynamism began to emerge in Ethiopian agriculture from the beginning of the twenty-first century. Productivity and output have consistently grown at near double-digit rates. Proactively including women has had and will continue to have significant impact on household nutritional status and increased women's contribution to the country's overall development.[8] Increased agricultural productivity and commercialization also provide employment opportunities for Ethiopia's youth as well as drive industrialization and create export growth. Consequently, accelerating agricultural growth in Ethiopia has had wide-ranging impacts beyond smallholder farmers and rural development.

Progress has been particularly more remarkable for the three main crops of *tef*, wheat, and maize, initially prioritized by the Agricultural Transformation Agenda. This has been made possible by close coordination between federal and regional public sector partners, extending to local-level cooperative promotion agencies and the nearly 50,000 extension workers that ensure that high-quality information and technologies are delivered to farmers. This strong coordination at the federal, regional, and local levels, as well as donor assistance has been fundamental to achieving the massive production gains seen over the past years.

A number of deliverables within the Transformation Agenda focus on ensuring that Ethiopia generates and effectively disseminates increasing amounts and types of data to inform decision making at all levels. The Ethiopian Soil Information System (EthioSIS) digital soil fertility mapping project has been working to project local, regional, and nationwide estimates of soil nutrient status. The EthioSIS project is collecting on-site physical information and soil samples across the country, performing soil analysis in digitized form. This data is then used to prescribe corrective action, and to provide more customized crop and fertilizer recommendations to help smallholder farmers increase their productivity. The EthioSIS project undertakes extensive demonstrations on farmers' plots and at Farmer Training Centers (FTCs).

The Soil Sector Development Strategy includes the promotion of agronomic practices designed to rehabilitate degraded soils while preventing further erosion; increasing the availability and access to improved soil nutrients needed to help smallholders maximize their growing potential; and the establishment of a comprehensive sustainable land management program.

A digital soil fertility map is being created, which will provide localized data on soil fertility throughout the country. This data will help indicate which soil nutrients should be utilized where, in order to increase production of various crops in different areas. In addition, fertilizer blending plants are being constructed in the regions to provide customized, farm-level blends of an expanded range of fertilizers to smallholder farmers.

Climate information is another area where data analysis and timely communication can be pivotal in providing extension workers and farmers with valuable decision-making information. As weather and seasonal climate forecasts of the National Meteorological Agency (NMA) cover wide areas, efforts are being undertaken to provide local, user-tailored forecasts to local areas. For example, a project to install plastic rain gauges at Farmer Training Centers (FTCs) and on selected model farmer plots has been tested in targeted local areas. The rain gauges empower FTCs to monitor rainfall in their respective areas, enabling farmers to undertake evidence-based agronomic decisions.

Rain gauges also ensure that farmers will not need to solely rely on traditional crop calendars to make decisions about planting dates or irrigation practices when rainfall is increasingly variable and inconsistent. An integrated Interactive Voice Recording (IVR) system, leveraging mobile technologies to disseminate agricultural information to smallholder farmers, is being established. The IVR system technology allows individuals to call into a hotline and access a wide range of relevant agronomic information. Through the IVR system, smallholders and development agents have direct access to pre-recorded messages, in a wide range of local languages, at their own convenience.

In the areas of access to inputs, innovations aim to improve the availability of high-quality seeds and fertilizers to farmers across the country. This project works with farmer local level cooperative unions to own and operate the blending facilities as commercial ventures. The Direct Seed Marketing (DSM) project seeks to expand smallholder farmers' access to inputs by introducing well trained private retailers as a complementary model to primary cooperatives in distributing improved seeds to smallholder farmers.

A pilot shallow groundwater mapping exercise has been initiated during the GTPII period. This project is to address the lack of water resource knowledge available to inform irrigation practices in Ethiopia. It will provide information on the depth of the water table, the amount of shallow groundwater resources available, and the command area, as well as the number of beneficiary households that are within reach of water.

Irrigation

The quality and availability of irrigation pumps in Ethiopia has suffered from the absence of national quality standards, low domestic manufacturing capability, and inefficient procurement and distribution channels. To address these issues, a set of comprehensive interventions, including the creation of national pump standards has been initiated. Mandatory standards ensure that pumps conform to basic quality guidelines, and help farmers gain improved access to spare parts and maintenance services. A set of mandatory national standards for engine-powered irrigation pumps has been approved by the National Standard Council. A testing and certifying facility has been established. A training curriculum is being developed for the country's Technical and Vocational Education Training Colleges (TVETC).

Ethiopia also plans to expand the production of high-value crops under irrigation. A software program has been developed for use by agriculture officials at the local level. It integrates agronomic and market infrastructure variables to determine the best crops for Ethiopia's farmers to grow under irrigation. A specific focus has been placed on vegetables that have been traditionally de-prioritized in extension efforts. These vegetables include onions, tomatoes, carrots, potatoes, head cabbage, and hot peppers. The Ethiopian Fruit and Vegetables Marketing S.C. (ETFRUIT) has been set up to market the vegetables. ETFRUIT is to source increasing outputs of fruits and vegetables from local cooperatives, at flexible prices determined by local market conditions at the time of purchase. ETFRUIT and other large commercial buyers are also to source greater amounts of produce from smallholder farmers for export markets, including to neighboring countries.

Efforts to develop and strengthen Ethiopia's seed system include strengthening the research and quality maintenance capability of research institutes; evaluation and restoration of the genetic material of key varieties of major staple crops (maize, wheat, *tef*, and barley); supporting producers to produce the right type and quantity of seed for their target market; improving and expanding the distribution of improved and certified seed through multiple outlet channels; and strengthening the seed regulatory system in order to ensure that farmers receive the highest quality seed possible.

Cooperatives are being developed up to the local level. A college has been established as a Cooperative Center of Excellence. This will equip Ethiopia's agricultural cooperatives with technical, financial, and managerial capacity necessary to offer their members a variety of higher value services.

Development of energy and power

Ethiopia is endowed with abundant renewable energy resources and has a potential to generate over 60,000 megawatts (MW) of electric power from hydroelectric, wind, solar, and geothermal sources. Of its overall energy potential, Ethiopia's hydropower potential is estimated up to 45,000 MW, the second highest in Africa next to the Democratic Republic of Congo (DRC). By 2015, the modern energy generation input mix of Ethiopia was 86 percent hydroelectric, 8 percent other renewables, and 6 percent thermal. The installed capacity was 2,261 MW with rural access of 8 percent, and a residential tariff of 3 cents (Ministry of Water, Irrigation, and Energy 2015).

In general, Ethiopia's terrain is advantageous for hydropower projects. With ten river basins (of which the Blue Nile, Omo, Wabe Shebelle, and Genale-Dawa are international rivers), hundreds of streams flowing into the major rivers dissecting the mountainous landscape in every direction; and each river basin covering massive catchment areas with adequate rainfall. Besides, the mountainous landscape makes many of the country's hydro resources suitable for hydroelectricity generation of varying sizes, ranging from *pico* hydro to small and large hydropower plants.[9] Small-scale hydro schemes are particularly suitable in remote areas, which are not connected to the national grid.

Ethiopia's ability to achieve its goal of becoming a middle-income country by 2025 requires huge amounts of power. This need for vast amounts of power is reinforced by the rapid growth of the country since the beginning of the twenty-first century. Thus, during the Growth and Transformation Plan (GTP I), Ethiopia's targets for increasing generation capacity to 10,000 MW was to be met by completion of two major hydropower plants in 2017 and 2018. GTP II has a new target to increase generation capacity to over 17,000 MW by 2020, with an overall potential of 35,000 MW by 2037. This would not only help sustain Ethiopia's continued economic growth, it would also enable Ethiopia to become a regional renewable energy hub in Eastern Africa.

Targets that were set during the first Growth and Transformation Plan (GTPI) were to reach the generating capacity from 2,000 MW to 10,000 MW, to increase transmission lines from 11,440 to 17,000 km, electric distribution lines from 126,000 km to 258,000 km, and re-installation of electric distribution lines from 450 to 8,130 km. The plan also targeted to reach millions more customers (GTP1).

Projects planned to achieve these goals included: Fincha Amertinshe hydropower (97 MW), Ashegoda wind farm (120 MW), Adama I wind farm (51 MW), Adama II wind farm (153 MW), and Gibe III hydropower (1,870 MW). About 324 MW electricity was to be generated from wind, which is a new source of power in Ethiopia. Genalle Dawa II (254 MW) hydropower and Repe (50 MW) dry waste were among the electric generation projects planned for completion by 2016. Projects that were started in the GTPI but not completed within the planned period included the Grand Renaissance Hydro Power Dam (GERD) with a capacity of generating 6,000 MW power and the 1,870 MW Gibe III dam that was being built in southern Ethiopia. The centerpiece of Ethiopia's plan is the 6,000 MW Grand Renaissance Dam was planned for completion in 2017/18. This has been the subject of a long-running row between Ethiopia and Egypt over a potential loss in the volume of the Nile water owing to evaporation in the dam's reservoir.

Over the volcano

One of the most ambitious schemes is a plan to install a geothermal power plant in the caldera of an active volcano in the Rift Valley, about 200 km south of Addis Ababa. The "Corbetti" scheme, which is being undertaken by Reykjavik Geothermal (an American-Icelandic company), will eventually produce 1,000 MW of power. Reykjavik Geothermal signed a twenty-five–year deal with the Ethiopian government in September 2014. According to Reykjavik Geothermal, Corbetti's potential is great because its geological conditions are ideal as geochemistry studies show the water to be exceedingly hot and studies suggest the reserve is vast.

The work will be undertaken in a number of stages. A 10 MW plant was expected to be operational by 2015, increasing to 100 MW in 2016 and to 500 MW by 2018, by which time about 100 wells will have been dug. The second 500 MW phase of the project is expected to be completed by 2021. Altogether, the work is expected to cost $4 billion. Ethiopia is believed to have over 10,000 MW of geothermal potential.[10]

Wind and solar power

Ethiopia is one of the largest wind-power generators in Africa. The government plans eventually to generate 800 MW of wind power. A 120 MW wind farm started turning in October 2013. The $290 million scheme was built by a French firm, Vergnet, and was financed by a low-interest loan from BNP Paribas and the French Development Agency. The Ethiopian government covered 9 percent of the cost. In 2017, the installed capacity was 820 MW consisting of 120 MW from the Ashegoda plant, 51 km from Adama I plant, and 151 km from the Adama II plant (Egziabher 2017).

In the solar field, two US companies have been awarded a contract to construct and operate three 100 MW photovoltaic power stations. Ethiopia has begun to manufacture photovoltaic panels. Total installed capacity in 2017 was 300 MW (Ministry of Water, Irrigation, and Energy, 2017).

Electricity export

Ethiopia is gearing up to export large amounts of clean power across Eastern Africa, starting with the neighboring countries of Djibouti, Kenya, and Sudan. By 2040, Ethiopia hopes to be exporting $1 billion of electricity to its neighbors and consuming a large amount in its own factories. In April 2016, the government announced that 29 percent of a new national transmission system had been built, which would provide power to nine industrial zones. That electricity exports accounted for over 7 percent of GDP, and that by 2018, it would export renewable energy to more neighboring countries (Woldegebriel 2013). However, Ethiopia is exporting electricity to Djibouti and Sudan only. The transmission line to Kenya is still under construction.

The Eastern Africa Power Pool (EAPP) aims to connect the power grids of at least ten countries, including Burundi, Democratic Republic of Congo (DRC), Djibouti, Ethiopia, Kenya, Rwanda, South Sudan, Sudan, Tanzania, and Uganda. It may also be extended to northern and southern Africa. Ethiopia is also planning to lay a cable on the Red Sea and export 100 MW of electricity a year to Yemen. Ethiopia may eventually supply Saudi Arabia with cheap and cleaner energy as the two countries have recently started to establish stronger economic relations.

Work is already underway to achieve the goal of energy export. A 283-km 230 kV Ethiopia-Djibouti transmission line enables Djibouti to import up to 60 MW of electricity, which is estimated to be earning Ethiopia at least $1.5 million per month. This has eased Djibouti's reliance on fossil-fuel power plants and generators. The African Development Bank (AfDB) provided $95 million for the project linking the two countries.[11]

A 296-km, 230 kV Ethiopia-Sudan transmission line links Ethiopia and Sudan, which is to export up to 100 MW of electricity to Sudan. The $41 million project, funded by the World Bank, started in 2008. The Ethiopia-Kenya electric transmission line will bring Ethiopia closer to the East African Community, linking the country to the East African Grid. The 500-kV transmission line connecting the Kenyan and Ethiopian grids was expected to be completed by the end of 2016 at a cost of up to $1.26 billion. It would make Kenya, which has the region's largest industrial base, the largest buyer of Ethiopian power at an eventual 400 MW, and could allow Ethiopia to export up to 1,600 MW to countries further afield. In June 2012, the Ethiopian Electric Power Company (EEPC) brokered its fourth power export agreement with South Sudan, to be undertaken in two phases. South Sudan, which has rich oil reserves, has depended on fossil fuels for its power supply.

The government of Ethiopia has determined that private sector investment is critical to achieve these aggressive power generation targets, but it lacks sufficient experience with Independent Power Projects (IPPs). It also faces other major challenges in expanding the country's energy system, including the need to rehabilitate an aged distribution system with high losses and ensure more efficient operation and maintenance of the expanded system. It must build the financial capacity to purchase electricity from IPPs, address foreign exchange constraints, reform tariffs to allow for full-cost recovery, and deliver more power to the majority of the population living off-grid.

Power Africa is supporting Ethiopia's energy development strategy through wide-ranging technical assistance in cooperation with Sweden, Norway, and the World Bank including the International Finance Corporation, European Commission, the UN, DFID, and other development partners. In addition, Power Africa is supporting the Eastern Africa Power Pool, which is based in Ethiopia. The power pool is mandated to facilitate cross-border trading of renewable energy at the lowest possible cost and to efficiently manage a regionally integrated system. Power Africa support includes development of common codes for the regional network, tracking interconnecting transmission lines, and training for power pool and member countries to analyze and operate the regional power system.

Concluding remarks and the way forward

Ethiopia is fundamentally an agrarian country. Although the transformation towards a more manufacturing and industrial economy is the ultimate goal, the agricultural sector continues to be the most dominant component of the economy. Furthermore, the majority of the agriculture sector is made up of smallholder farmers who live off of less than two hectares of land. As such, transformation of the agriculture sector is central in Ethiopia's key to reaching middle-income country status by 2025 and eventually becoming an industrial economy.

While many opportunities exist to accelerate growth and transformation in manufacturing, there are also many short to medium-term challenges that must be overcome. Ethiopia can become globally competitive in the apparel, leather products, and agribusiness industries, and compete with imports in the wood and metal product industries. The facilitating factors include very low wages combined with high trainability of workers; potential access to competitive sources of key inputs; continental infrastructure networks; a large and growing domestic market, and proximity to large export markets; and duty-free access to EU and US markets. Ethiopia has comparative advantage in the export of manufactures in sectors including textiles and garments, leather goods, and processed agricultural products.

Ethiopia's infrastructure development programs that will further its transformation include power production and distribution, roads, rails, airports, and industrial parks. The construction of a Standard Gauge Railway connecting Ethiopia to the Port of Djibouti is already finished and functioning. The plan to triple the capacity at the international airport in Addis Ababa to 25 million passengers will also help boost the country's trade; so is the expansion of the domestic airport network to nineteen airports. Air transport is essential in a country where mountains and deserts make developing and maintaining of a road network challenging.

Further government actions that will facilitate the process of industrialization include reduction or elimination of tariffs on key inputs; reduction of regulations; removal of restrictions on imported seeds and foreign exchange; and removal of restrictions that allow banks to overcharge on letters of credit and trade documentation.

In spite of the currently insignificant heavy industry in Ethiopia, the Agricultural-led based Industrialization Strategy, together with the strategies of agricultural transformation, and electrification will lay a firm foundation for heavy and general industrialization of Ethiopia. Rising incomes of the large population and human development will facilitate the process of establishing a self-sustaining industrial economy. This is especially so, given the country's ability for maintaining a high rate of sustained economic growth for about two consecutive decades.

Although Ethiopia has huge areas of arid land, it also has many large rivers. It can irrigate large areas and generate large amounts of hydroelectric power, some of which can be exported. Moreover, its mineral potential has hardly been tapped. Its recent program of greatly expanding graduate programs in its universities will enhance the development of the country's huge youthful human resources. With its fast-growing population, and large arid lands, industrialization is imperative for Ethiopia, as an industrial economy has greater capacity to sustain a large population.

Enhancing productivity growth, the demographic transition, and a large domestic market offer important potential. However, continued reliance on external financing for transformation may not eventually be sustainable in the long run. Over time, this reliance needs to be minimized and domestic financing substantially raised. Such a strategy will enable Ethiopia to independently prioritize its pattern of development and transformation.

Furthermore, the development process must be socially and geographically equitable. Nationals from various communities must be included to fully participate in their economy. Efforts must be made to facilitate various individuals and communities to acquire the necessary capital and skills so that all the diverse identities in the country can fully participate in the development of their country. This measure will be critical in the sustainability of the transformation process. Political leaders should also address political causes of social dissatisfaction as this can have serious negative effects on the country's economic progress.

Notes

1 World Bank. 2016. *An Annual Overview of the Economy of Ethiopia.*
2 Data on the plan targets are obtained from the specific documents of each plan, while performance data are obtained in the review parts of succeeding plans. The plan documents are for the SDPRP, PASDEP, GTPI, and GTP II.
3 *Kaizen* is a Japanese word which translates literally to *continuous improvement resulting from every team member in an enterprise making their own small contribution.* Late Ethiopian Prime Minister Meles Zenawi introduced it in Ethiopia in 2008 to motivate increase in productivity and product quality by focusing on working behavior, human resources development, and promotion of innovation. The goal is for continuous improvement to lead to big results from many small changes accumulated over time
4 For data on details of Ethiopian trade in 2015, see the same sources as for Nigeria and South Africa: https://globaledge.msu.edu/countries/ethiopia/trade and https://comtrade.un.org/ (Accessed February 19, 2017). Comprehensive trade data for DRC were not available from the same sources.
5 The SNNP stands for Southern Nations, Nationalities, and Peoples': a region bordering Kenya and South Sudan. It is one of the federal regions covering an area of about 112,323 km^2 with a population of about 18 million (2018) made up of about 45 ethnolinguistic groups.
6 Most of the data on the performance of the agricultural sector are obtained from the annual reports of the Ethiopian Agency for Agricultural Transformation (EATA), especially the one of 2013/14, which gives an overview of many years. The review parts of the GTPII also give an overview of past performances of agriculture as well as other sectors.
7 CAADP is a pan-African framework that provides a set of principles and broadly defined strategies to help African countries. It champions reform in the agricultural sector, setting broad targets: 6 percent annual growth in agricultural GDP and an allocation of at least 10 percent of public expenditures to the agricultural sector.
8 Women and youth programs have been explicitly included in Ethiopian development plans, especially in both phases of the GTP.
9 Ethiopia defines its power schemes by size in the following terminologies: large (> 30 MW), medium (10–30 MW), small (1–10), mini (501–1,000 kW), micro (11–500 kW), and pico ≤ 10 kW) (https://energypedia.info/wiki/Ethiopia_Energy_Situation (Accessed April 18, 2017).
10 The Corbetti geothermal scheme will be the first project to be developed under the US government's Power African Initiative, which was launched 2013 by President Obama in a speech at Cape Town University. This makes $7 billion available to support power schemes in Ethiopia, Ghana, Kenya, Liberia, Nigeria, and Tanzania.

11 This project is significant for both Djibouti and Ethiopia as Djibouti's port serves as the gateway for around 98 percent of landlocked Ethiopia's export-import trade, while domestic electricity generation is costly in Djibouti. Producing power with fuel-operated generators in Djibouti costs about $0.25 per kilowatt hour compared with around $0.07 per kilowatt hour of power imported from Ethiopia.

Bibliography

African Development Bank (AfDB). 2013. *Federal Democratic Republic of Ethiopia Country Strategy Paper 2016–2020.* Abidjan: AfDB.
———. 2011. *Federal Democratic Republic of Ethiopia Country Strategy 2011–201.* Abidjan: AfDB, April.
Altenburg, Tilman. 2010. "Industrial Policy in Ethiopia." Discussion Paper, Deutsches Institut für Entwicklungspolitik.
Berhan, Tewolde and Gebre Egziabher. 2017. *Renewable Energy Projects in Ethiopia.* Addis Ababa. https://unfccc.int/files/bodies/awg/application/pdf/3_ethiopia.pdf (Accessed October 20, 2017).
Central Statistics Agency of Ethiopia (CSA). 2010-2011. *Report on Small Scale Manufacturing Industries Survey.* Addis Ababa: CSA.
———. 2012. *Report on Large and Medium Manufacturing and Electricity Industries Survey.* Addis Ababa: CSA.
———. 2003. *Report on Cottage/Handicraft Manufacturing Industries Survey.* Addis Ababa: CSA.
Diao, Xinshen. 2010. *Economic Importance of Agriculture for Sustainable Development and Poverty Reduction: The Case Study of Ethiopia.* Paris: OECD.
Dinh, Hinh, Vincent Palmade, Vandana Chandra, and Frances Cossar. 2012. *Light Manufacturing in Africa: Targeted Policies to Enhance Private Investment and Create Jobs: Vol. I.* Washington, DC: World Bank.
Ethiopian Agricultural Transformation Agency. (ATA) 2014. *2013/14 and 2014: Transforming Agriculture in Ethiopia.* Addis Ababa: ATA.
Gebreeyesus, Mulu. 2013. "Industrial Policy and Development in Ethiopia: Evolution and Present Experimentation." *WIDER Working Paper No. 2013/125.*
Gebremeden, Yared. 2016. "Ethiopia: Energy Development to Ensure the Growing Economy." *The Ethiopian Herald,* March 3.
Girma, Zelalem. 2018. "Ethiopia: Industrial Parks Transforming Manufacturing Sector." *The Ethiopian Herald,* Addis Ababa, March 6.
———. 2016. "Ethiopia: Industrial Parks Fostering Sustainable Growth." *The Ethiopian Herald,* June 16.
Haile, Tewelde G. 2015. "Comparative Analysis for the SDPRP, PASDEP, and GTR of the FDR of Ethiopia." *Global Journal of Business, Economics, and Management* 5, no. 1: 13–14.
International Monetary Fund (IMF). 2017. *World Economic Outlook,* October.
———. 2011a. *The Federal Democratic Republic of Ethiopia: Joint Staff Advisory Note on Growth and Transformation Plan 2010/11–2014/15.*
———. 2011b. *IMF Country Report: The Federal Democratic Republic of Ethiopia: Poverty Reduction Strategy Paper: Growth and Transformation Plan 2010/11–2014/15: Vol. I.*
———. 2006. *IMF Country Report No. 6/27: The Federal Democratic Republic of Ethiopia: Poverty Reduction Strategy Paper-2003/04 Annual Progress Report.* Industrial Parks Development Corporation: www.ipdc.gov.et/index.php/en/ (Accessed August 20, 2017).
Kassahun, Chanie. 2018. "Ethiopia: Expanding Industrial Parks to Ensure Sustainable Growth." *Ethiopian Herald,* January 10.

Ministry of Finance and Economic Development (MOFED). 2010a. *The Federal Demo-cratic Republic of Ethiopia: Poverty Reduction Strategy Paper: Growth and Transformation Plan 2010/11–2014/15: Vol. I: Main Report.* Addis Ababa.

————. 2010b. *Growth and Transformation Plan (GTP), 2010/11–2014/15 Draft.* Addis Ababa, September.

————. 2010c. *Performance Evaluation of the First Five Years Development Plan (2006–2010) and the Growth and Transformation Planning (GTP) for the Next Five Years (2011–2015).* Addis Ababa, July.

————. 2006. *Plan for Accelerated and Sustained Development to End Poverty (PASDEP), (2005/06–2009/10).* Addis Ababa, September.

————. 2005. *Ethiopia: Sustainable Development and Poverty Reduction Program (SDPRP): Annual Progress Report (2003/04).*

————. 2002. *Ethiopia: Sustainable Development and Poverty Reduction Program (SDPRP).* Addis Ababa, July.

Ministry of Industry. 2002. *Industrial Development Strategy of Ethiopia.* Addis Ababa, August.

Ministry of Water, Irrigation, and Electricity. 2007. *The Ethiopian Power Sector: A Renewable Future.* Berlin Energy Transition Dialogue, March.

National Planning Commission. 2016. *Growth and Transformation Plan II (GTP II) (2015/16–2019/20): Vol. I: Main Text.* Addis Ababa, May.

Tekle, Tesfa-Alem. 2017. "Ethiopia Pushes Plan to Become Africa's Manufacturing Hub." *Sudan Tribune,* June 20.

United Nations Industrial Development Organization (UNIDO). (n.d.). *Programme for Country Partnership: Ethiopia, Summary.*

Woldegebriel, E. G. 2013. "Ethiopia Plans to Power East Africa with Hydro." *AlertNet: Thomson Reuters Foundation.* Addis Ababa, January 29.

World Bank. 2017. *Global Economic Prospects: A Fragile Recovery,* June.

————. Worldbank.org/en/country/ethiopia/overview/ (Accessed October 22, 2016).

Zerihun, A. 2008. "Industrialization Policy and Industrial Development Strategy in Ethiopia." In *Digest of Ethiopia's National Policies, Strategies and Programs,* ed. T. Assefa. Addis Ababa: Forum for Social Studies: 239–81.

6 The Nigerian economy

An overview

Nigeria has the natural and human resources to establish a diversified self-sustaining industrial economy. It has a large pool of educated human resources that can be trained into various experts, specialists, and technicians. It has tremendous agricultural potential. The large and growing population of over 180 million and large and growing GDP provide a large domestic market, which can absorb much of its domestic output. Its daily output of over two million barrels of oil per day (bb/day) should be able to provide it with huge revenues to finance a transformational national development program.

Nigeria is counted in two groups of countries that are projected to become major world economies. The two groups are the *MINT* countries (Mexico, Indonesia, Nigeria, and Turkey) and the *PINE* countries (Philippines, Indonesia, Nigeria, and Ethiopia). These economies are projected as among the emerging economies following the *BRICS* (Brazil, Russia, India, China, and South Africa) countries.

Nigeria's population is growing fast (about 3 percent per annum), with a high fertility rate. It has a large population of children aged 15 years and younger. Nigeria's population is projected to outstrip that of the other three MINT countries by 2050 and could by then be the fourth most-populous country in the world, with a population of about 402 million (UN 2015). On the other hand, Nigeria's overdependence on oil plus its major problem of electric power shortage and inefficiency greatly impair the country's viability as a modern economy. Industrialization, diversification, and rural development can address the issues of poverty, unemployment, and geographical and inter-personal inequalities. Such policies would considerably enhance the domestic market and the capacity of the country to absorb much of its national output. With the prospects of rising incomes, Nigeria offers a large consumer market. Development of the manufacturing sector, especially of the capital goods industries, would have tremendous impact on domestic supply and demand. The multiplier effects would extend to the whole West Africa and the rest of Africa through trade and investment.

Macroeconomic performance and structural changes

Nigeria rebased its economy in 2013, becoming the largest African economy (Sy 2015).[1] The rebasing of the Nigerian economy revealed a much more diversified economy than was previously thought. Nigerian GDP now includes previously uncounted industries like telecoms, information technology, music, online sales, airlines, and film production. GDP for 2013 totaled $509.9 billion (80.3 trillion naira). The agricultural sector contributed 35 percent to GDP prior to rebasing but was only estimated to account for 22 percent of GDP after rebasing. Meanwhile, the services sector's contribution increased from 29 percent to 52 percent of GDP, with the telecommunications sector rising from 0.9 percent to 8.7 percent of GDP. After rebasing, the manufacturing sector was estimated to contribute 6.8 percent to GDP, compared to just 1.9 percent previously. The oil and gas sector's contribution was revised down to 14.4 percent from 32.4 percent before rebasing. Industry accounted for 20.6 percent of Nigeria's real GDP in 2013, according to the Central Bank of Nigeria's (CBN). However, in compiling data the country lumps in manufacturing with upstream oil and gas production. Manufacturing itself accounted for 9.2 percent of real GDP for the same year, and the government plans the figure to rise to 10 percent by 2020. The Nigerian Bureau of Statistics (NBS) plans to rebase GDP figures every five years to ensure that estimates remain up to date (Kale 2015).[2] Table 6.1 summarizes the macroeconomic performances of the Nigerian economy during the first fifteen years of the twenty-first century. Nigeria registered high rates of growth of real GDP and per capita GDP throughout the whole period. The growth rates began to decline towards the end of the period because of a major fall in international petroleum prices. For example, in 2015, real GDP grew by 2.7 percent only, leading to the growth of real GDP per capita falling to 0.1 percent only. Inflation did not change much, hovering at about 12 percent. Nigeria's national savings by far exceed its rate of gross investment, which means that Nigeria financed its gross investment with its own resources. However, Nigeria also received much foreign investment, especially into its petroleum sector. Fiscal imbalances were negligible as in most years Nigeria's government revenue exceeded government expenditure. Again the exceptions were during years of low international oil prices.

The external sector

The general performance of the Nigerian foreign sector is illustrated in Table 6.2. The table shows that Nigeria's export earnings by far exceeded the country's imports. Hence, Nigeria experienced a surplus balance on both merchandise and current accounts throughout the fifteen-year period. Except at the beginning of the period, Nigerian terms of trade were favorable for most of the period. Changes in international petroleum prices have considerable impact on Nigeria's terms of trade. Nigeria had favorable reserve position for

Table 6.1 Macroeconomic performance (percent in real terms)

Item	2001–05	2002–06	2003–07	2004–08	2005–09	2006–10	2007–11	2008–12	2009–13	2010–14	2011–15
GDP Growth	5.7	6.2	7.3	7.0	7.0	7.5	7.4	6.8	6.7	6.2	5.0
Per Capita GDP Growth	2.9	3.5	4.5	4.2	4.2	5.3	4.5	4.0	3.9	3.3	1.9
Consumer Prices (2000 = 100)	15.7	13.8	15.1	11.6	11.1	10.3	10.8	12.2	11.5	10.7	9.7
Gross Investment	23.3	23.1	23.4	24.0	23.1	22.3	21.2	18.7	17.0	15.8	15.3
Gross Domestic Savings	34.3	36.7	40.5	38.1	39.0	34.7	29.8	24.7	21.0	18.8	17.1
Fiscal Balance (Including Grants)	1.3	4.0	5.1	7.6	3.9	1.2	-0.4	-0.6	-2.4	-1.6	-1.6
Fiscal Balance (Excluding Grants)	1.3	4.0	5.1	7.6	3.9	1.2	-0.4	-0.6	-2.4	-1.6	-1.6
Government Revenue (Excluding Grants)	25.0	25.2	26.0	32.6	25.1	21.9	20.0	17.5	13.3	13.2	12.3
Government Expenditure	23.7	21.2	20.8	25.0	21.2	20.7	20.4	18.2	14.7	14.8	13.9

Source: IMF Various years. Regional Economic Outlook: Sub-Saharan Africa. Five-year moving averages calculated from IMF annual data.

Table 6.2 The performance of the external sector (percent of GDP in real terms)

Item	2001–05	2002–06	2003–07	2004–08	2005–09	2006–10	2007–11	2008–12	2009–13	2010–14	2011–15
Export of Goods and Services	48.8	51.5	51.5	58.3	43.6	36.7	30.2	26.2	21.5	20.1	17.7
Imports of Goods and Services	37.7	37.9	35.3	28.5	29.4	26.1	23.3	21.0	17.7	17.0	16.0
Balance of Trade (Goods only)	19.5	21.4	24.1	22.9	22.0	18.0	14.3	11.5	8.7	7.5	5.9
Current Account (Including Grants)	0.8	2.6	8.2	−14.2	11.5	10.4	8.6	6.1	4.0	3.0	1.8
Terms of Trade (Index: 2000 = 100)	70.6	133.1	133.8	132.1	149.9	148.0	144.2	148.9	150.6	155.9	164.4
Reserves (months of Imports of Goods and Services)	6.7	7.7	8.7	9.8	10.5	9.4	7.9	7.3	6.0	5.7	5.9

Source: Five-year moving averages calculated from IMF annual data.

IMF, *Regional Economic Outlook: Sub-Saharan Africa* (various years).

the whole fifteen-year period. The lowest reserve position was 5.1 months of imports, while the highest was 7.2 months.

As of 2015, the value of Nigerian exports totaled $102.9 billion, while imports amounted to $46.5 billion, resulting in a huge surplus of $56.4 billion. The top ten exports constituted about 98 percent. Petroleum and petroleum products dominated the list with oil and mineral fuels contributing 90.9 percent of the total exports. The second item, ships and boats, was a distant 2.1 percent only. The rest were explosives (1.9%), cocoa (0.8%), textiles articles (0.7%), industrial machinery (0.6%), hides and leather (0.6%), oil seeds (0.5%), cotton (0.2%), and aluminum (0.2%).[3]

Nigerian imports are much more varied. The leading ten constituted about 71 percent, ($32.9 billion) while the remainder constituted about 29 percent ($13.6 billion). The ten top imports were oil and mineral fuels (16.3%), industrial machinery (15.6%), motor vehicles and parts (9.6%), electrical machinery (7.6%), cereals (5.3%), plastics (4.7%), iron and steel articles (4%), seafood (2.7%), and sugar and confectionery (2.1%).

Intra-industry trade exists in Nigeria's pattern of international trade, but it is not significant. It consists of oil and mineral fuels, and industrial machinery. This pattern of trade should increase as Nigerian industrialization increases and matures.

The destinations and origins of Nigeria's exports and imports have also become more diversified. In 2015, the ten leading export markets took 70 percent ($72.1 billion) of Nigerian exports. The remaining 30 percent ($30.8 billion) went to the rest of the world. India was Nigeria's leading export market, taking 14.6 percent of the country's exports. The remaining nine were the Netherlands (10.2%), Spain (9.3%), Brazil (8.1%), France (5.7%), the United Kingdom (5.1%), South Africa (5%), Italy (4.4 percent), Indonesia (3.9%), and the United States (3.8%).

Nigeria's ten top sources of imports in 2015 amounted to 68 percent. They were: China (22%), the United States (10.4%), Belgium (7.2%), the Netherlands (6.1%), India (6%), the United Kingdom (3.9%), Germany (3.8%), South Korea (3.7%), Brazil (2.5%), and France (2.5%).

Manufacturing in Nigeria

Nigeria's major manufacturing industries include rubber, wood, textiles, cement and other construction materials, food products, footwear, chemicals, fertilizer, printing, ceramics, steel, and shipbuilding and repair. The manufacturing sector contributes less than 10 percent to the GDP. It accounted for 9 percent of GDP in 2013. Growth in the sector has been rapid at a pace of about 18 percent per annum during 2011–2013, although it is hampered by supply bottlenecks, especially disruptions to electricity supply. Generally, industrialization is low outside of the oil and gas sector due to lack of competitiveness of manufactured goods compared to imported items. The cost of production, packaging options, and quality of products are some of the challenges facing Nigerian factories. As a result, manufacturing capacity utilization has been below 60 percent in recent years. It averaged 57 percent in 2011–2012 (kpmg.com/Africa)

Before rebasing, manufacturing constituted about 6.8 percent of GDP. After rebasing, this percentage rose to about 9 percent (NBS 2014) as a result of better measurement after reclassification of the sector. Prior to rebasing manufacturing included just three activities: oil refining, cement, and other manufacturing. After rebasing, the "other manufacturing" has been broken into eleven different activities, such that Nigerian manufacturing sector now consists of thirteen components.

The manufacturing sector is dominated by food, beverages, and tobacco, which constituted about 52.7 percent of the sector's total in 2013 (NBS 2014). This was followed by textiles, apparel, and footwear at about 18 percent. Cement contributed about 6.2 percent, and oil refining 5.7 percent. Other subsectors of manufacturing include wood and wood products, chemicals and pharmaceuticals, pulp, paper, and paper products, non-metallic products, and motor vehicles and assembly.

Nigerian manufacturing uses more domestic raw materials than imported ones (NBS 2014; kpmg.com/Africa). In 2010, basic metals, iron and steel had the greatest portion of locally sourced materials of about 95.8 percent of its raw materials. This was followed by chemicals and pharmaceuticals with 79.6 percent of its total raw material supply. For imported raw material, food, beverages, and tobacco had the largest share, about 72.3 percent. Plastics and rubber products imported about 46.9 percent of their raw material supplies (NBS 2014).

Growth in the Nigerian manufacturing sector is hampered by supply bottlenecks, particularly disruptions to electricity supply. Improving electricity generating capacity can substantially reduce the supply constraints. The power sector has been privatized and some transmission lines and substations have been completed in recent years.

Pharmaceutical production has received a boost from the World Health Organization (WHO) with the certification of three local companies in accordance with good manufacturing practice standards, with four companies able to produce medicines for malaria, HIV/AIDS, and tuberculosis for the international market (kpmg.com/Africa).

In 2013, there were about 130 pharmaceutical firms operating in Nigeria with five indigenous firms controlling about 58 percent of the manufacturing of pharmaceutical products. Being small in size, Nigerian firms cannot mobilize the huge amount of resources required for research and development as the oligopolistic firms in the major industrial countries (Ugbam and Okoro 2017).

The automotive industry has recently become a major focus and growth rates in the sector have reached double-digits. Consequently, automotive manufacturing is becoming a prominent subsector. A local company, Innoson Vehicle Manufacturing, produced its first passenger vehicles in 2014. Nissan delivered its first "*Made in Nigeria*" car in 2015. However, at present Nigeria still imports most of its automobiles. Toyota and Ford are the main suppliers. Other major automobiles exporters to Nigeria include Nissan, Mercedes-Benz, and Skoda (kpmg.com/Africa). Preference for foreign models inhibits the success of locally assembled models. In 2013, the government passed the New Automobile Industrial Policy Development Act. This entails higher tariffs on used vehicle imports, an improvement in industrial infrastructure, skills development, and promotion of investment. The objective is to promote investment in the assembly of inexpensive cars in Nigeria at prices that people in Nigeria can afford so as to substitute car imports with domestic made models. But this policy must be complemented with improvements in infrastructure, electricity supply, and general business climate in the country, if the objective is to be attained through private foreign investment.

Boosting Nigeria's non-oil industrial subsectors

After decades-long slump in manufacturing output, triggered by the scaling up of oil production in the 1970s, the country is working to reverse the trend and enable manufacturing and heavy industry to play a larger role in the economy. Success would diversify the economy and create job opportunities for many Nigerians. The Federal Ministry of Industry, Trade and Investment (FMITI) published its Nigeria Industrial Revolution Plan (NIRP) in 2012, with the main goal being to boost manufacturing from 4 percent of GDP to 10 percent by 2020, timed to match up with the Vision 20: 2020 plan, which aims to position Nigeria as one of the top-20 economies worldwide by year 2020. The NIRP's goals include fully replacing imports of metals, petrochemicals, and processed palm oils, among other products.

The target for the automotive sector is 50 percent of supply from domestic operations by 2020. The government also made local production a major factor in its own procurement procedures, such as in the automotive industry, where it is anticipated to buy locally made cars and trucks whenever possible for its own operations. The NIRP also includes capacity-building measures such as training funds and lending program through non-commercial outlets like the Bank of Industry (BOI). Plans to support small and medium-sized enterprises (SMEs) are found in the National Enterprise Development Program, a vehicle for providing finance, business development program, training, and turnkey facilities for companies at the SME level.

Opening up textile markets slashed the number of manufacturers in that segment from 124 in 1994 to 45 as of 2011, according to the Manufacturers Association of Nigeria (MAN), due to the difficulty local producers had in adjusting to the influx of cheaper goods. As a result, and in order to improve the scale of the domestic sector and allow it to better compete with imports, tariffs have been put in place in a number of sectors, from cement to automotive.

The tariffs, at least in certain sectors, appear to be having the intended effect. Private sector responses to import tariff increases have been swift. But while the new tax regimes have stimulated investment, they have also incentivized the smuggling of imports, which has the potential to derail the strategy. For example, rice tariffs, which vary by quality, have been rising ahead of a plan to ban imports by 2015. The country wants to grow enough to feed itself, boost its milling and processing sector, and cut down on its food import bill.

However, high tariffs or even prohibition, have not prevented smuggling of a number of goods to Nigeria. Hence, from August 2019, Nigeria began closing some of its borders in an attempt to prevent the importation of goods, which include rice, used clothes, poultry products, and vegetable oil.

Nigerian rice accounted for 75.5 percent of supply in the 1990s, 55.1 percent in the 2000s and 53 percent from 2010 to 2012. Domestic producers' inability to compete on price and taste explain the phenomenon. For example, the cost of production is about double that in Thailand, one of the world's main rice suppliers. Even with shipping costs and associated fees calculated in, Thai rice is cheaper in the Nigerian market. The tariffs and pending ban are intended to allow local producers to expand capacity in the long term. The tariff has been combined with public sector initiatives such as staple crop processing zones (SCPZs), which provide turnkey facilities and fiscal incentives to agro-industrial ventures.

The cement industry

Among Nigeria's various manufacturing subsectors, one of the most visible in recent years has been cement. The country's cement sector is dominated by a few large companies, with smaller firms importing and reselling. Dangote Cement, a local industrialist, is a major player and is now a global producer. Two other world leaders in cement production operating in Nigeria are Lafarge and Holcim. Cement output climbed 15.6 percent in 2013 to 21.2 million tons, outstripping the average increase in the past years of 10.9 percent. Nigeria's per capita consumption of cement was 126 kg (Global Cement Report 10th Edition). With the global average per capita consumption at 510 kg, Nigeria has plenty of room for growth of the industry. In 2012, the government estimated Nigeria had a housing shortage of 15 million to 20 million housing units. Infrastructure spending is also expected to serve as another demand driver. However, quality has been a concern in recent years, and the Standards Organization of Nigeria (SON) introduced new rules to reduce the risk of structures collapsing. It mandated different grades of cement for plastering, buildings, constructing building bridges, and for columns, slabs, and block molding.

Automobile assembly

Nigeria virtually imports nearly all of its cars, with an average of 50,000 new and 150,000 used vehicles entering the market through formal channels in recent years. However, according to Courteville Business Solutions, a total of 5 million vehicles were registered in 2013, implying a large informal market.[4] According to the National Automotive Council, a government agency, the import bill for vehicles and parts was $7.4 billion in 2013. The statistics available may not be accurate, however, given the size of the informal trade in vehicles and parts, and the challenge of collecting data in a large country where capacity for data collection and management is limited. The Nigerian Automotive Manufacturers' Association is reliant on manifests from ships carrying vehicles into the country for its information and warns that the numbers can be subject to distortions.

During the immediate post-independence era, Nigeria had a number of large-scale auto manufacturing facilities with government joint venture factories churning out vehicles from many foreign companies, especially UK's Leyland, France's Peugeot, and Germany's Mercedes-Benz. However, output has declined significantly in the decades since and most of these facilities were shut down. Nigeria's existing small production lines of commercial vehicles are complete or semi-knockdown assembly kits imported and constructed at local plants. The Automotive Industrial Policy Development Plan (AIPDP), approved in late 2013, was meant to reactivate the Nigerian domestic auto manufacturing sector. It established a 70 percent tariff on all imported passenger cars up to 2019, after which it will fall to 55 percent. Commercial automobiles will be taxed at 35 percent. The size of Nigeria's population makes it an important market for vehicles and it is likely to be of increasing importance as the population and income grow. The first made-in-Nigeria passenger cars, by Nissan, rolled off factory lots in Lagos State in June 2014. The Nissan models are made in a joint venture between the Japanese manufacturer and Nigerian conglomerate, Stallion Group. Nissan hopes to make Nigeria a manufacturing hub for the region, given the potential scale of the local market. Other international auto brands such as Kia and Tata have announced plans to assemble their products in Nigeria. According to Nigeria's National Automotive Council (NAC), as of June 2014, twenty-one (21) international auto-companies had already signed commitments with technical partners to set up Nigerian assembly operations (kpmg.com 2012).[5] To be competitive with imports, the Stallion and Nissan cars were expected to sell for between $7,375 (N1.2 million) and $9,219 (N1.5 million). Smuggled vehicles, typically second-hand cars, loom as the biggest potential problem for the domestic car industry. The government's efforts to use protectionism to support domestic industries have been challenged by the porous border in other areas as well such as in rice smuggling. The hiking of tariff on rice did stimulate local production, but in addition to a jump in total hectares of rice paddy, there was an increase in smuggled rice into the country.

Nigeria has been working on developing the new automotive policy with input from the South African Government. South Africa rolled out its Motor Industry Development Program (MIDP) in 1995 to boost production and improve export volumes. The program consisted of reducing import duties on both vehicles and components along with rebates and credits for components inputs (kpmg.com 2012).[6] Should Nigeria see similar improvements to production, the impact on job creation and export revenues for the country would be significant.

First "Made-in-Nigeria" cars

In 2014, Innoson Motors unveiled a new brand of vehicles, building on local assembly successes by Hyundai and Nissan. The company had earlier impressed with its trucks and buses. Seventy percent of the parts used in building the new brands of cars were locally sourced, heralding the emergence of a local car manufacturing industry. Innoson offered a sedan at $6,146 (N1 million). Innoson Vehicles Manufacturing Company continued to produce several ranges of vehicles from trucks and SUVs to mini-buses. The company plans to export its brands to neighboring countries in West Africa.

The range of Innoson vehicles is already enjoying patronage locally, unlike in the past when indigenous manufacturers were stifled by the lack of national appreciation of their products. The government of Anambra State became a frequent buyer of the locally made vehicles. Nigeria's Federal Road Safety Commission (FRSC) began to purchase pickups made by Innoson. In March 2016, Innoson Vehicle Manufacturing Company signed a Memorandum of Understanding (MOU) with the Nigerian Air Force to produce jet fighters' parts. According to the Chief of Air Staff, the collaboration between the company and the Air Force had kept its jet fleet running for months before the signing of the MOU. The Air Force Chief of Policy and Planning said, the MOU would further solidify the collaboration, improve local content and engineering as well as save the country a lot of foreign exchange used in importing expensive parts.[7]

However, establishing a large-scale local auto manufacturing will take some time. As with other attempts in the past, both for cars and other goods, the current effort at developing an automotive industry is reliant on protecting domestic players by taxing imports. Imports are typically cheaper than Nigerian products on account of the high costs of production within the country, due to factors like the need to import supplies, sporadic electricity, and poor roads, as well as other basic obstacles. The long-term surer way to success is by working to remove the structural impediments in the country.

Historical perspective on industrialization in Nigeria

During the period 1956–1960, rules and incentives were designed to stimulate domestic manufacturing. The government encouraged domestic manufacturing through engaging in joint ventures with foreign companies. However, development policy emphasis was placed on utilities, education, and basic infrastructure. After independence in 1960, the government drew up the 1962–1968 National Development Plan, in which resources were channeled to the directly productive sectors. In the 1960s and 1970s, the main industries included textiles, synthetic fabrics, footwear, soft drinks, beer, cement, soap and detergents, sugar confectionary, paints, and refineries. The manufacturing sector performed well during the 1960s and 1970s, but stagnated beginning from the 1980s onward as a result of several factors, which included a lack of access to foreign exchange and poor infrastructure. The apparent excellent performance of the manufacturing sector in the 1960s and 1970s hid serious defects that existed in the industrial sector. These included lack of technical and technological knowledge and skills. In addition, the sector lacked international competitiveness. In the 1980s, especially towards the late 1980s, many of the industries in the manufacturing sector performed poorly, operating much below capacity.

The post-civil war plans of 1970–1974 and 1975–1980 were ambitious given the opulence of oil wealth. The Nigerian Enterprises Promotion Act was enacted in 1973 with emphasis on self-reliance and reduction of foreign dominance in the industrial sector. Some businesses were reserved for Nigerian entrepreneurs. Foreigners were restricted to more technologically demanding industries and joint ventures. The government continued drawing up comprehensive development plans up to the 1980s, followed by rolling plans in the 1990s (Agbu: 28).

With the oil boom, manufacturing, like other economic sectors, was neglected. With the realization that dependency on an exhaustible resource such as oil with volatility in the world market, government policy was reshifted to emphasize manufacturing with definite emphasis on steel mills, petrochemical industry, machine tools, and other core projects targeted at building industrial complexes. The government became strongly committed to the promotion of a free market economy characterized by privatization and deregulation. Many state-run firms were privatized with mandates to operate as profitably as possible without recourse to the state for assistance. Before this policy, the government had invested in certain targeted industries including paper mills, assembly plants, iron and steel, petrochemical plants, oil refineries, fertilizer plants, liquefied natural gas plants, and cement plants. Most of these industries failed to generate significant foreign exchange or compete effectively with imported products, except for natural gas projects.

Since 2003, government industrial policy focused on targeting small-scale and medium-sized industries. The government drew up the National Economic Empowerment Strategy (NEEDS), which emphasized industrialization and the creation of jobs. Launched in May 2004, the NEEDS replaced the rolling plans of the 1990s. NEEDS followed the Poverty Reduction Strategy Paper of 2001. The Nigerian government also encouraged foreign investment. But most of the foreign investment continued to flow to the oil and gas sector. Recent Nigerian industrial development policy has particularly put emphasis on four sectors: agriculture, manufacturing, non-oil mining and mineral extraction, and export of manufactured products. Priority in manufacturing has been focused on agro- and agro-allied subsectors for which there are vast natural resources including food preparations, fruit drinks, milling feed, milk, and vegetable oil processing. Others include industries that support food production through local manufacture of chemicals, equipment, and light commercial vehicles, chemicals and petrochemicals. Other industries encouraged are those with greater multiplier effects such as flat sheet mills and machine tools industry that include foundries and engineering industries for spare parts production; basic industries for petrochemical and liquefied gas projects for which the government encourages foreign partners; and the processing of local agricultural produce and minerals into industrial raw materials as manufactured intermediate goods required by the existing industries.

The development of the iron and steel industry

Nigerian planners began to think of developing the iron and steel industry in 1958. After wide consultations with western experts, it was concluded that the country lacked the technology, infrastructure, and technical skills for such an industry. However, between 1961 and 1965, proposals were received for a project in the same industry, from foreign organizations and companies. The proposals ranged for projects in the order of 100,000 to 300,000 tons per annum. The initial attempt was to build rolling mills and establish the market potential for steel products. Later efforts were redirected to establishing an integrated iron and steel plant. In 1967, significant progress was made towards the establishment of an iron and steel plant in Nigeria. Following a bilateral technical/economic agreement between the governments of Nigeria and the Soviet Union, Soviet experts conducted a feasibility study for the establishment of iron and steel plants in Nigeria. However, the Soviet experts concluded that the then-known iron deposits in Nigeria were of poor quality. The Soviet team recommended further geological surveys for better ores. The Soviet survey team reported that there were high prospects for finding rich iron and coal in Nigeria. Consequently, Nigeria signed a contract in 1970 with a Soviet firm to provide specialists and equipment to carry out further geological survey in order to determine the quantity of iron ore and coal resources to be used in the proposed iron and steel industry. The Nigerian Steel Development Authority (NSDA) was established in 1971, and the first Nigerian furnace steel plant was founded at Ajaokuta.[8] The NSDA was charged with the responsibility of planning, construction, and operation of steel plants in the country. It was also to carry out investigations into geological surveys, market studies, and metallurgical research. The NSDA also embarked on short and long-term training of Nigerians both at home and abroad, in the operation and management of the iron and steel industry in Nigeria. In 1973, another Soviet firm was commissioned to prepare a preliminary project report on the iron and steel industry in Nigeria. The report recommended alternative steel production schemes based on both local and imported raw materials. The Soviets prepared a detailed report that was submitted to the Nigerian Government in 1977.

With the assistance of a firm of French consultants, the detailed Soviet report for the establishment of a steel plant was accepted in 1978. The Detailed Project Report (DPR) specified broadly the general layout, composition, and requirements as well as a tentative master schedule of the Ajaokuta Steel Plant, and in 1979 Nigeria signed a contract with a Soviet firm for the construction of the Ajaokuta Steel Plant.

The signatories committed themselves to the development of an iron and steel industry in Nigeria. The Nigerian government dissolved the NSDA and established the Ajaokuta Steel Plant and five other limited liability companies. The other five companies were the Delta Steel Company Limited at Aladja, the Jos Steel Rolling Mill, the Oshogbo Steel Rolling Mill, the Katsina Steel

Rolling Mill, and the Associated Ores and Mining Company Limited. The last one was changed to the National Iron Ore Mining Company (NIOMCO) at Itakpe.

By the 2000s, Nigeria had added to the aforementioned firms the following: the Nigerian Metallurgical Development Center in Jos, the National Steel Raw Materials Exploration Agency in Kaduna, and the Nigerian Metallurgical Training Institute at Onitsha. In 1979, contracts were signed for the three rolling mills at Katsina, Jos, and Oshogbo. Kobe Steel of Japan served as technical partners during the erection of the Katsina plant, while German companies constructed the Jos and Oshogbo plants. The steel companies, rolling mills, and the mining company were incorporated as limited liability companies and were expected to be self-funding. Research and training centers were funded by the government.

The Nigerian government plans to privatize these enterprises. In addition to the public sector firms, there are mini steel private firms engaged in the re-rolling of billets, with capacities ranging from 50,000 to 100,000 tons. The productivities of these firms have been constrained mainly by operational efficiency, lack of working capital, and insufficient and intermittent electric power. Their total annual output has never exceeded 300,000 tons (Agbu 43–44).[9]

Raw materials

The availability of raw materials is a key consideration in the establishment of an iron and steel plant. Nigerian authorities started early to look for sources of raw materials within the country in order to be able to select the appropriate technologies that could be used and ensure that the industry is viable. The Soviet specialists and the NSDA exploration division worked extensively over a large area of the country, exploring for deposits of iron ore, coking coal, limestone, dolomite, and refractory clays. The discovery of the Itakpe iron ore in 1973 by the Soviet aero-magnetic survey team catalyzed the development of the steel industry in Nigeria. More iron deposits were found at Agbaja, Ajabanoko, and Chokochoko. A British firm found more iron ore deposits at Agbaja and Udi. Coal was discovered in large quantities at Enugu and limestone at Jakura. More coal was discovered in Nigeria. Some of the Nigerian coal was found suitable for coking using the direct reduction method in steel making. Establishment of a sponge iron mill was recommended to be fired by Nigerian coke. It was also found that tar and coke could be produced at competitive prices in the country.

The overall findings were that there were sufficient local raw materials. These included iron ore, coal, limestone, dolomite, refractory coal, water, and natural gas. The other material would have to be imported, including scrap, bauxite, and manganese. The National Iron Ore Mining Company (NIOMCO) became responsible for exploration, exploitation, processing, and supply of iron ore concentrate to the steel plants at Ajaokuta and Aladja.

The Ajaokuta steel plant

The Ajaokuta plant was a multifaceted industry with at least twenty-one com-panies encapsulated within it. The principal units of the plant included the iron making plant, steel making plant, the rolling mills repair facilities, auxiliary facilities, and the electric power supply system. At inception, the project was envisaged to produce 1.3 million tons at its first stage, 2.6 million tons at its second stage, and 5.2 million tons per annum, at the third phase, of long and flat products.

Due to scarcity of skilled human resources in Nigeria for the steel industry at that period, a strong emphasis was placed on personnel training right at the inception of the industry. Various training agreements were entered into, which resulted in the training of large numbers of the steel sector workforce abroad. The manpower estimate for the operation of the Ajaokuta plant at peak was 9,000. The training contract with the Soviet firm was about 1,500 Nigerian engineers, technicians, and operational staff. Many NSDA staff were sent for preliminary training in steel- design and operations in various countries (Soviet Union, Italy, Canada, United States, Japan, France, Britain, and India). There was also local training in metallurgy and related fields in some of the local uni-versities. The Metallurgical Training Institute (MTI) was set up in Onitsha in 1981, as well as the Training Institute of the Ajaokuta Steel Company Limited (ASCL), with a capacity output of 2,000 students, offering courses in twenty-seven specialties. While the trained Nigerians performed their work well, poor remuneration and poor job satisfaction led to many leaving for jobs in the private sector. Some returned to Nigeria to find that the jobs they had been trained for were not ready.

With the return to elected government in 1999, the Obasanjo administration revived interest in the Ajaokuta Steel Project, which had waned since the mid-1990s. However, by then some plant facilities had deteriorated. A total amount of about $460 million was needed to rehabilitate and complete the first phase of the project. The Ajaokuta Steel Company Limited (ASCL) formed a joint venture company with a German firm, Ferrostaal AG (ASFERRO), to operate commercially. The workshops included the forge and fabrication shop, machine tools shop, foundry and pattern making shop, steel structural workshop, and power equipment repair shop.

The rolling mills at Ajaokuta, consisting of Light Section Mills (LSM), Wire Roll Mill (WRM), and Medium Section and Structural Mill (MSSM) were down for about fourteen years until the government allocated more resources for the company with about $899.13 committed to the mills. Due to the pau-city of the mills, the government invited the private sector through conversion agreements, negotiated and signed with a number of private entrepreneurs, whereby they buy billets and get them rolled at Ajaeokuta for a fee. To make the commercialization effort attractive, the government approved the adjustment of tariff on all types of rolled steel products from 30 percent to 65 percent and billets from 10 percent to 5 percent from the fiscal year 2011.

Initially four private steel producers responded to the privatization endeavor (Russian, USA, Japanese, and Austrian). The TPE (Russian) made a commercial offer of $421.125 million, while the Solgas (USA) offer was $986 million. Kobe Steel (Japanese) proposed the introduction of the FASTMELT process of steel making technology into the plant, which it claimed was capable of using Nigerian non-coking coal. Its figure was about $916 million for a three-unit plant having 1.5 million tons capacity. A joint venture was proposed with ASCL for production and marketing of steel blooms and/or billets in a ratio of 60/40 for ASCL and Kobe. Solgas (USA) was chosen.

The Nigerian government entered into a ten-year agreement with the Solgas Energy. A $282 million agreement was signed in 2003. Solgas was to rehabilitate, complete, commission, and operate the steel plant. It was expected to build and operate a gas processing plant, as well as an electricity generating plant with all plant coming to stream within two years. The electricity plant was to generate about 2,300 MW within 18 months and provide 11,000 jobs, while the steel and gas processing was to provide 9,000 and 10,000 jobs respectively. Solgas was also to provide all the financing for the projects. However, Solgas was an energy company with little or no experience in steel production. It did not have the required technical capacity to deliver on its promises, and hence, the agreement was terminated.

In 2004, the Nigerian government handed the management and operation rights of the project to Ispa Industries of India under Mittals. Mittals acquired control over Ajaokuta Steel Company, with assets valued at about $3 billion for a period of ten years, renewable for another ten years. The Ajaokuta Steel Plant consisted of a power plant, a sponge iron plant, and a coke oven battery, in addition to its manufacturing of light and medium structural and wire rods. By early 2006, the plant had started to export steel products to other West African countries.

Delta steel company limited at Ovwian-Aladja

In 1977, the Federal Government of Nigeria signed a turnkey contract with a German-Austrian consortium for a Direct Reduction (DR) plant to be located in Ovwian-Aladja, Warri. In March 1979, it was established as an integrated plant, and designed to produce steel, using iron ore through the Midrex Reduction cum Electric Arc Furnace technology. It was wholly owned by the Nigerian Government until the government signed an agreement with GSHL of India in 2005.

Delta Steel produces Cold Briqettes Iron (CBI), Direct Reduced Iron (DRI), and billets. Insufficient working capital, from its commissioning in January 1982 until May 1996, never allowed the plant to produce beyond 25 percent designed capacity (Agbu: 52). The Obasanjo government went into some arrangement with the original builders, Voest Alphine, and Osaka Steel (Japan) under a partial privatization program to refurbish and operate the plant. The plan of the government was to sell off all the steel plants and the rolling mills to private sector operators. The Nigerian government made a commitment of $45 million, while Voest Alphine component of the consortium promised to source a loan of $55 million to repair the plant. Osaka Steel was supposed to come up with a working capital of $40 million. The Nigerian Government provided its own component of finance, but Voest Alphine had problems in sourcing its loan. By late 2005, the Nigerian government agreed with Global Steel Holdings (GSHL) of India for the revitalization and operation of the Delta Steel Plant, with GSHL acquiring 80 percent stake in the plant values at $30 million. GSHL also holds 6 percent stake in Ispat Industries. The Delta Steel Company plant manufactures longs and structural, has a two million ton pelletization plant, a 1.4 million tons per annum directly reduced iron (DRI) plant, and a 1.8 million ton per annum electric arc furnace.

Global Steel Holdings (GSHL) also took over the management of the Ajao-kuta Steel Company in August 2004 and negotiated iron mining leases of the Nigerian Iron Ore Mining Company (NIOMCO). The iron ore linkages were expected to be used for both the Delta and Ajaokuta plants. All the key parts of the plant – the power plant, oxygen plant, lime plant, and the steel making shop – are all producing at high capacities. The plant exports finished Nigerian steel products. Delta Steel is producing largely from indigenous raw materials. The raw materials, in particular iron, are being supplied by the Nigerian Iron Ore Mining Company LTD (NIOMCO). Delta Steel appointed a concession-aire to manage NIOMCO along with ASCL. NIOMCO maintains in stock two million tons of raw iron, while mining is still going on. Mining at Ajaba-noko, Enugu, Itakpe, and other mines will supply both Delta Steel and ASCL for at least twenty-five years. A viable Delta Steel plant will mean the smaller rolling mills all over Nigeria will no longer have to rely on imported billets since Delta Steel will be able to supply them all.

Power and credit shortages

Most Nigerian industrialists and researchers observe that the greatest obsta-cle to manufacturing and other sectors of the Nigerian economy is inad-equate and unreliable electricity supply. Erratic supply from the national grid requires backup generators, which typically are powered by diesel fuel and produce power at a more expensive rate than grid supply. The Manufactur-ers Association of Nigeria (MAN) members spent N470 ($2.87) billion on generators in 2011 (Ibikunle 2014).[10] The group estimates that the goal of getting 10 percent of GDP from manufacturing by 2020 will require current electricity production to jump from an average annual level of 3,000 MW to 50,000 MW in that same time period.

Addressing this issue, the government launched a privatization process for generating and distributing assets in 2013 and 2014. In addition to expanding supply, the new stakeholders will have to tackle some of the remaining bottle-necks in the power sector, including too-low tariffs that cannot attract sufficient capital to the sector; and historically low collection rates of existing distribution companies. As a result, manufacturers will continue to rely on diesel generators for some years. Large-scale power users often build their own captive power plants, with the possibility of selling the surplus into the national grid.

Access to finance is also a challenge for manufacturers, in particular small and medium enterprises (SMEs). The Nigeria Export-Import Bank disbursed N9.44 billion ($57.58 million) in 2013, a 30 percent rise over N7.31 billion ($44.59 million) in 2012, with manufacturing getting 50.14 percent of the total, or N4.73 billion ($28.85 million). The Bank of Industry (BOI), which has a mandate of helping to promote and develop the domestic industrial sector, approved and disbursed N154.48 billion ($942.33 million) and N32.72 billion ($199.59 million), respectively, in 2013. Of the total disbursed, 5.2 percent was allocated to microcredit, with the rest being for long-term loans.[11] There are also two SME-targeted lending schemes, the SME Credit Guarantee Scheme and the SME Manufacturing Refinancing/Restructuring Fund, both formed in 2010. By 2013, the former has provided guarantees to over forty ventures, while the latter has allotted N235 billion ($1.43 billion) in credit to some 535 projects (MAN 2014).

There have been other sector-specific initiatives to improve access to credit. The Textile Intervention Fund, being managed by the BOI, received N100 million ($610,000) in seed capital from the government in 2010 to support manufacturing uses for indigenous cotton. In early 2013 the fund was saving 8,070 jobs, boosting capacity from below 40 percent to 61 percent and helping half of the country's textile ventures become profitable.

Minerals and Industrialization

Nigeria is endowed with vast reserves of solid minerals, including but not limited to precious metals, stones, and industrial minerals. In the area of non-oil mining and mineral extraction, Nigeria has exploitable quantities of barites, coal, diatomite, lignite, columbite, and iron ore. The country was a major exporter of tin, columbite, and coal in the early 1970s. However, activities in the mining sector declined because of the narrow focus on the oil sector only. With the refocusing on diversifying and industrializing the Nigerian economy, a new national focus and strategy on mining evolved such that in 2007, the Nigerian Minerals and Mining Act was enacted to revitalize the Nigerian mining industry.

Exploitation of many of Nigeria's minerals will aid in the country's process of heavy industrialization. The Ministry of Mines and Steel Development has designated coal, bitumen, iron ore, limestone, barites, gold, lead, and zinc as strategic assets. In addition, the country has deposits of gemstones, tungsten, bauxite, copper, kaolin, feldspar, gypsum, granite, marble, soda ash, talc, zircon, phosphates, rutile, monazite, and limonite. In fact, Nigeria has over forty different types of minerals spread across the country. However, not all the minerals are available in commercial quantities. As part of the strategies to reform the sector, the Ministry of Mines and Steel Development (MMSD) has identified seven strategic minerals for priority development. These are coal, bitumen, limestone, iron ore, barites, gold, and lead/zinc.

Iron ore deposits have been found in various locations in Nigeria. Iron ore deposits in Nigeria typically occur in the form of hematite, magnetite, meta-sedimentary, bands of ferruginous quartzite, sedimentary ores, limonite, magh-emite, goethite, and siderite. Rich ore constitutes more than 4.5 percent of the total reserves, with medium grades estimated at 85.4 percent and lean ore at 13.1 percent. Estimates of reserves in these locations have been put at about 883 million tons (KPMG 2012).

Nigerian coal has been found suitable for boiler fuel, production of high caloric gas, domestic heating, briquettes, formed coke, and the manufacture of a wide range of chemicals including waxes, resins, adhesives, and dyes. Coal has been found in the central, middle-east and south-east regions of the country. A total estimate in these regions has been put at 396 million metric tons, while unproven reserves are estimated to be about 1,134 million tons. In addition to its use in the iron and steel industry, coal can also provide fuel for power genera-tion and domestic use. Consequently, the coal resources were marked out into ten prospective blocks and placed for bid by companies with proven financial and technical competence. Nine of the blocks were put up for bidding. Five blocks have been earmarked for power generation.

The largest and purest deposits of limestone are found in the south-west and middle belt of the country. Limestone in the south-west region of Nigeria has been estimated at 31 million tons. Most limestone mining activities are mainly for cement production.

In Nigeria, bitumen typically occurs both on the surface and sub-surface. The estimated probable reserves, in the south-west, are about 16 billion barrels. Tar sands and heavy oil is estimated at 42 billion barrels. The probable reserve of bitumen and heavy oil in the entire tar sand belt is expected to be about 84 billion barrels. The bitumen belt has been marked out into six blocks with an average of 600 km^2 each, and sold to investors.

Currently, the bitumen used in Nigeria is processed from imported heavy crudes, in addition to bitumen imported to supplement local consumption. Heavy and extra heavy crude can be extracted from Nigerian tar sands, and sulfur and phenol can be derived from these crude grades. They are also suit-able for production of lubricants for plain and roller bearings. Barites are suitable for manufacturing glass, paint, and paper making. It is also used in petroleum well-drilling. Proven reserves are estimated at over 21 million tons. Lead/zinc ores are usually found together. They are often associated with cop-per and silver. Nigerian proven commercial reserves of lead/zinc are well over 100,000 tons of lead and 80,000 tons of zinc. Lead/zinc ores are used in the production of batteries, electrical cables, solders glass, and protective coatings for other metals.

Gold is associated with the north-west, central, and south-west regions of Nigeria, although there are smaller occurrences beyond these major areas. The preliminary exploration and identification of deposits which is still ongoing has confirmed ten sites to be holding reserves of over 50,000 ounces of high-quality gold. Licensees have been issued to co-operative societies and companies for mining of gold in the country. Most of the concessions are still at the exploration stage.

Challenges in the Nigerian mining industry

The major challenges faced by the mining industry are similar to those facing other sectors of the Nigerian economy: electricity, railways and roads, and project funding. Insecurity and illegal mining also challenge the sector. Access to the sites of mineral deposits is a major challenge. Due to the long period of inactivity and the slow implementation of the Federal Government's reform agenda in the sector, multinational corporations have been reluctant to fund major mining projects in the country. However, the progress made in the regulatory reform, so far, is expected to stimulate activities by new investors in the sector.

The ongoing privatization of the national utility and reform of the power sector, which started in 2005, is intended to address the infrastructural challenges and stimulate private investment in the mining sector. Meanwhile, mining investors can meet their power needs by engaging independent power producers for captive generation and supply of energy to the mines. Furthermore, access roads will ultimately improve with ongoing investments by the Federal and State Governments in road infrastructure. The ongoing rehabilitation of the rail lines will also facilitate product evacuation across the country for export.

Security concerns are among the major problems for investors, especially when the local communities where the minerals are located believe that they are not benefiting from the exploitation of their resources. This was/is the case with oil in the Niger Delta. This can be minimized if the government and investors put in place a robust corporate social responsibility program to address the needs of their host communities. The feeling of being cheated from one's natural resources has increased the act of illegal mining and community challenges. Policymakers and their private sector partners must wake up to the reality that the goal of development is to improve the living conditions of the population, beginning with the local populations where the projects are located. Profit motivation has to be synchronized with the general welfare of all stakeholders in any enterprise.

The potential for developing mining activities in Nigeria is significant, according to the Extractive Industries Transparency Initiative (EITI), of which Nigeria is a member country. However, according to the EITI, illegal exporting and a general lack of regulation are causing the domestic sector to lose out on potential revenue. The group recommended adopting a taxation system similar to Nigeria's petroleum sector, in which companies pay profit taxes. It also recommended regular reviews of the mining cadaster to remove licenses from players that are not mining or exploring but merely holding these rights in hopes of reselling them. The EITI found that an estimated 70 percent of mining licenses were held by speculators as of 2011.

The importance of agricultural development

As for most economies, development of the agricultural sector is crucial in the industrialization strategy of the Nigeria economy. Nigeria's wide range of climate variations allows it to produce a variety of food and cash crops. The staple food crops include cassava, yams, corn, coco-yams, cowpeas, beans, sweet potatoes, plantains, bananas, rice, sorghum, and a variety of fruits and vegetables. The leading cash crops include cocoa, citrus, cotton, groundnuts (peanuts), palm oil, palm kernel, benniseed, and rubber.

Nigeria has over 84 million hectares of arable land with only about 40 percent cultivated. It has about 263 billion cubic meters of water, with two of the largest rivers in Africa: the Benue and the Niger. Development of this potential will supply food and raw materials as well as reduce heavy dependence on the importation of agricultural products. Development of the agricultural sector will also reduce the country's level of unemployment (as the sector is labor intensive) and reduce poverty. Consequently, this will help curb rural-urban migration and raise incomes at all levels of society (Adesina 2013).

Nigeria was largely food self-sufficient in the 1960s and was well known for its global position in the production and export of major agricultural commodities. Before the emphasis on oil in the 1970s, Nigeria was the world's biggest exporter of peanuts and palm oil. But since then farming has been neglected and yields have stagnated. The oil boom of the 1970s led to the neglect of all other sectors of the Nigerian economy. Hence, the country became a net food-importer, spending on average $11 billion per annum on importing wheat, rice, sugar, and fish alone (Adesina 2013).[12]

To unlock the great potential of agriculture to once again drive the economy, Nigeria has embarked on a major transformation of the agricultural sector through the rapid transformation of key agricultural value chains. It launched the Agricultural Transformation Agenda (ATA) in 2011, with the goal of adding 20 million tons of food to the domestic food supply by 2015 and stimulating the creation of 3.5 million jobs along the agricultural value chains. It is encouraging all levels of agricultural activity: small-, medium-, and large-scale farming. It aims at import substitution of the various agricultural imports that gained prominence since the 1970s.

The government launched the Growth Enhancement Scheme (GES) to provide subsidized inputs to farmers. To reach farmers directly with seeds and fertilizers, the Federal Ministry of Agriculture developed an Electronic Wallet System, which allows farmers to receive subsidized electronic vouchers for their seeds and fertilizers on their mobile phones. In 2012, 1.5 million small-holder farmers got their subsidized seeds and fertilizers using their mobile phones. This had an impact on 7.5 million persons. In 2013, over 3.5 million farmers received their subsidized inputs via the Electronic Wallet Scheme. The GES program is being expanded beyond crops to provide support for fisheries, livestock, and mechanization services. The electronic system eliminates corrupt officials who used to sell the inputs to traders. Subsidies for agricultural development have existed for more than three decades but red tape and corruption hampered distribution and limited production.

The country has import substituted much of its rice imports. To reduce the almost $4 billion import bill on wheat annually, Nigeria embarked on a cassava flour substitution policy to replace some of the wheat flour used in bread and confectionaries. Several of the major Nigerian bakers shifted to the incorporation of 20 percent high-quality cassava flour in producing bread. The whole cassava value chain is being transformed by substituting starch imports through cassava starch, and sweeteners to reduce sugar imports. Nigeria has contracted with China to export a total of 3.2 million MT of cassava chips earning the country an annual income of $800 million. As for the development of wheat, Nigeria has developed new tropical wheat varieties that are heat tolerant, which give yields of 5–6 tons per hectare, which is 500–600 percent more than the yields obtained previously by farmers. The plan was to produce at least 2.5 million MT of wheat annually, and this was to reduce wheat imports by 50 percent by 2015. As the commercialization of cassava bread reaches its peak, it will reduce the country's wheat import bill by at least almost $800 million annually. To accelerate the production of high-quality cassava flour, the government is supporting the private sector to access cheap financing to import and establish large-scale cassava-processing plants. To further scale up nationwide production and commercialization of cassava bread, the government established a $60 million cassava-bread fund. Promoting cassava as a wheat substitute could reduce wheat imports substantially. Nigeria also plans to import substitute orange juice, pineapple and mango concentrates, and tomato paste by processing its local produce. In 2011, a local private firm established a $6 million plant to process oranges into concentrate. Another local private firm was investing $35 million in the establishment of a tomato processing plant. The company was also investing $45 million to set up a 6,000-hectare pineapple plantation and processing plant.

To develop the export market for fresh produce from Nigeria into Europe, a fresh produce value chain development program has been launched in partnership with the Ministry of Aviation. The country is building cargo airports to enhance its competitiveness in the export of fresh produce. Nigeria has embarked on restoring its prominence in palm oil production. It is recapitalizing its plantations by providing millions of high yielding improved seedlings of oil palm to smallholder farmers and plantation estates in the country free of charge. In addition, private sector investments are expanding with new palm oil processing plants.

In cocoa, the country's target was to double production by 2015. The government distributed 3.5 million pods of high yielding cocoa hybrids to smallholder farmers, all free of charge, in addition to support for production inputs. In 2012, smallholder cocoa farmers earned $900 million in foreign exchange. The private sector has expanded its processing capacity for value addition to cocoa beans. Nigeria plans to make chocolates locally.

In the livestock sector, Nigeria's *halal-certified* beef with cold chain logistic systems is now being exported.[13] Nigeria is also working to become self-sufficient in fish production by encouraging aquaculture, inland fisheries, and marine fisheries.

To further build the resilience of its food system, Nigeria is expanding the number of silos for strategic food reserves. These silos are now being provided under concessions to the private sector, for the establishment of agricultural commodity exchanges. Development financing institutions, including the World Bank, African Development Bank, and International Fund for Agricultural Development are supporting Nigeria's agricultural transformation. Nigeria's Agricultural Transformation Agenda (ATA) brought about reforms in the input delivery through the Growth Enhancement Support (GES) Scheme, agricultural financing, value chain development, including the Staple Crop Processing Zones, and farm mechanization. All these efforts have yielded an abundant harvest for farmers and great gains for the country. For example, between 2011 and 2014, national food production grew by 21 million MT. This led to a sharp reduction in food imports. Nigeria's food import bill fell from N3.19 trillion in 2011 to N635 billion in 2013; a 403 percent reduction. Direct farm jobs rose by 3.56 million in the period 2012 to 2014 due to the Agricultural Transformation Agenda (ATA).

Government policy focuses on attracting private sector agribusinesses to set up processing plants in zones of high food production, to process commodities into food products. The government put in place appropriate fiscal, investment, and infrastructure policies for Staple Crops Processing Zones. These policies include tax breaks on import of agricultural processing equipment, tax holidays for food processors that locate in these zones. Government also invested in infrastructure such as roads, railway, storage facilities, power, irrigation, flood control, and marketing. The Staple Crop Processing Zones are to link farmers to food manufacturing plants.

Concluding remarks and the way forward

Nigeria has made significant progress in socio-economic terms over the last fifteen years. However, the country continues to face massive development challenges, which include reducing the dependency on oil and diversifying the economy, addressing insufficient infrastructure, and the building of strong and effective institutions, as well as governance issues, public financial management systems, human development indicators, and the living conditions of the bulk of the population.

A transformed industrial Nigeria has the capacity to serve as a growth and development pole in West Africa and the rest of the continent. However, the growth of any major African economy cannot have profound positive effects on the rest of the countries without vibrant industrialization spearheaded by growth in the capital goods industries such as iron and steel; and also at the same time meeting the basic needs of the local population so as to create a massive domestic market for manufactured goods.

Before the oil industry came to dominate the Nigerian economy, the country produced its own food supplies and exported large quantities of cocoa, cotton, cattle, hides and skins, groundnuts, palm oil, and palm kernels. Reemphasis on the development of the agricultural sector would raise incomes, reduce poverty and inequalities, expand the domestic market, and further enhance the national efforts to build a self-sustaining industrial economy.

The Nigerian iron and steel industry has been beset by major constraints including inadequate financing, poor planning, and implementation. Hence, many of the early steel facilities either failed to take off or have been performing below capacity. However, in the process of their implementations, a lot of lessons have been learned.

Increasing domestic competitiveness to allow for a reduction in imported goods will take some time, however, and to help improve local capacity the government has explored a handful of protectionist policies, which is not unusual in the history of industrializing economies. For example, in 2014 domestic production of passenger cars commenced, partly due to a government policy of hiking tariffs on imported automobiles. The government launched a number of initiatives to create industrial supply chains by boosting activity in areas such as mining and petrochemicals, as well as assisting industrial activity in a broader sense by addressing economy-wide obstacles. These include problems such as the lack of reliable electricity supply, corruption, bureaucracy, and transport infrastructure.

Power infrastructure has been the major challenge facing Nigeria's economy. Even privatization of the power sector is yet to yield the desired result to resolve perennial electricity shortage and disruptions in the country. By the mid-2010s, the power generation capacity stood at between 4,000 and 5,000 MW, which is quite insufficient for a population of over 180 million. To further improve power supply and sustainability, the Federal Government has approved billions of dollars for power transmission infrastructure and manpower development and training of thousands of human resources in the field.

Allocation of investment funds to the power sector seems not to be the main problem; but implementation of the power plan is the issue. In the short to medium run, the federal government should grant manufacturers licenses to generate their own power, as refusal to give manufacturers approval to generate electricity for their own use is affecting their operations. Furthermore, some states should be free to generate their own power, rather than depending on the Federal Government. The long-term solution is to establish an efficient power system, including joint investment and sourcing of power from the Grand Inga Complex of the Democratic Republic of Congo (DRC).

Insufficient working capital is another problem. Manufacturers need loans with a repayment period of between seven to ten years, with the interest rate in single digits, about 5 percent. Short-term loans from commercial bank with interest rates as high as 25 percent are hard to enable infant manufacturers to establish and be competitive. Also, the Standards Organization of Nigeria (SON) should be adequately funded and equipped with standard laboratories for products testing and subsequent certification. For instance, for a locally made product to be accepted in the international market, the product must meet specific quality certification in export market standards. Although changing, local market attitude to national manufactures is still a problem. Even though some locally made products are far better than imported goods, the local consumers prefer the imports. The state should spearhead the development of the steel industry, especially at its early stages of establishment. But the criteria for project selection should be based on economic feasibility such that a project must yield some positive rate of return. Developmental states have been able to achieve industrialization through direct state intervention in the process. Raising the level of living of the population through agricultural and local development will contribute to equitable development and reduce poverty, inequalities, unemployment, and instability. A large but poor and segmented population is not a viable domestic market that can sustain high rates of growth of manufacturing, as the different segments of society have different demand patterns. Hence, the focus on agricultural, rural, regional, and local development will positively contribute to the industrialization of the Nigerian economy.

Notes

1 In addition to Nigeria, other African countries rebased their economies as follows: Kenya (2013), Tanzania (2013), Uganda (2014), and Zambia (2010).
2 Yemi Kale was the Statistician General (professional head) of the Nigerian National Bureau of Statistics at the time of rebasing the Nigerian national income in 2013. Also see National Bureau of Statistics (April 2014).
3 The details of Nigeria's 2015 trade data were obtained from the same sources for Ethiopia and South Africa: https://globaledge.msu/countries/ethiopia/trade and https://comtrade.un.org/ (Accessed February 19, 2017). Comprehensive trade data for DRC were not available from the same sources.
4 Courteville Business Solutions was a private firm that provided motor vehicle registry services in twenty of thirty-six Nigerian states.
5 www.vanguardngr.com/2016/03/innoson-signs-pact-air-force-produce-jet-fighters-parts/ (Accessed October 20, 2017).
6 See www.vanguardngr.com/2016/03/innoson-signs-pact-air-force-produce-jet-fighters-parts/ (Accessed October 20, 2017).
7 See Chapter 7 on South Africa's Motor Industry Development Program (MIDP).
8 The Ajaokuta Iron and Steel industry is one of the most studied industries in writings on Nigerian industrialization.
9 Most of the data on iron and steel are mostly based on the works of Agbu (2007); Lawal (2015); and Nigerian Metallurgical Society (NMS) (2016).
10 www.vanguardngr.com/2014/10/problems-crippling-manufacturing-nigeria-ibikunle-ipwa-plc-md/; https://punchng.com/manufacturers-keen-to-tap-idle-electricity-as-generation-wobbles/; https://guardian.ng/business-services/industry/manufacturers-generate-13000mw-from-alternative-energy-sources/ (Accessed October 20, 2017).
11 The Nigerian Bank of Industry (BOI) targets businesses that engage in manufacturing and processing activities. It only finances enterprises or companies and not an individual person or group of persons. It was principally set up to finance industrial equipment used in manufacturing. The bank does not disburse the loan to the borrower in cash but to the vendors and suppliers of the equipment for which the loan application is made.
12 Most of the figures on agricultural performance, quoted below, are available in Adesina's presentation. Also see *The Economist*, May 4, 2013.
13 Halal is the Muslim view on animals slaughtered in an Islamic way.

Bibliography

Adeniyi, R. 2015. "ECOWAS CET: FG Smuggles 70% Duty, Tax on Used, New Vehicles." *National Daily* (online), April 27. www.nationaldailyng.com/business/maritime/3736- (Accessed March 8, 2016).

African Development Bank (AfDB). 2015. *Economic Report on Nigeria: 2015 Special Edition.* AfDB.

Agbu, Osita. 2007. *The Iron and Steel Industry and Nigeria's Industrialization: Exploring Cooperation With Japan Institute of Developing Economies.* Osaka: Institute of Developing Economies. Japan External Trade Organization, March.

Akinwumi, Adesina. 2013. "Transforming Nigeria's Agriculture." Speech delivered by Minister of Agriculture and Rural Development Federal Republic of Nigeria, at the Inauguration of the Agriculture and Food Security Center of the Earth Institute of Columbia University, New York, USA, September 10.

Chete, L. N., J. O. Adeoti, F. M. Adeyinka, and O. Ogundele. 2014. *Industrial Development and Growth in Nigeria: Lessons and Challenges.* The Brookings Institution, African Development Bank, World Institute for Development.

Furlonger, D. 2014. "Nigeria Joins Race to Expand Motor Industry." *Business Day Live,* October 27. www.bdlive.co.za/africa/africanbusiness/2014/10/27/nigeria-joins-race-toexpand- motor-industry (Accessed May 10, 2015).

Kale, Yemi. 2015. *Reviewing the Structure and Capacity of the Nigerian Economy for Improving Government Revenue.* Abuja: National Bureau of Statistics.

KPMG. 2012. *Cutting Through Complexity, Nigerian Mining Sector. Manufacturing in Africa.* February, 2015.

Lawal, Ganiyu Ishola. 2015. *Nigeria's Quest for Industrial Development: The Iron and Steel Quagmire.* Lagos: University of Lagos Press.

Manufacturers Association of Nigeria. 2014. *Speech by Tella Sulaiman Ibikunle, Chairman of Paints Manufacturers of Nigeria and Managing Director of Manufacturers of Industrial Coatings, Marine, and Building Paints.* Quoted in www.vanguardngr.com/2014/10/problems-crippling-manufacturing-nigeria-ibikunle-ipwa-plc-md/ (Accessed October 20, 2017).

Mike, A. Jide. 2010. "The Structure of the Manufacturing Industry." Paper presented at the National Workshop on Strengthening Innovations & Capacity Building in the Nigerian Manufacturing Sector. (Ikeja, Lagos). (Mike was then the Secretary General of the Manufacturers Association of Nigeria).

National Bureau of Statistics (NBS). 2014a. *Nigerian Manufacturing Sector: Summary Report: 2010–2012.* Abuja: National Bureau of Statistics, October.

———. 2014b. *Rebasing of National Accounts Statistics: Methodology Notes on Gross Domestic Product (GDP) Rebasing Exercise.* Abuja: National Bureau of Statistics, April.

National Planning Commission (NPC). 2009. *Nigeria Vision 20:2020: Economic Transformation Blueprint.* Abuja: National Planning Commission.

———. 2007. *Nigeria: National Economic Empowerment Development Strategy (NEEDS2).* Abuja: National Planning Commission.

———. 2004. *Nigeria: National Economic Empowerment and Development Strategy.* Abuja: National Planning Commission.

Nigeria Export Processing Zones Authority (NEPZA). 2013. www.nepza.gov.ng (Accessed October 20, 2017).

Nigerian Metallurgical Society (NMS). 2016. *Book of Proceedings 32nd Conference and Annual Meeting: 26th–29th October.* Kaduna.

Sy, Amadou. 2015. *Are African Countries Rebasing GDP in 2014 Findings Evidence of Structural Transformation?* Brookings, March 3.

Ugbam, Ogechukwu C. and Ephraim A. Okoro. 2017. "A Strategic Study of the Nigerian Pharmaceutical Sector: Organizational Leadership, Market-share, and Competitive Performance." *International Journal of Business, Humanities and Technology* 7, no. 1 (March).

United Nations Industrialization Organization (UNIDO). 2011. *Pharmaceutical Sector Profile: Nigeria.* Vienna: UNIDO.

World Bank. 2017. *Nigeria Economic Update: Beyond Oil, Key Drivers for Sustainable Growth,* May.

———. 2012. *World Development Indicators.* Washington, DC: World Bank.

United Nations, Department of Economic and Social Affairs, Population Division.

7 The South African economy

A macroeconomic overview

South Africa is a middle-income industrial country with an abundant supply of natural resources. The country has well-developed financial, legal, communications, energy, and transport sectors. The country's modern infrastructure supports a relatively efficient distribution of goods to major urban centers throughout the Southern Africa region.

South Africa's economy was traditionally rooted in the primary sectors, that is, it is the result of a wealth of mineral resources and favorable agricultural conditions. From the second half of the 1900s, structural shifts began to take place in output. Mining and manufacturing began to dominate output. Since the early 1990s, economic growth has been driven mainly by the tertiary sector, which includes wholesale and retail trade, tourism, and communications. South Africa is becoming a knowledge-based economy with a greater focus on technology, e-commerce, and financial and other services.

Economic growth has decelerated in recent years, slowing to an estimated less than 1 percent from 2014. Because of the minimal growth of GDP, per capita GDP growth has fallen below zero in some years. Even though apartheid formally ended in 1994, the economic impact of the system has hardly eased, in spite of substantial government efforts to alleviate the situation. Recorded poverty fell from 33.8 percent in 1996 to 16.9 percent by 2008 (*World Bank 2018*). However, in spite of progress, unemployment, poverty, and inequality remain high. The unemployment rate is highest among the youths. The rate of inflation is low, about 5 percent.

Gross domestic investment is relatively higher than gross national savings. The gap is filled with capital inflow. Fiscal imbalance is negligible as the difference between government revenue and expenditure has been small. Government revenue ranged from about 24 to 28 percent of GDP, while government expenditure ranged from about 25 to 32 percent.

The structure of the economy

The economy is diversified, with no sector contributing more than 25 percent of GDP. Among the key sectors that contribute to the GDP are

Table 7.1 Macroeconomic performance (percent in real terms)

Item	2001–05	2002–06	2003–07	2004–08	2005–09	2006–10	2007–11	2008–12	2009–13	2010–14	2011–15
GDP Growth	3.9	4.3	4.7	4.9	3.5	3.1	2.8	2.1	1.8	2.4	2.1
Per Capita GDP Growth	2.4	3.0	3.2	3.5	2.0	1.5	1.1	0.7	0.3	0.9	0.5
Consumer Prices (Index: 2000 = 100)	5.1	4.9	4.5	5.6	6.8	6.9	7.0	6.7	3.6	5.4	5.4
Gross Investment	17.0	18.2	19.2	19.9	21.0	21.1	20.6	20.4	19.9	19.8	19.8
Gross Domestic Savings	18.6	18.4	17.3	14.7	16.7	16.8	16.6	16.7	16.5	16.1	15.3
Fiscal Balance (Including Grants)	−1.4	−1.0	−0.5	0.2	−0.8	−1.6	−2.5	−4.4	−4.3	−4.1	−4.0
Fiscal Balance (Excluding Grants)	−1.4	−1.0	−0.5	0.2	−0.8	−1.6	−2.5	−4.4	−4.3	−4.1	−4.0
Government Revenue (Excluding Grants)	23.9	24.6	25.9	28.2	27.8	28.0	28.1	27.5	27.1	27.4	27.9
Government Expenditure	25.3	25.6	26.4	28.0	28.6	29.6	30.5	31.1	31.4	31.5	31.9

Source: Five-year moving averages calculated from IMF annual data.

IMF:Various years. *Regional Economic Outlook: Sub-Saharan Africa.*

Table 7.2 Structure of the economy, 2013

No	Sub- sector	Percentages
1	Agriculture, forestry, and fishing	2.2
2	Mining and quarrying	4.9
3	Manufacturing	15.2
4	Electricity, gas, and water	1.8
5	Construction	3.0
6	Wholesale, retail and motor trade, catering and accommodations	12.5
7	Transport, storage, communications	9.0
8	Finance, real estate, business services	21.5
9	General government services	13.7
10	Personal services	5.4
11	Taxes less subsidies on products	10.8
12	**Total**	**100.0**

Source: Statistics South Africa: *South Africa's economy: Key Sectors.*

manufacturing, retail, financial services, communications, mining, agriculture, and tourism.

Agriculture

Covering 1.2 million square kilometers of land, South Africa has seven climatic regions, ranging from Mediterranean to subtropical to semi-desert. This biodiversity, together with a coastline of 3,000 kilometers long and served by seven large commercial ports, gives rise to the cultivation of a wide range of marine and agricultural products, ranging from deciduous, citrus, and subtropical fruit to grain, wool, cut flowers, livestock, and game. Agricultural activities range from intensive crop production and mixed farming in winter rainfall and high summer rainfall areas, to cattle ranching in the bushveld, and sheep farming in the arid regions.[1]

While 13 percent of South Africa's land can be used for crop production, only 22 percent of this is high-potential arable land. The greatest limitation is the availability of water. Rainfall is distributed unevenly across the country, with some areas prone to drought. Almost 50 percent of water is used for agriculture, with about 1.3 million hectares under irrigation.

South Africa is not only self-sufficient in virtually all major agricultural products but is also a net food exporter. Farming remains vitally important to the economy. South Africa has both well-developed commercial farming and more subsistence-based production in the rural areas.

In 1960, agriculture constituted 9.1 percent of the total economy; this has decreased to only 2.2 percent in 2013. This means that the secondary and tertiary sectors have become more important. Maize is most widely grown, followed by wheat, oats, sugar cane, and sunflowers. Citrus and deciduous fruits are exported, as are locally produced wines and flowers. The government has been developing programs to promote small-scale farming and to boost job creation.

The major problem with agriculture is the continued pattern of apartheid-era land ownership. Land reform efforts have not achieved much success.

Mining and quarrying

South Africa has abundant mineral resources, accounting for a significant proportion of both world production and reserves. South African mining companies dominate many sectors in the global industry. Mining and quarrying contributed 4.9 percent to GDP in 2013.

South Africa is the world's biggest producer of gold and platinum, and one of the leading producers of base metals and coal. The country's diamond industry is the fourth largest in the world, with only Botswana, Canada, and Russia producing more diamonds each year. The country produces 10 percent of the world's gold and has 40 percent of the world's known resources (kpmg.com/Africa).

Although well over a century old, South Africa's mining industry is far from fully tapped. While holding the world's largest reserves of gold, platinum-group metals, and manganese ore, the country has considerable potential for the discovery of other world-class deposits in areas yet to be exhaustively explored. The sector spans the full spectrum of the five major mineral categories: precious metals and minerals, energy minerals, non-ferrous metals and minerals, ferrous minerals, and industrial minerals.

In addition to its prolific mineral reserves, South Africa's strengths include a high level of technical and production expertise, and comprehensive research and development activities. The country has world-scale primary processing facilities covering carbon steel, stainless steel, and aluminum, in addition to gold and platinum.

With the growth of South Africa's secondary and tertiary industries, as well as a decline in gold production, mining's contribution to South Africa's GDP has declined over the past few decades. However, this may be offset by an increase in the downstream or beneficiated minerals industry, which the government has targeted as a growth sector. Opportunities exist for downstream processing and adding value locally to iron, carbon steel, stainless steel, aluminum, platinum group metals, and gold. A wide range of materials is available for jewelry, including gold, platinum, diamonds, tiger's eye, and a variety of other semi-precious stones (kpmg.com/Africa).

South Africa's mining industry is continually expanding and adapting to changing local and international world conditions, and remains a cornerstone of the economy, making a significant contribution to economic activity, job creation, and foreign exchange earnings. The Mineral and Petroleum Resources Development Act of 2002 enshrines equal access to mineral resources, irrespective of race, gender, or creed.

Wholesale and retail trade

The Statistics South Africa monthly survey of retail trade generally covers retailers in specialized food, beverages, tobacco, pharmaceutical and medical goods, cosmetics and toiletries, general dealers, textiles, clothing, footwear, leather goods, household furniture, appliances and equipment, hardware, paint, and glass, as well as various other dealers in miscellaneous goods. According to the survey, general dealers, other retailers and retailers in textiles, clothing, and footwear and leather goods are the major contributors to the increase in retail trade sales. Real retail trade is sensitive to changes in interest rates and overall performance of the economy.

Tourism

Tourism has been earmarked as a growth industry in South Africa. The industry is ideally suited to adding value to the country's many natural, cultural, and other resources. On the average, tourism directly and indirectly constitutes approximately 7 percent of GDP and employment in South Africa.

Some 74 percent of all visitors in 2006 were from mainland Africa and about 26 percent from overseas. About 7.9 million of the 8.5 million foreign travellers (92 percent) visited the country for a holiday and approximately 196,951 (2.3 percent) for business in 2006. South Africa's international tourism receipts amounted to $7.3 billion in 2005. Its share of total African tourist arrivals and tourism receipts was over 34 percent in 2005. In 2010, Fifa's World Cup event boosted the South African tourist industry (Statistics South Africa 2012; World Tourism Organization).

Finance and business services

South Africa has a sophisticated financial sector. With the formal end of apartheid and the country's re-integration into the global sphere in 1994, corporate governance rules, disclosure, transparency, and accountability became an integral part of doing business in South Africa. Consequently, regulations governing the financial sector, and particularly risk management, have undergone considerable refinement to align them to internationally recognized standards and best practice.

The financial, real estate, and business service sector accounted for 22 percent of the country's real value added in 2006 and, together with other services sectors, has proved to be a pillar of the country's economic growth over the years. The sector boasts dozens of domestic and foreign institutions providing a full range of services: commercial, retail, and merchant banking; mortgage lending, insurance, and investment. South Africa's banking sector compares favourably with those of industrialized countries. Foreign banks are well represented, and electronic banking facilities are extensive, with a nationwide network of automatic teller machines (ATMs). Internet banking is becoming increasingly important.[2]

Communications

The communications sector, which together with transport and storage accounted for almost 10 percent of GDP in 2006 and has been one of the fastest growing of the South African economy, reflects the rapid expansion of mobile telephony across the country. Fixed-line penetration is estimated at 10 percent while mobile penetration is significantly higher at around 93 percent. In 2007, the estimated revenue generated in the telecommunications sector was $18.5 (R126) billion and telecommunications (hardware and software) contributed an estimated additional $4 (R27) billion.

Telkom, a listed company in which the government is the biggest shareholder, was until recently the only licensed provider of public fixed-line telecommunications services. Telkom is also a key player in an optical fiber undersea cable project that is catering for Africa's growing telecommunications needs. In late 2006, the government awarded Neotel a license to become the second fixed-line operator. A second transatlantic cable, Seacom, and small other service providers, were licensed for business in 2009.[3]

South Africa's cellular phone market has grown phenomenally since its inception in 1994. It is also the fourth fastest growing Groupe Speciale Mobile (GSM) market in the world. Cellular services have been provided largely by three licensed operators: Vodacom, MTN and Cell C. In June 2006 a virtual cellular service provider, Virgin Mobile, was brought to life in partnership with Cell C. Research firm World Wide Worx predicted Internet users would reach 8.5 million in 2013 and 9 million users in 2014.

Information and communications technology

The South African information and communication technologies (ICT) sector is characterized by technology leadership, particularly in the field of mobile software and electronic banking services. South African companies are global leaders in pre-payment, revenue management, and fraud prevention systems, and in the manufacture of set-top boxes, all of which are exported successfully to all parts of the world. Export growth and internationalization of South African companies is supported by the Department of Trade and Industry via the South African Electrotechnical Export Council (SAEEC).[4]

According to the SAECC, in 2013, the South African ICT market was estimated at US$42.6 billion (R468.4 billion) with IT accounting for US$15.08 billion (R164 billion) and communications US$27.18 billion (R297 billion). The sector contributed approximately 8.2 percent to South Africa's GDP.

Several international corporates, recognized as leaders in the IT sector, operate subsidiaries from South Africa, including IBM, Unisys, Microsoft, Intel, Systems Application Protocol (SAP), Dell, Novell, and Compaq. Testing and piloting systems and applications are growing businesses in South Africa, with the diversity of the local market, first rate know-how in business and a developing country environment making it an ideal test lab for new innovations.

The electronics industry has repeatedly demonstrated world-class innovation and production. The industry is characterized by a handful of generalist companies with strong capabilities in professional electronics, while small to medium companies specialize in security systems and electricity pre-payment meters.

Investment opportunities lie in the development of access control systems and security equipment, automotive electronic subsystems, systems and software development in the banking and financial services sector, silicon processing for fiber optics, integrated circuits, and solar cells. There are also significant opportunities for the export of hardware and associated services, as well as software and peripherals.

The foreign sector

Exports and imports are more or less balanced at about 30 percent of GDP. Hence, the merchandise trade has been balanced. The current account deficit did not exceed 5.5 percent. The terms of trade were favorable throughout the period, 2000–2015, ranging from 104 to 144 percent. Foreign reserves can finance imports for about 2.5 to 5.5 months.

In 2015, the value of South African exports totaled $69.6 billion, while imports amounted to $79.6 billion, resulting in a deficit of $10.0 billion. The top ten exports constituted about 72 percent of its total. Most of the major exports originated from two sectors: mining and manufacturing. Exports from the mining sector included precious stones and metals (15%), ores (10%), and aluminum (1.7%), while those from the manufacturing sector included motor vehicles and parts (11.5%), industrial machinery (7%), iron and steel (6.6%), electrical machinery (2.7%), and beverages (1.87%). Other major exports included oil and mineral fuels (11.7%) and fruits and nuts (4.1%).[5]

South Africa's ten leading imports in 2015 constituted about 70 percent of the total, amounting to about $55.3 billion. They mainly consisted of manufactures goods. These included industrial machinery (13.4%) and electrical machinery (10.8%), motor vehicles and parts (8.2%), plastics (2.8%), precision instruments (2.5%), pharmaceuticals (2.4%), chemical products (1.8%), and organic chemicals (1.7%). Oil and mineral fuels were the leading items totaling about 17.5 percent. Intra-industry trade is mainly in the major manufactured products: industrial machinery, electrical machinery, motor vehicles and parts, and oil and mineral fuels.

Both the export destinations and origins of South African imports were diversified. The ten leading export markets took about 57 percent of South African exports, while the ten leading import sources supplied over 63 percent of South African imports. China was the leading export market (8.9%), followed by the United States (8.0%), Germany (6.5%), Namibia (5.9%), Botswana (5.8%), Japan (5.6%), India (4.8%), United Kingdom (4.7%), Belgium (3.5%), and Zambia (3.3%). The major sources of imports included China (18.6%), Germany (12.0%), United States (6.8%), Nigeria (5.8%), India (5.0%), Japan (3.9%), United Kingdom (3.2%), Saudi Arabia (2.8%), Italy (2.6%), and Thailand (2.3%).

The manufacturing sector

South Africa has a strong manufacturing base from which to build its economy. Manufacturing is dominated by industries such as agro-processing, automotive,

Table 7.3 The performance of the external sector (percent of GDP in real terms)

Item	2001–05	2002–06	2003–07	2004–08	2005–09	2006–10	2007–11	2008–12	2009–13	2010–14	2011–15
Export of Goods and Services	28.9	28.9	28.7	30.2	30.5	30.7	34.9	30.5	29.5	30.2	30.7
Imports of Goods and Services	27.2	28.7	29.7	32.0	32.4	32.2	31.5	30.9	29.7	30.9	31.8
Balance of Trade (Goods only)	2.0	0.6	–0.6	–1.0	–1.1	–0.5	0.3	0.3	0.4	–2.5	–0.8
Current Account (Including Grants)	–1.5	–2.8	–4.4	–5.2	–5.5	–5.0	–4.1	–3.7	–3.4	–4.0	–4.6
Terms of Trade (Index: 2000 = 100)	104.3	105.6	108.7	116.3	119.5	128.1	136.7	141.7	144.4	143.8	137.1
Reserves (months of Imports of Goods and Services)	2.5	2.7	2.9	3.1	3.8	4.0	4.3	4.7	4.8	5.0	5.5

Source: Five-year moving averages calculated from IMF annual data.

IMF, Regional Economic Outlook: Sub-Saharan Africa (various years).

chemicals, information and communication technology, electronics, metals, textiles, clothing, and footwear. The manufacturing sector provides a locus for stimulating the growth of other activities, such as services, and achieving specific outcomes, such as job creation and economic empowerment, thus accelerating the country's growth and development. The sector also enables the building of key national infrastructure such as electricity generation and municipal services, and also provides a viable means of beneficiating natural resources extraction.

Manufacturing employs around two million people, and accounts for about 15 percent of GDP. For every rand invested in manufacturing there is about R1.13 of value addition to the South African economy. In 2015 manufacturing production increased by 5.6 percent, driven mostly by a 39.6 percent production rise in the automotive industry and a 17.4 percent rise in the metals and machinery industry (kpmg.com/Africa 2014, 4).[6]

Three major categories of manufacturing can be identified in South Africa. First, there are capital-intensive sectors. These generally comprise the capital- and energy-intensive "*Minerals-Energy Complex*" sectors which convert primary resources into semi-processed ones (kpmg.com/Africa 2014, 4). These sectors include steel, chemicals, and aluminum. Due to economies of scale, there is little scope to substitute labor for capital. The role of these sectors with regard to employment is less to create employment directly as such, but to enable greater employment in sectors that are medium and highly labor intensive by supplying intermediate inputs to them at competitive prices. This would also ensure that the underlying advantages of the country's resource endowments are passed on to a broader group of sectors, employees, and consumers.

The second group of sectors comprises those in which *capital and labor are complements rather than substitutes*. For example, in sectors such as the fabrication of metals and plastics or capital and transport equipment, there is no contradiction between increasing levels of fixed investment and employment intensity. In these industries, employment rises as capital investment rises. Substantial parts of the agro-processing sector also exhibit this trait. In addition to promoting greater investment in agro-processing, it is necessary to increase agricultural output and exports. This will stimulate agricultural employment directly and provide higher levels of feedstock for further local processing. Parts of the automotive value chain also have significant scope to raise employment in conjunction with increased investment. This includes increasing the volume of the vehicle assembly segment (which is highly capital intensive), while simultaneously increasing the breadth and depth of domestically produced automotive components (which generally are much less capital intensive than assembly). Similarly, the manufacture of components for the renewable energy sector provides opportunities to raise employment.

The third group of the sector are *intrinsically labor intensive*, such as the production of clothing and footwear. These are the most challenging sectors in the context of the massive global increase in unskilled labor and hence competition from imported, low-priced labor-intensive goods. South Africa also faces competition in these sectors from countries such as China that offer low monetary wages because the wages are counterbalanced by more extensive provision of *"social infrastructure"* than in South Africa. The *"social infrastructure"* includes cheap housing close to the source of employment, cheap public transport, and affordable health care.

The South African government is keenly focused on factories and heavy industry as an employment creator despite operational and profitability challenges in the secondary sector. Top growth and employment multipliers in South Africa include the manufacturing of footwear, textiles, and leather products; automotive, machinery, and related equipment, as well as food and furniture production. South Africa's steel industry is the largest on the continent. Automotive production produces complete vehicles, components, and parts for local, regional, and international markets. The chemical subsector has developed an upstream component, with gas-to-oil processing the dominant activity.

The Industrial Action Plan launched in April 2013 focused on value-added production, with state support centered on nurturing and defending industrial development. The plan also emphasized re-aligning the country's value-added exports towards other developing economies in Africa and emerging markets.

South Africa's strong manufacturing sector has had, and continues to have, an important impact on development in Africa, especially in southern, eastern, and central Africa. However, South Africa needs to spread the benefits of its economy widely at home through land reform, mass education, and training. Although much has been done since the end of apartheid in 1994, much more effort needs to be exerted in the creation of a post-apartheid economy. For development to be viable and sustainable, the bulk of the population must participate in, and benefit from it. A dynamic, internally stable, industrial South Africa will reduce dependence of many countries in the region on long-distance imports of development inputs from outside the continent, and hence accelerate development in the region and continent.

The structure of manufacturing

Manufacturing in South Africa is dominated by the following industries: (i) agro-processing; (ii) automotive; (ii) chemicals; (iii) ICT and electronics; (iv) metals; and (v) textiles, clothing, and footwear industry.

Agro-processing

The agro-processing industry spans the processing of freshwater aquaculture and mari-culture, exotic and indigenous meats, nuts, herbs, and fruit. It also involves the production and export of deciduous fruit; production of wines for the local and export market; confectionary manufacturing and export; and the processing of natural fibers from cotton, hemp, sisal, kenaf, and pineapple.

World-class infrastructure, counter-seasonality to Europe, vast biodiversity, and marine resources, and competitive input costs make the country a major player on the world's markets.[7] In 2013, the agro-processing sector was worth

$4.7 (R49) billion and created as many as 207,893 jobs in the third quarter of that year (kpmg.com/Africa 2014). It is also significant in sustaining the environment and growing the economy. Since 2008, food processing grew by over more than the manufacturing sector as a whole. The government's New Growth Path (NGP) and National Development Plan (NDP) had both identified agro-processing as a sector with high growth potential, despite the challenges of imports competition, loss of market, and the unstable currency and exchange rate.

The automotive cluster

This is the most important subsector of South African manufacturing, with firms operating along all levels of the value chain. The sector accounts for about 12 percent of South Africa's manufacturing exports. Major international automobile manufacturers are at the center of the country's export-oriented auto cluster. Vehicle manufacturers such as BMW, Ford Motors, Volkswagen, Daimler-Chrysler (Mercedes-Benz), Toyota, Nissan, Mazda, and others have production plants in the country, while component manufacturers have established production bases in the country. Their presence has spawned the creation of supporting suppliers. The country exports auto components, particularly catalytic converters and leather upholstery.

The South African automotive supply chain includes manufacturing, distribution, maintenance, and servicing. Over the years, it has transformed itself from a mainly importing industry to an increasingly self-sufficient one. It has been able to increasingly integrate its operations throughout the entire value chain. Suppliers for the manufacturing process include both domestic and international firms. The cluster's value chain begins by utilizing basic materials from mining and livestock (steel, aluminum, leather, rubber, plastics, and glass)

Table 7.4 The structure of manufacturing in 2014 (percent)

No	Subsector	Percent
1	Food and beverages	24.7
2	Petroleum, chemical, rubber and plastic products	23.0
3	Metal and metal products	19.6
4	Wood and paper products, publishing and printing	9.2
5	Vehicles, parts and accessories	8.8
6	Glass and non-metallic mineral products	4.1
7	Textiles, clothing, leather and footwear	2.6
8	Electrical equipment	2.3
9	Audio visual, communication and professional equipment	1.8
10	Furniture	1.2
11	Other manufacturing groups	2.6
12	**Total**	**100.0**

Source: kpmg.com/Africa. 2014. *Manufacturing in Africa*, p. 4.

which are manufactured into various components to be assembled and then distributed for final sale either in the domestic market or as exports.

The auto cluster faces intense competition from a global industry whose center of gravity is increasingly shifting to emerging economies with low labor costs and greater proximity to major export markets. Because automobile production is a bulk-gaining industry, transport costs of the final product to the consumer are significant, so there are advantages to locating near the end market. Furthermore, many emerging market countries maintain tariffs or incentives to favor domestic automobile production. Given economies of scale in the auto industry, South Africa's domestic market, while significant, is not large enough for production there to be economical without significant exports to outside markets. As a result, South Africa exports a far greater proportion of its automobile production than China, India, and Brazil. Medium-sized countries comparable to South Africa export to neighboring large markets such as the US and Europe.

The restrictions during the apartheid period led to development of domestic components and market. This created a fairly integrated but small and locally oriented automobile industry. With persistent increase in domestic sales of vehicles has been an increase in the number of original equipment manufacturers (OEMs), component producers, and proliferation in the number of models.[8]

With the end of apartheid, South Africa became exposed to the global market. The government helped the auto cluster adjust to international competition through the support of the Motor Industry Development Program (MIDP). The MIDP was introduced to help the small protected auto industry integrate with the global market within the context of economy-wide liberalization following the end of apartheid. Initially it was planned to be phased out by 2002 but was extended a number of times until 2012. The central objective of the program was to develop a globally competitive auto industry with strong spillovers in employment, vehicle affordability in the domestic market, and catalyzing the economy in general.

The key elements of the MIDP were gradual reduction in protection and export facilitation. The reduction in protection involved abolition of the domestic content component requirement and gradual reduction in import tariffs. The export facilitation program involved duty free on imported components in exchange for an equivalent value of domestic content exported; trade in export credits among producers, and duty free incentive for the production of smaller fuel-efficient vehicles.

Over the course of its lifetime the MIDP was extended twice, and under it vehicle exports grew from a negligible number in 1995/96 to 277,893 units in 2012, while in value terms the nation exported around R4 billion ($490 million) per year at the start of the program against around R86.9 billion ($10.6 billion) in 2012. The South African automotive industry has emerged as the largest local manufacturing sector, accounting for 80 percent of South Africa's total production.[9]

The outcome of the policy included strong export growth rates to countries such as Germany, UK, Japan, USA, and Australia, which were the main countries of South African OEMs. There was improved re-orientation of the global market, employment generation, and lower cost for domestic consumers.

The MIDP was replaced by the Automotive Production and Development Program (APDP) in January 2013. The main objective of the APDP was to build local manufacturing capacity and to meet the World Trade Organization's (WTO) requirement on subsidies. The program seeks to improve international competitiveness through a re-orientation of incentives towards local manufacturing capacity building. Its key elements included return on investment on new plant or machinery, allowances for cost incurred on R&D, training, and technology transfer, and import tariff rebate based on value of total production. It is aimed at affecting second and third tier suppliers, and original equipment manufacturers. Because of the APDP, the volume of cars manufactured in South Africa was projected to increase to 1.2 million annually by 2020 as well as to diversify the automotive components chain. According to the National Association of Automobile Manufacturers (NAAM), production, particularly that of light motor vehicles, will rise from 2014 onward because of the APDP.

The Motor Industry Development Council (MIDC) was established in 1996 as a co-operative forum between government, industry, and labor to recommend policy and discuss cluster-wide issues. However, the country must address the problems of labor unrest, lack of skilled technicians, low levels of R&D, and insufficient supplier depth. There are few technicians and researchers compared with global peers.

The market size and financial services, including access to consumer credit, helps the auto cluster by supporting domestic demand. During apartheid, it was mainly the domestic market that supported the auto industry.

Companies with production plants in South Africa are placed to take advantage of the low production costs, coupled with access to new markets as a result of trade agreements with the European Union and the Southern African Development Community (SADC) free trade area. Opportunities also lie in the production of domestic materials such as automotive steel and components.

Europe remains the local industry's largest export market, despite the effects of slow growth and recession in the Eurozone. In 2012, 66,929 vehicles were sold to Europe, 6,000 more than were sold in Africa (kpmg.com/Africa).[10]

Chemicals industry

The chemicals industry has been shaped by the political and regulatory environment that created a philosophy of isolationism and protectionism during the apartheid years. This tended to foster an inward approach and a focus on import substitution in the local market. It also encouraged the building of small-scale plants with capacities geared to local demand, which tended to be uneconomic.

Through isolation of the industry from international competition and high raw material prices as a result of import tariffs, locally processed goods have generally been less than competitive in export markets. In post-apartheid South Africa, South African chemical companies are focusing on the need to be internationally competitive and the industry has been reshaping itself accordingly.

The South African chemicals sector has two noticeable characteristics. Firstly, while its upstream sector is concentrated and well developed, the downstream sector, although diverse, remains underdeveloped. Secondly, the synthetic coal and natural gas-based liquid fuels and petrochemicals industry is prominent, with South African being world leader in coal-based synthesis and gas-to-liquid (GTL) technologies.

The industry is highly complex and widely diversified, with end products often being composed of a number of chemicals that have been combined in some way. The primary and secondary sectors are dominated by Sasol (through Sasol Chemical Industries and Sasol Polymers), AECI, and Dow Sentrachem. These companies have recently diversified and expanded their interests in tertiary products, especially those with export potential. In 2013, the chemical sector was South Africa's fourth-largest employer with 200,000 jobs and contributed about 5 percent to the country's GDP.[11]

ICT and electronics industries: The South African information technology (IT) industry growth outstrips the world average. South Africa established a sophisticated indigenous information and communication technology (ICT). The electronics sector comprised more than 3,000 companies. It has already access to cutting edge technologies, equipment, and skills and has the advantage of access to the rapid expansion of telecommunications and IT throughout Africa. South African software developers are recognized as world leaders in innovation, production, and cost efficiency backed by an excellent local infrastructure. This sector consists of telecommunications, electronics, and information technology.

The telecommunications subsector is thriving, contributing more than 7 percent to South Africa's GDP. Growing at a rate of 50 percent per year and the fourth fastest growing cellphone market in the world, South African GSM cellphone market has three major operators: Vodacom, MTN, and Cell-C. Some of the world's leading telecommunication brands like Siemens, Alcatel, SBC Communications, Telecom Malaysia, Cell C, and Vodaphone have made significant investments in the country.

The South African electronics and ICT subsectors have repeatedly proved themselves in terms of world-class innovation and production. The electronics industry is characterized by a handful of generalist companies specializing in security systems and electricity pre-payment meters. Investment opportunities lie in the development of access control systems and security equipment, automotive electronic subsystems, systems and software development in the banking and financial services sectors, silicon processing for fiber optics, integrated circuits, and solar cells. There are also significant opportunities for the export of hardware and associated services as well as software and peripherals.

Metals industry

The metal industry is a large, well-developed sector, representing about a third of South Africa's industry. It is based on vast natural resources and a supportive infrastructure. It comprises basic iron ore and steel, basic non-ferrous metals, and metal products. The iron and steel basic industries involve the manufacture of primary iron and steel products from smelting to semi-finished stages. Primary steel products and semi-finished products included billets, blooms, and slabs, forgings, reinforcing bars, railway track material, wire rod, seamless tubes, and plates. South Africa is a net exporter of steel and steel products.

In recent years, the international and South African steel industry has changed dramatically. Several steel companies have fallen away and protectionism has increased. To survive in these harsh conditions, the South African primary steel industry has taken major steps to become more efficient and competitive. Many South African steelworks have engaged in restructuring and productivity improvements.

South Africa's non-ferrous metal industries comprise aluminum and other metals such as copper, brass, lead, zinc, and tin. South Africa is ranked eighth in world production of aluminum. Although the other non-ferrous metals are small, they are still important for exports and foreign exchange earnings. The country's copper, brass, and bronze industries have declined in recent years. It is hoped that new mining and reclamation technologies will allow the exploitation of previously unviable deposits.

Textiles, clothing, and footwear industry

Owing to technological developments, local textile production has evolved into a capital-intensive industry, producing synthetic fibers in ever-increasing proportions. The apparel industry has also undergone significant technological changes and has benefited from the country's sophisticated transport and communications infrastructure. The clothing and textile industry offers the full range of services from natural and synthetic fiber production to non-woven, spinning, weaving, tufting, knitting, dyeing, and finishing. Exports mainly go to the US, through the *African Growth and Opportunity Act (AGOA)*, and European markets. The South African textile and clothing industry aims to use all the natural, human, and technological resources at its disposal to make it the preferred international supplier. Though the textile and apparel industry is small, it is well placed to make this vision a reality. In 2013, textiles and clothing accounted for about 14 percent of manufacturing employment and represented South Africa's second largest source of tax revenue (Statistics South Africa). The textile industry is the most cost-effective way of creating jobs.

With the US's African Growth and Opportunity Act (AGOA) renewed in 2015, the South African textile industry is set to benefit even more than before. But, in spite of this, the industry remains vulnerable to cheap imports. China's inclusion in the World Trade Organization in 2001 rocked local manufacturers as South African businesses began importing cheaper textiles and clothing from China. Additionally, a relatively strong rand from 2003 onwards led to the industry's decline. As a result, the number of jobs decreased. However, the government's rescue plan for the textile and clothing industry, which was outlined in 2009, has done exceptionally well to recover the industry in recent years and is in the best position it has been in a decade.

Deindustrialization and revitalizing manufacturing

For years, South African industry had been in a state of decline, facing challenges around productivity, costs, labor issues, skills shortages, efficiency, and new technology. To bolster the contribution of manufacturing to GDP, the country embarked on overcoming some of the fundamental challenges, which include low productivity, compared to international competitors, such as China and Germany; high input costs, especially labor costs and efficiency, which render the South African manufacturing sector uncompetitive; a lack of alignment between government and the manufacturing sector on how to promote growth in the industry and, a shortage of skills at all levels in the manufacturing industry. The main focus has been on shifting South African manufacturing globally, from traditional labor-intensive manufacturing practices to the latest technological, especially digital, advances.

These new models require skill sets which are in short supply in the South African manufacturing sector. In order to meet the National Development Plan targets by 2030, South Africa needs to increase the training of artisans by producing 30,000 artisans a year. At present, the country produces 13,000 artisans a year across all trades, and 72 percent of these are trained by private institutions (OECD 2013). South Africa plans to place itself into a regional manufacturing hub.

To stem out further deindustrialization, the Preferential Procurement Policy Framework Act regulations came into force in December 2011, empowering the Department of Trade and Industry (DTI) to designate the products that should be sourced locally. These included items such as busses, uniforms, power pylons, canned vegetables, rolling stock, pharmaceuticals, furniture, set-top boxes, cables, and solar water heaters. An aggressive export drive in Africa and strive to remain globally competitive were emphasized. For South African manufacturing companies to be globally competitive, they require forward thinking that considers technological advancements and global trends, and not only the immediate needs of the enterprise and current demand in the economy. Hence, a strong export dimension was incorporated into the latest version of the Industrial Policy Action Plan (IPAP), while the Department of Trade and Industry (DTI) was pushing ahead with negotiations for a trilateral free trade area involving the Southern African Development Community, the East African Community, and the Common Market for Eastern and Southern Africa. In 2012, Africa surpassed the European Union as the largest market for South African manufactured products. Total exports to the continent more than doubled from $10.9 (R100) billion in 2008 to well over $24.1 (R200) billion in 2012 (Mavuso 2014).

A number of plans were put in action. The overarching plan for dealing with the deindustrialization threat is the *Industrial Policy Action Plan (IPAP)*, which details key actions and timeframes for the implementation of the initial round of industrial policy. IPAP sets out transversal and sector-specific program and action plans to retain, grow, and diversify South Africa's industrial base. It also aims to bring about structural change in the economy by focusing on value-adding activity in the production sectors, particularly labor-intensive and export-orientated sectors, led by manufacturing.

IPAP is built on the vision of the National Industrial Policy Framework, which is based on the notion of broadening participation in the economy. This plan is complemented by the medium-term *New Growth Path*, which also emphasizes the importance of a production-led growth trajectory.

Each year, the Department of Trade and Industry (DTI) launches a revised three-year rolling IPAP with a ten-year outlook in the context of rapid economic change and significant global uncertainty. To achieve and consolidate these objectives, new platforms would need to be built continuously to strengthen existing stakeholder engagement and deepen trust and cooperation between government, private sector, and organized labor.

The Department of Trade and Industry (DTI) continues to support investments in the Manufacturing Competitive Enhancement Program and the Automotive Incentive Scheme. However, a major area of concern for many manufacturers remains the hostile industry-labor climate, with the metals and engineering sectors having experienced a protracted and, at times, violent strike. For South Africa to turn its economy into high growth and job creation again, it must focus on building its skilled labor force through a dramatic expansion of vocational training, and forging a true development partnership between government, business, and labor.

The DTI has identified five key policy measures, which are advanced manufacturing, infrastructure productivity, natural gas, service exports, and agricultural transformation. South Africa can draw on skilled labor to grow into a globally competitive manufacturing hub focused on high-value-added categories such as automotive, industrial machinery and equipment, and chemicals. To realize this opportunity, however, South African manufacturers will have to pursue new markets and step up innovation and productivity. The country is investing heavily in infrastructure, but big gaps remain in electricity, water, and sanitation. By forging a true partnership, the public and private sectors can together drive three strategies to make infrastructure spending up to 40 percent more productive: making maximum use of existing assets and increasing maintenance; prioritizing the projects with greatest impact; and strengthening management practices to streamline delivery.

South Africa's electricity shortage has constrained growth, and despite new capacity, another shortfall is projected between 2025 and 2030. Natural gas plants, which are fast to build, entail low capital costs, and have a low carbon footprint, can provide an alternative to diversify the power supply. With the necessary regulatory certainty, South Africa could install up to 20 GW of gas-fired power plants to diversify base-load capacity by 2030. Gas can be provided through imports, local shale gas resources, or both. South Africa is also collaborating with the Democratic Republic of Congo (DRC) to develop the Inga III hydroelectric project.[12]

South Africa has highly developed service industries, yet it currently captures only 2 percent of the rest of sub-Saharan Africa's market for service imports, which is worth nearly half a trillion rand (or $ 37 billion). With the right investments, service businesses could ramp up exports to the rest of Africa, and government can help by promoting regional trade deals. In construction, the opportunity ranges from design to construction management to maintenance services. In financial services, promising growth areas include wholesale and retail, banking, and insurance.

With consumption rising in markets throughout sub-Saharan Africa and Asia, South Africa plans to triple its agricultural exports by 2030. This could be a key driver of rural growth of South Africa's smallholder farming should land reform be accelerated.

South Africa offers various attractive investment incentives, targeted at specific sectors or types of business activities. These include *The Enterprise Investment Program manufacturing program (EIP – manufacturing/tourism)* The EIP (manufacturing) is a cash grant for locally based manufacturers who wish to establish a new production facility, expand an existing facility, or upgrade an existing facility in manufacturing industries. The EIP (tourism) is an investment incentive grant, payable over a period of two to three years, to support the development of tourism enterprises, to stimulate job creation and encourage the geographical spread of tourism investment throughout South Africa. Tourism-related activities supported by the grant include: (i) accommodation services; (ii) passenger transport services; (iii) tour operators; (iv) cultural services; and (v) recreational and entertainment services. *The foreign investment grant* seeks to compensate qualifying foreign investors for the cost of moving qualifying new machinery and equipment from abroad to South Africa.

The critical infrastructure fund is a cash grant for projects designed to improve critical infrastructure in South Africa, including the following: (i) transport systems (road and rail systems); (ii) electricity transmission and distribution systems (power flow and regulation systems); (iii) telecommunications networks (cabling and signal transmission systems); (iv) sewage systems (network and purification); (v) waste storage, disposal, and treatment systems; and (vi) fuel supply systems (piping for liquid, gas, and solid fuel conveyer transportation).

Industrial development zones are purpose-built industrial estates linked to international ports that leverage fixed direct investments in value added and export-oriented manufacturing industries. These zones provide the following benefits: (i) quality infrastructure; (ii) expedited customs procedures; and (iii) duty-free operating environments.

The location film and television production incentive program consists of a *Large Budget Film and Television Production Rebate Scheme,* whereby foreign-owned qualifying producers are rebated a maximum of R10 million for the production of large budget films and television productions. The South African *film and television production and co-production incentive financial assistance* is extended to South African feature films, tele-movies, television drama series, documentaries, and animation. The objective is to contribute to the local film industry. Production budgets are required to be more than R10 million, with the rebate being 35 percent, capped at R10 million.

The *export marketing and investment assistance* (EMIA) scheme partially compensates exporters in respect of activities aimed at developing export markets for South African products and services, and to recruit new FDI into South Africa. The scheme provides assistance in the form of: (i) air travel expenses; (ii) subsistence allowances; (iii) freight-forwarding of display materials; and (iv) exhibition space and booth rental costs.

The *business process outsourcing and offshoring investment incentive* (BPO&O) comprises an investment grant, and a training support grant, towards costs of company-specific training. The incentive is offered to local and foreign investors establishing projects that aim primarily to serve offshore clients. The *automotive production and development program* has four key elements: (i) tariff reduction freeze from 2013 until 2020; (ii) local assembly allowance; (iii) production incentives; and (iv) automotive investment allowance.

Generally, South Africa's attractiveness as an investment destination is supported by the National Development Plan, the New Growth Path, and the Industrial Policy Action Plan. Through the New Growth Path the mining, agriculture, tourism, infrastructure development, green economy, and manufacturing sector are being boosted.

Land reform: reduction of poverty, unemployment, and inequality

At the beginning of majority rule in South Africa in 1994, about 90 percent of land in the country was owned by the 10 percent white population. The new government of Nelson Mandela and the African National Congress (ANC) vowed to redistribute land to the majority dispossessed black population. The land reform policy envisaged that by 2014, one-third of the country's land would be shifted from white farmers to blacks. However, by 2014, less that 7 percent of the land had been redistributed (Lahiff 2007).[13]

The deadline for the one-third redistribution has been postponed to 2025. Furthermore, much of whatever little land has been redistributed lies unutilized because of lack of capital and skills by the new owners. In addition, there is dire lack of support services to the new owners who are expected to suddenly turn from landless peasants to commercial farmers to maintain the standards of the previous landowners, who had been commercial farmers for decades with support from the apartheid state.

There was a restitution policy from 1994 to 1998 by which those evicted from their land during the apartheid era could reclaim their land. Under the restitution policy most claimants settled for the short-run benefit of cash compensation, so not much land changed ownership. By 2009, about 2.6 million hectares of land had been transferred.

The redistribution program continued beyond the five years of the restitution. It was based on the *"willing buyer/willing seller"* approach, which depended on voluntary market transactions. As should be expected, this method proved unsuccessful as many whites did not want to sell and many blacks lacked the resources to buy land at the high prices demanded. No measures were taken against uncooperative landowners as all transactions were required to be voluntary.

Then under the *"Area Based Land Reform and Proactive Land Acquisition"* policy, the state was to approach landowners on behalf of would-be buyers, instead of leaving the potential buyers to fend for themselves in a land market with unequal powers between the seller and buyer. This pushed up prices as the sellers charged higher prices knowing that the state has more resources than the individual buyers. This reduced the effectiveness of the state land budget, therefore limiting the amount of land that could be purchased for redistribution. A policy of compelling landowners with excess land to sell a portion of the excess land at affordable price was considered but not implemented.

Support for land reform beneficiaries after settling on the land has been consistently weak due to small budgets and split of responsibilities. The national Department of Rural Development and Land Reform is responsible for land acquisition, while the provincial departments of agriculture are responsible for agricultural support services. Another complicating factor has been the wrong advice given to the new farmers who were expected, all of a sudden, to become large-scale commercial farmers.

The commercial farming plans of the support agencies exacerbated the lack of capital and skills that has been the major problem of land reform in South Africa. Unfeasible business plans required levels of capital and skills far beyond the capacity of most new participants have been imposed. Breaking up large estates into family-size farms and adopting low-input labor-intensive methods have been discouraged by state agencies as they have been determined to maintain the commercial nature of South African agriculture as the previous white owners who have been commercial farmers for decades.

As marginal land has been the one mostly traded, gradual development of the productive capacities of the new farmers would not affect South African food production. The latter takes place in the most productive land, usually under irrigation.

In July 2014, the *Restitution of Land Rights Amendment Bill* reopened the claims process that had ended in 1998. It gives people who were forcibly removed from their land five years to lodge new claims. Like before, if successful, claimants are given the option of getting their land back or receiving financial compensation; most of the claimants prefer the short-term, cash compensation option.

As the land reform issue in South Africa drags on, its political significance has risen. In early 2015, President Zuma outlined land reforms plans. Under these proposals, foreigners will only be allowed to lease land, not to own it. Local farmers will not be allowed to own more than 12,000 hectares of land (Reuters 2015).

Some politicians are calling for taking over land from white farmers without compensation, evoking practices of land acquisition during the apartheid period. Another recent government proposal is to transfer 50 percent share of commercial farmland to workers in proportion to the amount of time they have worked on the farm.

The South African government should robustly be engaged in the land reform process and provide high levels of support to the new farmers. Unequal power and patterns of land ownership are unlikely to resolve themselves on market basis. Dragged on for decades, the issue may become politically violent as radical land seizures become inevitable when the reform process begins to be seen as a failure. All parties should cooperate in the resolution of the issues given its historical roots and national significance. All parties stand to gain from cooperating on a land reform that is seen as just in addressing the emotional historical legacies of European settlement, colonialism, and apartheid.

Some expropriation may be inevitable.[14] Differentiation in the provision of support services to the new beneficiaries should be devised depending on their initial resources and skills. Obsession with large-scale, commercial production should be discontinued. Small, medium, and large owners should be progressively treated differently as the state support should be based more on social need rather than on commercial criteria. Raising the levels of living of the poor and landless households will have long-term benefits for the South African economy as a whole. Training, credit, and marketing infrastructure should be availed in the locations of smallholders. The type and scale of farming should be consistent with the interests and backgrounds of the new farmers. Prosperity of the resettled landless is a new frontier for the expansion of the South African internal market and dynamism in the economy. Growth in an industrial market economy needs a growing market.

The creation of a new source of domestic market is particularly important as the old large landowners have large savings in the large South African financial sector and abroad. Their farm earnings do not have to be directly channeled into immediate spending. Their marginal propensities to consume are low and they have less incentive to invest in the real economy, or create real jobs, because they can live comfortably off the interest accrued from their financial assets. Prosperity of the new landowners can provide new dynamism to the South African economy as this new source of demand will probably be channeled to domestic spending. Such increase in domestic demand will generate more investment and growth in the South African economy, and hence create more jobs.

Concluding remarks and policy implications

South Africa remains a dual economy with one of the highest inequality rates in the world, perpetuating both inequality and exclusion. The government is acutely aware of the immense challenges it needs to overcome in order to accelerate progress and build a more inclusive society. Its vision and the priorities it is making to address these challenges are outlined in the *2030 National Development Plan, which comprises the two main strategic goals of eliminating poverty and reducing inequality from 0.70 to 0.60 by 2030.*

The country faces structural constraints that also limit economic growth, such as skills shortages, declining global competitiveness, and frequent work stoppages due to strike action. The government faces growing pressure from urban constituencies to improve the delivery of basic services to low-income areas, to increase job growth, and to provide university level-education at affordable prices. Land reform remains a burning issue.

Unstable electricity supplies retard growth. Eskom, the state-run power company, has built new power stations and has installed new power demand management programs to improve power grid reliability. It is revamping South Africa's nuclear power generating capabilities. South Africa is cooperating with the Democratic Republic of the Congo (DRC) and other regional countries to implement the Inga III Power Project. Other major reforms include accelerated implementation of ongoing public and private infrastructure projects, investing in basic and tertiary education, promoting competition and small and medium enterprises (SMEs) growth, and increasing the flexibility and efficiency of factor markets.

Manufacturing plays an irreplaceable role in driving growth and economic development. However, South African manufacturing continues to be heavily dominated by resource-processing sectors that are capital and energy intensive. Some structural shifts towards higher growth in more value-adding and higher labor-absorbing manufacturing sectors is essential for South Africa to shift to a development path which generates more growth and higher levels of employment.

South Africa's growth since 1994 has not been underpinned by expenditure that is due to rapidly rising incomes, but by rising levels of household debt, most notably during the mini boom of 2004–2008. The short-term capital inflows that fueled the overvaluation of the currency during this period were an important part of the credit extended for rising debt-based consumption. The overvaluation of the currency fueled a flood of cheap imports which hurt employment in the manufacturing sector. As a result, employment gains in debt-driven service sectors were insufficient to make any serious dent in unemployment over this period.

Unlocking the further growth and employment potential of services requires the revitalization of the manufacturing sector so that real national income can be raised. This occurs predominantly through the stimulatory effect on real national income and the associated derived demand that is then generated for the bulk of non-tradable services. Rising national income as the driver of services growth and employment is fundamentally more sustainable than when the growth of services is fueled by increases in household debt levels.

The South African manufacturing sector, although relatively diversified, is dominated by a few large subsectors, specifically chemicals, metals, and machinery, as well as food processing. The chemicals and food processing sectors expanded their respective shares of manufacturing value-add since 1994, while those of metals and machinery have remained unchanged.

While many manufacturing subsectors are domestic-market orientated, others rely heavily on export markets. Competitiveness is, thus, critical to their success. Consequently, several factors affect subsector performance over time, including domestic and external demand conditions, currency movements, input costs and pricing practices, technological upgrading, policy support, infrastructure and logistics, regulatory aspects, and tariff protection, as well as competition issues.

At the subsector level, the largest gains in real value-add during the 1994 to 2012 period among the manufacturing industries were recorded for petroleum products, motor vehicles, parts and accessories, machinery and equipment, basic chemicals, and electrical machinery.

Over the period 2004–2014, there had been persistent concern about deindustrialization in South Africa, as well as locally produced manufactured products having been increasingly displaced by imports. The very future of manufacturing has been called into question, despite a series of government interventions designed to not only stem the deindustrialization tide, but to place the manufacturing sector back on a positive growth path. An overview of the South African economy report by the Industrial Development Corporation (IDC), released in 2013, showed that, while the manufacturing sector accounted for 20.9 percent of the country's gross domestic product (GDP) in 1994, its contribution has since declined to around 12 percent.

From 1994 to 2004, the local manufacturing sector's contribution to GDP had declined by 0.76 percent, while there was a 5.2 percent average decline in contribution between 2004 and 2013. The global economic crisis accelerated this adverse trend, particularly owing to weakened demand in traditional markets, such as Europe, as well as difficult trading conditions domestically. The fierce competition in domestic and world markets that the manufacturing sector faces has also affected the sector's ability to grow.

Besides the demand-side stresses, the sector also has to deal with substantial cost pressures, arising in the areas of wages, inputs, among others. But its competitiveness has been further undermined by other challenges, such as electricity shortages, currency volatility, skills constraints, and a poor rate of productivity improvement. However, the sector has experienced short periods of relative strength, with some subsectors having registered good growth between 2004 and 2007 as a result of robust export demand backed by solid domestic demand.

To greatly improve the growth of GDP, and particularly of manufacturing, a number of measures need to be undertaken. Education needs to be transformed to train people for highly skilled manufacturing jobs. The country needs to evolve from being a producer of primary, and exporter of processed primary, products to becoming producers of value-added products.

The South African government has planned to spend billions of rand over the next few years to help manufacturers upgrade their factories, improve products and train workers. Additionally, the South African government has instituted two key national strategies that affect the manufacturing sector. These are the *New Growth Path* and the *Industrial Policy Action Plan II (IPAPII)*. The New Growth Path is a framework that seeks to address the issues surrounding unemployment, inequality, and poverty, through strategy implementation relating to job creation and aims to create five million jobs by 2020; through restructuring the South African economy to improve performance in relation to labor intensive and an improved growth rate. The Industrial Policy Action Plan (IPAP), on the other hand, is a step towards transforming South Africa's manufacturing sector, which aims to ensure that stronger cohesion exists between macro and micro economic policies that relate to exchange and interest rates, inflation, and trade balance requirements.

According to the Department of Trade and Industry (DTI), there was no single contributing factor that could be identified as being responsible for the decline of manufacturing in the country. Instead, the decline was a result of a range of factors that had to be dealt with collectively if the country wanted to raise the levels of diversified manufacturing and employment.

Two major factors that could have boosted productive capacity and domestic market; and hence economic growth in South Africa are a post-apartheid baby-boom and land reform. The post-apartheid baby-boom has been completely missed because of the HIV/AIDS pandemic that befell the country in the immediate post-apartheid period. Rapid growth of population since the end of apartheid would have increased the size and altered the age structure of the population. Such changes would probably have increased the rate of economic growth as well as the structures of demand and growth.

A major land reform that benefits the majority of the poor landless could substantially raise incomes with significant multiplier effects on the rest of the economy, particularly on the consumer goods subsector of manufacturing. This would have increased economic growth, particularly in the labor-intensive and mass consumer goods sectors. This can still be undertaken. As happened in the old industrial economies, the manufacturing sector creates more jobs than the service sector. Hence, South Africa should re-energize its manufacturing sector as it emphasizes on massive job creation.

Notes

1 Although other sources give more details on the sectors represented in Table 6.2, most of the details on the various sectors are contained in: www.southafrica.inf/business/economy/sectors/manufacturing.htm (Accessed May 20, 2016).

2 Statistics South Africa, *South Africa's Economy: Key Sectors*. Also see reports of the Financial Services Board and the South African Reserve Bank (various years).

3 www.southafrica.inf/business/economy/sectors/manufacturing.htm (Accessed May 20, 2016).

4 The South African Electrotechnical Export Council (SAEEC) is a non-profit company established as a Public-Private Partnership between South African business and the Department of Trade and Industry to facilitate the export growth and internationalization of its members in the fields of Electrical Engineering, Electronics, Information Technology, and Telecommunications.
5 The details of South Africa's 2015 trade data were obtained from the same sources for Ethiopia and Nigeria: https://globaledge.msu/countries/ethiopia/trade and https://comtrade.un.org/ (Accessed February 19, 2017). Comprehensive trade data for DRC were not available from the same sources.
6 KPMG is an international investment and consulting company with offices in many countries all over the world. In South Africa, it has offices in several cities, including Cape Town, Durban, Johannesburg, and Pretoria.
7 South Africa is in the Southern hemisphere, so the seasons alternate with those of its European major farm products exports.
8 Original equipment manufacturers are foreign car companies from which South Africa companies have imported technology.
9 See   www.southafrica.inf/business/economy/sectors/manufacturing.htm   (Accessed May 20, 2016).
10 The main manufacturing subsectors in South Africa. Available: www.southafrica.inf/business/economy/sectors/manufacturing.htm (Accessed May 20, 2016).
11 See previous section on communications and ICT.
12 See Chapter 4 on details of South Africa's involvement on the Inga III project in the DRC.
13 Although many articles have been written on this emotional issue, Edward Lahiff has been the major contributor on it.
14 For example, when in February 2017, Julius Mulema, leader of the Economic Freedom Fighters Party (EFF), proposed a motion that would have amended section 25 of the Constitution of South Africa to allow for expropriation of land without compensation, it was resoundingly defeated, 261 to 33 votes. However, a year later, and with a new South Africa president, Cyril Ramaphosa, the call for expropriation without compensation had gained steam. With some amendments proposed by the African National Congress (ANC), the motion was approved by a wide margin. The stage was set for allowing the South African government to take land without compensation and reallocating it as they see fit.

Bibliography

Automotive Industry Export Council (AIEC). 2015. *South Africa: Automotive Export Manual 2015.* Arcadia: AIEC.
Barnes, Justin and Anthony Black. 2013. "The Motor Industry Development Programme 1995–2012: What Have We Learned?" *International Conference on Manufacturing-led Growth for Employment and Equality,* Johannesburg, May.
Bhorat, H., A. Hirsch, R. Kanbur, and M. Ncube, eds. 2014. *The Oxford Companion to the Economics of South Africa.* Oxford: Oxford University Press.
Black, Anthony. 2001. "Globalization and Restructuring in the South African Automotive Industry." *Journal of International Development* 13, no. 6: 779–96.
Black, Anthony and Sipho Bhanisi. 2006. "Globalization, Imports and Local Content in the South African Automotive Industry." *The Birchwood Hotel and Conference Center,* Johannesburg, October 18–20.
Farole, T., T. Naughtin, and N. Rankin. 2014. "South Africa's Super-Exporters." *Manufacturing-Led Growth for Employment and Equality International Conference,* Johannesburg. www.developmentdialogue.co.za.49.

Fine, B. and B. F. Z. Rustomjee. 1996. *The Political Economy of South Africa: From Minerals-Energy Complex to Industrialization.* New York, NY: Routledge.

Finn, A., M. Leibbrandt, and M. Oosthuizen. 2014. "Poverty, Inequality, and Prices in Post-Apartheid South Africa." *WIDER Working Papers, No. 127*, UNU-WIDER.

Hall, Ruth and Edward Lahiff. 2004. "Budgeting for Land Reform." *Policy Brief Debating Land Reform and Rural Development No. 13*, August.

Kepe, Thembela and Ben Cousins. 2002. "Radical Land Reform in Key to Sustainable Rural Development in South Africa." *Policy Brief Debating Land Reform and Rural Development No. 3*, August.

KPMG. 2013. "The Role of Mining in the South African Economy." www.sablog.kpmg.co.za/2013/12/role-mining-south-african-economy/ (Accessed October 14, 2015).

Lahiff, Edward. 2007. "Willing Buyer, Willing Seller: South Africa's Failed Experiment in Market-Led Agrarian Reform." *Third World Quarterly* 28, no. 8 (December). Available PDF.

Lahiff, Edward and Guo Li. 2012. *Land Redistribution in South Africa-A Critical Review.* Washington, DC: World Bank, May 28.

Minerals Council. Various years. *Mining in South Africa: Annual Reports, Fact Sheets, and Facts and Figures.*

National Planning Commission. 2012. *National Development Plan: Vision for 2030.* Pretoria: National Planning Commission.

———. 2011. *National Development Plan 2030: Executive Summary.* Pretoria: National Planning Commission.

National Treasury. 2015. *Budget Review 2014 and 2015.*

Organization for Economic Cooperation and Development (OECD). 2015. "Barriers to SMEs in South Africa." *OECD Economics Department Working Papers.* Paris: OECD Publishing.

———. 2013. *OECD Economic Surveys: South Africa.* Paris: OECD Publishing.

———. 2010. *OECD Economic Surveys: South Africa.* Paris: OECD Publishing.

Reuters. 2015. "South Africa's Zuma Outlines Land Reform Plans." Report on President Juma's Speech to Parliament, February 14.

Statistics South Africa. 2014. *Poverty Trends in South Africa-An Examination of Absolute Poverty Between 2006 and 2011.*

———. 2012. *South Africa's Tourism Industry.* South African Iron and Steel Institute (various reports)

World Bank. 2018. *South Africa: Overview,* April 19.

———. 2014. "South Africa Economic Update: Fiscal Policy and Redistribution in an Unequal Society." *South Africa Economic Update, No. 6.* Washington, DC: World Bank.

———. 2012. *South Africa Economic Update: Focus on Inequality of Opportunities.* Washington, DC: World Bank, Reads 18,012.

Yager, Thomas R. 2016. *U. S. Geological Survey, 2013 Mineral Yearbook: The Mineral Industry of South Africa,* July.

Zalk, Nimrod. 2014. "What Is the Role of Manufacturing in Boosting Economic Growth and Employment in South Africa?" 11 February. www.econ3x3.org/article/what-role-manufacturing-boosting-economic-growth-and-employment-south-africa (Accessed October 14, 2017).

8   Developing infrastructure
networks

Introduction

Infrastructure plays a vital role in economic growth and transformation. The lack and deficiencies of infrastructure affect productivity and raise production and transaction costs, which hinder growth by reducing competitiveness and the ability to pursue economic and social development policies. General infrastructure development will be especially crucial as African economies undergo structural transformation from being primarily resource-driven to having bigger manufacturing and service sectors. Given the small sizes of most of Africa's economies, shared regional infrastructure is the only solution to problems of lack of economies of scale. Therefore, for the *Regional Development Poles Strategy* to succeed so that development from the poles can readily diffuse to the other countries, the various African countries will have to be linked with various networks of infrastructure. These infrastructural assets will not be aimed at just linking the countries, but also to consciously promote direct development along the corridors, or areas through which the infrastructure networks pass, so as to pursue inclusive development, reduce inequalities, and considerably reduce poverty continent-wide. Special attention should be paid to border areas, which are usually isolated from the capital cities, and hence lag behind other parts of most countries in all aspects of development including agriculture, education, health, water supply, transportation, and communications. The positive news is that Africa has already begun the development of joint continental infrastructure networks, which are embodied in the *Program for Infrastructure Development in Africa (PIDA)*.

PIDA is an African Union Commission (AUC) initiative, in partnership with the NEPAD Planning and Coordinating Agency (NPCA), the African Development Bank (AfDB), the United Nations Economic Commission for Africa (UNECA), the African Regional Economic Communities (RECs), and the various African national governments.[1] PIDA aims at accelerating infrastructure development across the continent. It provides new analysis and insights to bring together, under one coherent program, existing or previous continental infrastructure initiatives such as the African Highway Program, NEPAD Short Term Action Plan, and NEPAD Medium to Long Term Strategic Framework, the African Union (AU) Infrastructure Master Plans, and the African water vision. It fills in gaps and, based on previous lessons, assigns appropriate weight to the value of local ownership, the necessity of both hard and soft interventions, the need for diverse financing and the importance of sound implementation strategies.[2]

PIDA is a blueprint for African infrastructure transformation for the period 2012–2040. The program was adopted by African leaders in January 2012 and provides a strategic framework for priority infrastructure projects expected to transform the continent into an interconnected and integrated region. PIDA's overall strategic objective aims at accelerating regional integration of the continent and facilitating the creation of African Economic Community as planned by the Abuja Treaty.[3] By improving access to integrated regional and continental infrastructure networks, PIDA will allow countries to meet forecast demand for infrastructure services and boost their competitiveness by increasing efficiencies, accelerating growth, facilitating integration in the world economy, unleashing intra-African trade, and hence improving living standards.

The short-run program of PIDA, the Priority Action Plan (PIDA-PAP), will end in 2020. It comprises fifty-one programs divided into 433 projects covering transport, energy, information and communication technology (ICT), and trans-boundary water sectors (SOFRCO n. d.). Projects and programs under the PAP represent the first batch of agreed priorities resulting from the analysis and consultations on the RECs master plans. The PAP will be updated regularly to reflect progress and make way for new priorities as Africa's needs continue to evolve. This reflects the need to ensure coherence with RECs master plans and consistency with the PIDA strategic framework.[4]

The capital cost of PIDA's long-term implementation through 2040 has been estimated at more than $360 billion, while the cost of PIDA-PAP is expected to be nearly $68 billion, that is, about $7.5 billion annually. Energy and transport projects and programs represent around 95 percent of the total cost, demonstrating the critical need for transformative investments in both sectors to support African trade, promote growth, and create jobs. Investment needs for ICT and water represent the remaining five percent (SOFRECO n. d.).

The outcomes of PIDA will be as follows: reduction in energy costs and increase in access, slash in transport costs and boost in intra-African trade, water and food security, and increase in global connectivity. Energy savings are projected to be about $30 billion per annum or a total of $850 billion by 2040, while power access will increase from 39 percent to 70 percent by 2040, providing access to an additional 800 million people. Transport efficiency gains will be at least $172 billion in the African Regional Transport Integration Network (ARTIN). The opening of trade corridors will even generate more savings as these will facilitate more intra-African trade. Port throughput will rise from 265 million tons in 2009 to more than two billion tons in 2040. PIDA will boost broadband connectivity within Africa by 20 percent (SOFRECO n. d.).

PIDA and the Regional Development Poles Strategy

Three of PIDA's programs are more directly linked to the spread effects of the *Regional Development Pole Strategy*. These are the transport, energy, and ICT programs. While PIDA's water development program is vital, especially as regards trans-boundary water resources, it has limited consequences for the diffusion of development from the development poles. PIDA's *water vision* is to promote and enhance integrated water resource management through the development of trans-boundary water infrastructure to service the growing water demand, and strengthening institutions for efficient cooperation on shared water resources.[5]

However, unlike the trans-boundary water projects, the transport, power, and ICT networks will link the various regions and countries in the continent. This will greatly promote African economic integration and enhance regional and global competitiveness. Transportation costs and general transaction costs will be greatly reduced. Demand presently being suppressed by inefficiencies in the transport system will be unlocked by improvements in the system. Structural changes in African economies will foster more value-added industries, changing the profile of goods traded and increasing regional integration. Demand for air passenger services will rise with per capita income and urbanization. Containerized cargo will come to dominate port traffic and port traffic growth, increasing the importance of multimodal transport of containers along African Regional Transport Integration Network (ARTIN) corridors. Transit traffic from landlocked countries will increase more than tenfold by 2040. Bulk traffic growth will increase with mineral development.[6]

The various tiny African countries have compartmentalized their abundant energy resources. Hence, these resources are mostly underutilized resulting in scarcity of energy in most parts of the continent. The whole of Africa has just 125 GW of generating capacity and just 90,000 km of power transmission lines. Gas and petroleum product pipeline system are limited.

PIDA's projection of energy demand in Africa is an increase by about 5.7 percent annually through 2040 to 3,188 TWh. Modernization of African economies, coupled with social progress and commitment to widening access to electricity, will boost Africa's per capita energy consumption, raising it from its level of 612 kWh per capita in 2011 to 1,757 kWh per capita by 2040. Total demand for industry is projected to increase from 431 TWh in 2011 to 1,806 TWh by 2040.[7]

The ICT will continue to grow rapidly over the coming decades. Operators in every country will have access to international bandwidth through competitive gateways to submarine cable landing stations. The regional fiber optic infrastructure will be free of missing links. Countries must harmonize their technical and regulatory practices. Africa will strive to develop its own Internet Exchange Points (IXPs) and data centers to lower bandwidth costs.

Africa will install end-to-end fiber optical cable capable for carrying data from one country to a submarine landing station in another country, as well as networks that use national infrastructure to obtain better connectivity and improve broadband services for consumers. For regional infrastructure to meet the criteria of open access and promotion of competitiveness, it must possess an interconnection point where operators can physically connect their equipment to the regional infrastructure. It must have sites along its entire length that allows operators to install amplifiers or other equipment required for transmission. An interconnection catalogue must provide prices and technical specifications for the use of the regional infrastructure.

Transport programs and projects

PIDA's *transport vision* is an Africa where transportation services enable the free movement of goods and people through efficient, safe, affordable, and reliable transportation services through connecting cities with modern roads and railways and developing modern African Regional Transport Infrastructure Network (ARTIN) corridors, through the development of world-class ports and air transport services (www.au-pida.org). Regional surface transportation networks include road and railway corridors, inter-city highways, and land bridges that link hinterlands to ports, some of which will link the east and west coasts of the continent, so that the interior is brought closer to the Atlantic and Indian oceans. Major international airports should be safely linked for faster and safer freight and business travel. Major regional ports should be able to handle large modern ships and be efficiently linked to their hinterlands for faster, efficient, and cheaper transshipment to inland destinations for both coastal states and landlocked countries. Logistic systems and the regulatory frameworks that govern access should be made as efficient as possible to reduce delays and costs.

The twenty-four PIDA-PAP transport programs are summarized on table A2 (a) of the Appendix. Summarized in the table are also the immediate countries and regions of Africa as well as the regional economic communities (RECs) in direct charge of implementation together with NEPAD. Most of PIDA's *transport programs* and projects are completion, rehabilitation, or extension of the initial African highways that were initiated in the 1970s. However, new projects are also evolving such as the *one-stop border posts (OSBPs)* and *the Single African Air Transport Market (SAATM)*; the latter initiated by the Yamoussoukro Decision of 1999. Since the establishment of the first OSBP at Chirundu, between Zimbabwe and Zambia in 2009, the concept and development of OSBPs have expanded rapidly as one of the major tools to tackle impediments to intra-African trade growth. By 2017, there were about 80 OSBPs all over the continent, in various stages of implementation, while a small group of them were already operational.[8]

In Southern Africa the major PIDA transport program is the North-South Multimodal Corridor involving road, rail, ports, and OSBPs in South Africa, Botswana, Zimbabwe, Zambia, Malawi, and Mozambique. The North-South Corridor is joined with the implementation of the Beira and Nacala

Development Corridors. The Southern Africa Hub Port and Rail Program focuses on ports on both the east and west coasts of Southern Africa.

The major transport programs in Eastern Africa include the Northern Multimodal Corridor, the Central Corridor, the Lamu Gateway (LAPSSET), and the Djibouti-Addis Corridor. The Northern Corridor is to cover Kenya, Uganda, South Sudan, Rwanda, Burundi, and the Democratic Republic of Congo (DRC). It will connect the east and west coasts of the continent at Mombasa on the coast of the Indian Ocean and Banana at the DRC coast of the Atlantic Ocean. The Lamu Gateway will connect the Lamu Port on the Indian Ocean to Douala Port on the Atlantic Ocean. The direct beneficiaries of the Lamu Gateway will be Kenya, Ethiopia, South Sudan, the Central African Republic (CAR), and Cameroon. Ethiopia will be joined to the LAPSSET by road and rail from Kenya.

The Central Corridor will be based on the modernization of the Port of Dar es Salaam and the railway emanating from there to the interior, to include rail and road developments to Burundi, Rwanda, DRC, and Uganda. Transportation on and around Lake Tanganyika will also benefit Zambia.

In Central Africa, the transport projects include the Kinshasa-Brazzaville Road and Railway Bridge. This involves the construction of a railroad bridge across the Congo River to link Kinshasa and Brazzaville. In addition, the project will involve construction of a 1,000 km railway to connect the cities of Kinshasa and Ilebo (in central DRC) as well as development of road networks on both sides of the Congo River to link the two countries to the bridge. Other major projects in Central Africa include the Douala-Bangui/Doula-N'damena Corridor, the Pointe Noire-Brazzaville-Kinshasa-Bangui-N'djamena Multimodal Corridor, and the Central African Capital Connectivity, the Central Africa Air Transport, and the Central Africa Hub Port and Rail Program.

In West Africa, the transport projects include the Dakar-Bamako Rail Revitalization Project, of the 1,228 km line Dakar-Niamey Multimodal Corridor, with modern equipment. Another major coastal-interior project is the Abidjan-Ouagadougou-Bamako Multimodal Corridor. The acceleration of the Abidjan-Lagos Corridor and the Praia-Dakar-Abidjan Multimodal Corridor will modernize transportation along the entire West African coast. Two other major projects in West Africa are the West Africa Transport and Hub Port and Rail Programs.

Energy programs and projects

PIDA's energy vision is to develop efficient, reliable, affordable, and environmentally friendly energy networks and to increase access to modern energy services for all Africans through the development of continental clean power generation and transmission projects, implementation of high-capacity oil and gas pipeline projects, and developing renewable energy resources (www.au-pida.org).

According to PIDA, greater and smarter investment in the energy sector is key to faster and sustained economic growth in Africa if the continent is to attain its Agenda 2063.[9] PIDA is to achieve this by developing energy projects, oil refineries as well as oil and gas pipeline projects. For PIDA's Priority Action Program (PIDA-PAN), fifteen energy priority projects to be implemented by 2020 are summarized on Table A2 (b) of the Appendix.

The PIDA energy priorities focus on major hydroelectric projects, the interconnection of regional power pools, including regional petroleum and gas pipelines. PIDA estimates that through these projects, Africa will save $30 billion on electricity production costs and access to power will rise to nearly 70 percent by 2040, benefitting more than 800 million people.

Energy demand is constantly on the increase, be it electricity or gas for household use or petroleum and diesel products for transport and manufacturing. Africa has abundant energy resources in oil, gas, coal, and especially hydropower. Africa also has huge geothermal, wind, and solar energy resources. These resources are unevenly distributed across the continent, often going unexploited. Only through joint investments can they be economically exploited with the realization of economies of scale both in construction and distribution.

Furthermore, electricity connectivity on the continent remains relatively low. This means that for projects like Ethiopia's Grand Renaissance Hydro Power Dam to make sense, access to international markets must be guaranteed. A key part of the Ethiopian project is the planned interconnector line linking the power station to the grids of neighboring countries and eventually to both the Eastern Africa Power Pool and the Southern Africa Power Pool.

Joint investment and taking advantage of economies of scale will also help lower the cost of power in Africa. At present the average tariff per kilowatt hour in the region is $0.14, compared to $0.04 in Southeast Asia. It is estimated that investing in regional grids and hydropower will save the continent up to $2 billion annually. Hence, African countries have begun the process of integrating their power sector infrastructure, via regional power pools. The Southern African Power Pool (SAPP) was established in 1995; the North African Power Pool, Comité Maghrébin de l'Electricité (COMELEC) in 1998; the West African Power Pool (WAPP) in 2000; the Central African Power Pool (CEAPP) in 2003; and the Eastern Africa Power Pool (EAPP) in 2005. These are all initiatives to establish regional power markets and help harmonize energy policies (Niyimbona 2005).

Harmonization of energy policies among African countries will necessarily involve greater liberalization of their power sectors, especially with regard to power generation and distribution. There is also an urgent need to invest in interconnector infrastructure to ensure that power can be transmitted efficiently to market. Transmission may not be at full potential level due to lack of efficient transmission capacity. Furthermore, there is need to connect the regional power pools. This will create bigger markets, including potential export markets in the Middle East and Europe as has been envisaged with the development of the Grand Inga Complex in the Democratic Republic of Congo (DRC).

For many reasons, most African countries have been facing a power deficit, but the most compelling reasons are the poor planning and lack of maintenance of existing facilities. Although financing has been key impediment to increase generation capacity, the level of the deficit could have been reduced significantly if adequate planning and maintenance were applied. In addition, little involvement of private sector and low capacity of public institutions to address those issues have also been key negative contributing factors. Also, regional programs and regional planning has not been integrated adequately.

Nonetheless, current PIDA efforts indicate a positive outlook for African infrastructure, particularly for the power sector. The rapid growth of energy demand, accompanied by a growing middle class on the continent, has pushed individual countries and RECs to act strategically and to take regional planning and integration more seriously. This is why the African Union Commission focus of PIDA is on regional projects and programs. For the energy sector, the PIDA Priority Action Program (PIDA-PAP), if implemented, will boost the energy trade within the power pools and between the power pools. This will have a positive impact on the cost of the kWh due to economies of scale by the implementation of big projects serving many countries; energy mix such that countries with dominant hydro potentials supplying those with dominant thermal (gas and coal) potentials; increased access to modern energy services, which in turn will trigger increased access to clean water and improved health care system.

The 2011–2040 PIDA Energy Outlook foresees the increase of energy demand from 590 TWh to 3,100 TWh and installed capacity to grow from 120 GW to 700 GW (considering only units above 50 MW). To meet the future demand, total projected investment needs by 2040 have been estimated at $43 billion per annum, whereby investment needs for regional transmission lines are $5.4 billion per annum. Regional integration would save about $33 billion per annum. Considering the above financing needs, the involvement of different sources of financing, including the private sector is critical. Public spending in 2011 was estimated at only $5 billion per annum (SOFRECO Phase III n. d.).

The major PIDA-PAP energy projects and programs in West Africa are the *Kaleta, Sambagalou,* and the *West Africa Power Transmission Corridor.* The objective of the transmission program is to extend by a 2,000-km line the existing Nigeria-Ghana coastal line, with a capacity of 1,000 MW. The direct beneficiaries of this program are Guinea, Guinea-Bissau, Gambia, Sierra Leone, Liberia, Cote d'Ivoire, and Ghana.

The implementation of the Kaleta Hydropower Dam, in Guinea, has increased energy access by adding 240 MW in 2015 to the 2012 levels of 128 MW. In addition, about 30 percent of Kaleta's output is intended to go to neighboring Gambia, Guinea-Bissau, and Senegal through feeding into the West Africa Power Pool (WAPP). The project was also established to facilitate the construction of more mining refineries for Guinea's natural resources and hence, creating further economic growth and more employment opportunities.

The 128 MW Sambangalou hydropower plant will have a 185 square km reservoir that will also be used for irrigation and fishing. It will supply power to Gambia, Guinea, Guinea-Bissau, and Senegal.

There are two major PIDA -PAP power projects located in Central Africa: Inga III and the Central Africa Interconnection line. The Inga III project on the Congo River in the DRC, initiated as a 4,200 MW capacity run of river is now planned to generate electricity of more than 10,000 MW. The Agency for the Development of Inga was established in December 2015 and the feasibility study for the dam was updated with World Bank support in July 2016. With the support of the DRC and the South African governments, the agency will work closely with the African development agencies to establish the regional institution framework to coordinate the project development. NEPAD will support the financial and technical packaging of the transmission line, as well as the coordination and prioritization of the phased development of Inga-related transmission lines to the Central, Eastern, Northern, and Western African Power Pools. Inga III will be phased to the development of the Grand Inga Dam, which will generate over 44,000 MW and can power most of Africa plus surplus export of power outside Africa.

The Central Africa Interconnection is a 3,800 km transmission line from the Inga to South Africa through Angola and Namibia; and north to Gabon, Equatorial Guinea, Cameroon, and Chad. These lines will facilitate the exportation of Inga power to the other African regional power pools.

The 145 MW Ruzizi III hydroelectric plant will benefit the DRC in Central Africa as well as Burundi and Rwanda in Eastern Africa. It has been sponsored by the Economic Community of the Great Lakes (CEPGL) with membership of the three countries.

Another joint Eastern-Southern Africa energy project is the Zambia-Tanzania-Kenya (ZTK) Power Interconnector. This is a high voltage power transmission line connecting Zambia, Tanzania, and Kenya. The project aims to connect the power grids and create a link between the Southern Africa Power Pool (SAPP) and the Eastern African Power Pool (EAPP). The project's main objective is to provide opportunities to conduct power trade in the eastern and southern Africa regions and facilitate the creation of a Pan-African power market from Cape Town to Cairo. Covering a distance of 2,206 kilometers, the interconnector will have a capacity of 400 MW, and will be constructed as a double circuit 400 kilovolt (kV) line in sections from Zambia to Kenya; and as a 330 kV line within Tanzania. Ultimately, the ZTK interconnector will allow countries in eastern and southern Africa to share surplus electricity. Surplus power from Ethiopia will be exported to East and Southern African countries through this linkage.

The PIDA-PAP projects located entirely within Eastern Africa include the Rusumo 61 MW hydroelectric plant to benefit Burundi, Rwanda, and Tanzania. The other one is the Uganda-Kenya Petroleum Products Pipeline. This is a 300 km pipeline to provide a lower-cost transport of petroleum products.

In Southern Africa, the PIDA-PAP energy projects include the Batoka Gorge Hydropower project and the Mphamda-Nkuwa hydroelectric power plant. The Lesotho Hydro/Water project has a hydroelectric component although it is also meant for exporting both power and water to the Johannesburg/Pretoria Area, which is the industrial and mining heartland of South Africa.

The Mphamda-Nkuwa is a 1,500 MW plant on the Zambezi River in Mozambique that will mainly feed its power to the Southern Africa Power Pool (SAPP).

Construction of the Batoka Gorge hydropower station on the Zambezi River is expected to add 1,600 MW of electricity, enough to ease shortages in Zambia and Zimbabwe. The Batoka project entails the construction of a 181-meter gravity dam and the installation of eight 200 MW units with the power shared equally between the two countries.

Information and Communications Technology (ICT)

PIDA's ICT vision is to enable all Africans have access to reliable and affordable ICT networks through meeting Africa's demand for broadband at an affordable cost, increasing access and security of access to internet services, and the promotion of intra-African e-commerce. The vision envisages a continent that is on an equal footing with the rest of the world as an information society and an integrated e-economy in which every government, business, and citizen has access to reliable and affordable ICT services (www.au-pida.org).

PIDA's projection to 2020 was that as Africa catches up with broadband, ICT demand will swell by a factor of 20. The African demand of about 308 gigabits per second in 2009 would reach over 6,000 gigabits per second by 2018. Consequently, PIDA planned to boost African global connectivity by 20 percent. It was estimated that by increasing broadband penetration by 10 percent, GDP would increase by one to two percent by strengthening connections between goods and markets and between people and jobs (UNECA 2017).

When PIDA was launched, the Internet penetration rate in Africa was only about 6 percent compared to an average of 40 percent elsewhere in the developing world. But Africa's ICT sector has been growing very fast and it continues to grow rapidly. The largest share of investment has been coming from private enterprise. Those investments can have immense economic benefit, as healthy competition brings prices down and helps close the digital divide.

From 2012, with the landing of two more cables on the west coast of Africa, all coastal countries have access to at least one submarine cable; there would be hubs with four or more landing stations in all the regions. On land however, a few important gaps remained in fiber connections between neighboring countries and between regions. PIDA has been striving to fill those connections to complete Africa's global connectivity.

With ample intercontinental bandwidth available offshore, the expansion of access to high-speed Internet in Africa will depend on the degree of competition in the delivery of that bandwidth to telecommunications companies; the presence of land-based optical infrastructure capable of moving large quantities of data between the submarine cable landing stations and the appropriate transmitters that serve consumers in the absence of wired networks; and governments' willingness to grant licenses to competitive telecommunications operators and to make spectrum available at an affordable price. This will require that monopoly control on land-based infrastructure and international gateways is ended, with provisions for landlocked countries to reach submarine cable landing stations.

Taking advantage of the present opportunity to close the digital divide within Africa and between Africa and the rest of the world requires further legal and regulatory reforms in many countries, both to attract new investment and to optimize the use of existing infrastructure. Further liberalization will encourage construction of fiber-optic backbones and other cross-border infrastructure, to which all operators, including those in landlocked countries, should have free and non-discriminatory access.

The three ICT sector projects in the PIDA-PAP are *ICT Enabling Environment* (\$25 million), *ICT Terrestrial for Connectivity* (\$320 million), and *Internet Exchange Point (IXP) program* (\$130 million). The three projects are aimed at establishing an enabling environment for completing Africa's terrestrial fiber-optic infrastructure and installing Internet Exchange Points (IXPs) in countries that lack them. Each country is to be connected to two different submarine cables. Countries are to be interconnected and Internet exchange points are to be established (Progress Reports 2015, 2016, 2017).

The African Internet System Project (AXIS) objective is the establishment of Internet Exchange Points in the various regions of the continent. Africa has been paying overseas carriers to exchange intra-continental traffic. This is both costly as well as an inefficient way of handling exchange of African Internet traffic. Hence, the African Union Commission initiated the African Internet Exchange System Project (AXIS) to promote keeping of intra-Africa's internet traffic within the continent by supporting the establishment of National Internet Exchange Points (IXP) and Regional Internet Exchange Points (AXIS) in Africa.

The AXIS project aims to keep Africa's internet traffic local by supporting the establishment of domestic internet infrastructure, national and regional IXPs, as well as continental internet carriers. AXIS provides capacity building to Internet community stakeholders, technical assistance to regional IXPs, and policy and regulatory reform at a regional level. Through the support of the African Internet Exchange System (AXIS) project, African Union Member States, with Internet exchange points (IXPs), had increased from eighteen in 2012 to thirty-three by the end of 2017 (Progress Report 2017).

With many IXPs in Africa exchanging intra-country traffic locally and intra-regional traffic being exchanged within the continent, this will reduce costs by eliminating the international transit through overseas carriers. The project has also been supporting Regional Economic Communities (RECs) to develop regional interconnection policy frameworks. The East African Community (EAC) cross-border interconnection regulations and the Southern African Development Community (SADC) IP Interconnection Policy Framework have been developed (UNECA 2017).

Following three calls for proposals issued through open tendering, grants were awarded to eight internet exchange points to grow to become regional internet exchange points: Kenya and Rwanda in Eastern Africa; South Africa and Zimbabwe in Southern Africa; Congo and Gabon in Central Africa; Nigeria in Western Africa; and Egypt in Northern Africa. The support includes, but is not limited to the following: upgrade of IXP infrastructure to have the capacity to carry regional traffic; enhance technical capacity of staff through training; study visits to IXPs with large-scale operations to equip them with the skills to become, and run a large-scale IXIP; and promotion of the IXP as a Regional IXP.

Within Africa, regulators and policymakers have expressed concerns about international mobile roaming (IMR), especially regarding prices. Considerable dialogue has taken place between regulators, policymakers, and industry, which has at times been challenging due to the economic, commercial, and technical complexities of international mobile roaming. Under a grant awarded to the Kenya Internet Exchange Point, the African Union Commission supported the establishment of the first Global GSM Roaming Exchange (GRX) in Africa in 2017. By joining forces and pooling their roaming traffic, operators using the facility will benefit from lower rates and be able to make more attractive offers on mobile roaming data.

For Internet Exchange Points to have sustainable impact in contributing to reduction of access costs and promote growth of internet usage, it is critical that users have fast and affordable access to locally hosted content. Locally hosted content refers to content that is hosted in-country, either on servers, in caches, or delivered by content delivery networks (CDNs) with a presence in the country. In Africa, there is very little Internet content hosted locally, with the bulk of it hosted outside Africa. Post-AXIS support should focus on a project to bring back Africa's Internet Content to Africa by working with content developers, hosting service providers and country code top level domain names, to locally host Africa's internet content that is currently hosted outside Africa.

PIDA's challenges

Implementing infrastructure is always complex. This is more so for regional projects with many stakeholders. Two of the most binding constraints to implementing PIDA projects are project preparation and financing. Implementation relies on all actors, at all levels of the African development process, taking coordinated action: the AUC, NPCA, RECs, and the individual countries on whose territory the projects will be constructed. But as the RECs and national governments lack adequate human and technical capacity to fulfil their roles, NEPAD and its various institutions are helping them to address these challenges.

Regional and national agencies have to rely on experienced developers to carry out implementation on the ground. They have to marshal the resources and build the capacity essential for preparing, implementing, operating, and maintaining projects. But the responsibility for updating PIDA rests with the

NPCA in close cooperation with the RECs and their specialized institutions. Periodic planning exercises are to be undertaken at least every five years, with a revised outlook for the future.

Because of various implementing agencies at different levels of different countries, multiple challenges arise. These include differing implementation capacities of cooperating countries, poor coordination of national projects with a regional dimension, and failure to prioritize regional operations in national development plans and budgets. A tension often exists between national priorities and regional ones, especially in budgeting. Political considerations complicate the sharing of costs and benefits. For instance, the cost of expanding port infrastructure is often fully borne by a coastal country, but the collective benefits accruing to landlocked countries are higher. Countries located on regional transit routes may bear most of the cost of construction and maintenance of regional highways but fail to maximize access benefits to local communities or fully recover expenditure through transit fees.

Large regional infrastructure projects often involve multiple financiers who need to be carefully coordinated to ensure cost-efficient transactions. Regional project finance structuring also entails markedly higher transaction costs and complex risk factors for potential financiers compared to single country investments. Therefore, effective cooperation is necessary among countries at both bilateral and regional levels, and the harmonization of policies, rules and regulations, as well as procurement processes.

Although between 42 and 47 percent of the infrastructural funding has been committed by African governments, foreign funding is also significant (ICA Report 2013, 15; 2014, 9; 2016, 11). In the 2000s, China has become the major single foreign financier. China's engagement in Africa is often supported by strategic partnerships negotiated between African governments and the Chinese government, offering concessions to develop infrastructure in exchange for natural resources. China's financing of African infrastructure has been reinvigorated by the Belt and Road Initiative as discussed toward the end of this chapter.

The private sector has also played an evolving role in African infrastructure projects. Its sectoral focus has changed from several years of ICT dominance to growing interest in the energy sector. Other emerging instruments include diaspora bonds; local and foreign currency infrastructure bonds; infrastructure private equity funds that specifically target regional infrastructure projects; syndicated loans extended by regional banks, often in partnership with direct foreign investments; and regional foreign direct investments.

Official development assistance (ODA) will continue to play an important role. But the ODA resources will not be enough, nor should they be relied on solely for a coherent financing strategy. Consequently, countries have been called upon to mobilize their own public and private domestic resources and promote public-private partnership (PPP) risk management.

Some African institutions have put important funding instruments in place for development, including infrastructure bonds and loan guarantees. Some RECs are also playing an important role in innovative financing. ECOWAS has been implementing a 0.25 percent *community levy* for decades. This ECOWAS excise tax yields a steady revenue stream. SADC's Project Preparation Development Facility is targeted at supporting the PIDA-PAP. The COMESA-EAC-SADC Tripartite Project Preparation and Implementation Unit will, among other things, prepare tripartite infrastructure projects in the Southern and Eastern Africa regions to a bankable stage. Such resource pooling helps to neutralize the heterogeneity of project preparation capacities across cooperating countries.

RECs are also taking on new roles aimed at facilitating implementation of PIDA and regional infrastructure development plans, such as maintaining up-to-date databases of preparation status and project costs and marketing projects to private investors. This is in addition to their traditional roles of facilitating the harmonization of policies and regulations, and the coordination of regional cooperation on projects.

Addressing the PIDA challenges

A number of instruments have been devised to address the challenges facing PIDA. They include the Service Delivery Mechanism, Continental Business Network, Policy, and Regulations Framework, Presidential Infrastructure Champion Initiative, and Maintenance and Evaluation Information Management.

The Service Delivery Mechanism (SDM) addresses the lack of capacity for early stage project preparation at the national and regional levels. Its core mission is to make PIDA's projects technically sound, economically feasible, and politically acceptable. It provides institutional advisory services support that encompasses institutional design of special purpose vehicle (SPV) that oversees preparation, construction, operation, management, and maintenance of projects. It's legal advisory support drafts and vets legal instruments needed to develop a SPV. The communications backing unit prepares project brochures, flyers, publications, and communication strategies for projects. The capacity building support involves workplace training, workshops, and the drafting of practical manuals, lessons learned, and best practices.

The SDM works as a pool of resources seeded to jumpstart the procurement of high quality expertise and to provide project preparation, origination, and enabling environment advisory services. It assists national and regional lead agencies to get their projects technically ready for feasibility studies by deploying technical infrastructure experts to support project preparation.

The Continental Business Network (CBN) has been set up as an infrastructure investment advisory platform for government and the private sector. It serves to interface with high-level African policymakers and the private sector in promoting of the financing of African infrastructure projects. In 2016, the CBN issued its report of "*De-risking Africa's Infrastructure and PIDA Projects.*" The CBN aims at increasing private sector investment in PIDA from 1.5 to 5.0 percent in five years. This is to be achieved by increasing *African pension and sovereign investment funds* into PIDA.

In a dialogue with the African Development Bank, Economic Commission for Africa, and African investors, the CBN proposed the mobilization of African Pension and Sovereign-Wealth Fund capital for PIDA projects at NASDAQ in New York (Progress Report 2016). Sovereign-wealth fund leaders assessed domestic and regional-investment opportunities, including investment laws, governance, portfolio, and political risk considerations to optimize infrastructure investments and allocations. It explored potential funding for PIDA projects, including lending soft loans and grants, and strategic ways to mobilize sovereign-wealth and pension-fund capital.

The meeting concluded that *Africa needs to transition from a narrow focus on individual countries and domestic markets to a regionalized approach to infrastructure investment*. Key recommendations from the meeting included the need to mobilize domestic capital, central bank reserves, pension and sovereign–wealth assets for the continent to take the lead in infrastructure financing; the need to improve bankability and project packaging to gain increased access to capital; megaprojects must be broken down into smaller initiatives or phases, with shorter timelines, to make them more manageable; and the need to craft new ways to support strategic infrastructure that promotes growth, trade and development, while redressing the poor state of physical trade-facilitation infrastructure facilities throughout the continent.

During the 2016 NEPAD Africa Week, CBN and key African diaspora in infrastructure, banking, insurance, investment, and construction sectors launched the *De-Risking Report*. The dialogue also leveraged the support of the strategic partnerships that the agency is nurturing with financial institutions, such as Standard Bank and Barclays Africa.

Overall, the *outcomes of the CBN de-risking process and dialogues noted* the need to ensure recruitment of competent infrastructure experts to better prepare and package PIDA projects; standardize and ensure predictability of regulatory frameworks; improve incentives for institutional investors and increase transparency of funding plans; increase transparency of infrastructure development and expansion plans at the national level, as well as provide accurate datasets and detailed feasibility studies; further develop local capital markets; and consolidate political will and support for the development of infrastructure projects.

The Policy and Regulatory Framework (PRF) addresses soft issues that have important impact on infrastructure development. In 2016, PRF support focused on collaboration with the Economic Commission for Africa on the harmonization of policies, laws, and regulations to enhance private sector investment in African infrastructure. It also cooperated with the African Forum for Utility Regulators (AFUR) to expand the scope of its work to cover all PIDA sectors and the establishment of the African Center for Excellence for Infrastructure Regulation (ACEIR).[10]

The Presidential Infrastructure Champion Initiative (PICI) was adopted to accelerate regional infrastructure development through political championing of projects. It assigns a head of state and government to promote the implementation of a particular project. The champions bring visibility, unblock bottlenecks, coordinate resource mobilization, provide leadership, and ensure rapid project implementation within a specified threshold period.

The PICI ensures that projects are implemented within five years. Implementation refers to the progression of project from prefeasibility to feasibility phase, or from feasibility to construction, or that demonstrable evidence of progress is available. The champions report the progress of their projects every six months during bi-annual Heads of State and Government Orientation Committee meetings. A comprehensive project status report is also presented by the chair during the annual AU Assembly.

The Maintenance and Evaluation Information Management (MEIM) framework is aimed at monitoring progress in the implementation of PIDA projects. All PIDA actors participate in the evaluation: at the national, sub-regional, regional, and continental levels.

The PIDA MIEM framework aims to track and report information on PIDA project implementation progress on a yearly basis; report on interventions that have been provided by all stakeholders to advance project implementation; facilitate sharing information and learning on PIDA project implementations, including success stories and lessons learned, and increases stakeholder participation in advancing the realization of PIDA-PAP.

The impact of the Belt and Road Initiative on PIDA

As noted earlier, China became the single major African economic partner since the beginning of the twenty-first century. The role of China in financing African development, especially of infrastructure, has greatly increased with the launching of the global Chinese Belt and Road Initiative.[11]

China aims to strengthen its relations and friendship with Africa under the Forum on China-Africa Cooperation (FOCAC) and the Belt and Road Initiative, which will see African countries benefiting from trade and infrastructure development funded by the Chinese government. The Chinese government subsidizes its companies that undertakes the implementations of these projects in Africa.

The Belt and Road Initiative (BRI) projects in Africa started since President Xi Jinping put forward China's policy towards the continent in 2013. However, China was already investing in Africa, mainly in infrastructure, oil, and minerals. In 2013, President Xi Jinping proposed developing relations with Africa with *sincerity, real results, affinity, and good faith.* At the second summit of the Forum on China-Africa Cooperation (FOCAC), held in Johannesburg in March 2013, China announced it would roll out ten major plans to boost cooperation in three years, in areas including infrastructure. At the close of the 2018 China-Africa Forum for Cooperation Summit held in Beijing, China announced a new fund of $60 billion for Africa's development.[12] The disbursements from this fund are to be channeled to projects aligned to the Belt and Road Initiative. The fund is to cover areas such as telecommunications, construction of railways, roads, bridges, and seaports, energy, and human capacity. These projects are consistent with the African priority projects of PIDA. But Chinese projects in Africa also cover industrial parks, Special Economic Zones (SEZ), tourism, and urban development. Many of the BRI branded projects had already been started before 2013 but gained momentum under the Initiative. On the infrastructure projects, China is mainly financing PIDA's national and regional integration projects. PIDA also has projects implemented at the continental level.[13]

Although the maritime branch of China's Belt and Silk Road joins the African coast at Mombasa in Kenya, China's projects are distributed to virtually all African countries. In Kenya, the major projects are the construction of Mombasa Port berths, Mombasa-Nairobi Standard Gauge Railway, the Lamu Gateway Development – commonly known as the LAPSSET – and the Garissa power plant. The Garissa power plant is located in northeast Kenya. It costs $135 million and is the largest photovoltaic (PV) power plant in East Africa. It is to generate more than 7,600 kilowatt hours of power each year and will reduce a yearly carbon dioxide emission of 64,190 metric tons.

The Lamu Gateway Development is a massive port, oil pipeline, railway, and road project north of Mombasa. It will link the Indian Ocean to the Atlantic Ocean in Cameroon, passing through South Sudan and the Central African Republic (CAR). A road and rail routes branch from Kenya to Ethiopia, to join the Djibouti-Addis Ababa, Chinese-built electric Standard Gauge Railway.

The Mombasa-Nairobi Standard Gauge Railway is now being extended to the Uganda border. The plan is to extend it to Uganda, Rwanda, Burundi, South Sudan, and the DR Congo. This forms the PIDA Northern Multimodal Transport Corridor centered on the port of Mombasa. The Northern Corridor is planned to connect the Indian Ocean and the Atlantic Ocean at the port of Banana at the mouth of the Congo River in the DR Congo.

The Northern Corridor is to be linked with the Central Multimodal Corridor anchored on the port of Dar es Salaam, with railways and roads radiating from Dar es Salaam to Kenya, Uganda, Rwanda, Burundi, the DR Congo, Zambia, Malawi, and Mozambique. The railway will join the Tanzania-Zambian Railway (TAZARA) financed by China in the 1970s. The TAZARA, the old railway, is to be renovated by China.

The largest Chinese financed project, on the East African Coast, is the Bagamoyo Port and Export Development Zone (EDZ). Located about 60 miles north of Dar es Salaam, the Bagamoyo Port project also includes the construction of an industrial city, railway, and road. It connects the Maritime Silk Road with other East African countries such as Mozambique, Malawi, Zambia, the DRC, Burundi, Rwanda, Uganda, Kenya, South Sudan, Comoros, Madagascar, and the Seychelles (Leautier, Schaefer, and Shen 2015).

Another Chinese project in Tanzania is the Kigamboni Bridge that connects the Dar es Salaam business district with Kigamboni Creek in the Indian Ocean. This is a 680-meter bridge, 32 meters wide, with six lanes, three in each direction. It includes 2.5-meter-wide pedestrian and cyclist lanes on each side, the first of its kind in eastern and central Africa.

Djibouti is another hub of the Belt and Road Initiative at the strategic meeting on the Indian Ocean and the Red Sea, a major international shipping route. A branch of the Silk Road International Bank is located in Djibouti. The most significant project has been the Djibouti-Addis electric Standard Gauge Railway. China is also funding the new port of Doraleh, two airports, a gas pipeline, and a pipeline for drinking water from Ethiopia to Djibouti. It is planning a series of power plants and a free-trade manufacturing zone. China, like the United States, France, Germany, Italy, and Japan have military bases in Djibouti. Djibouti is modelling itself on Dubai as an entrepôt city. But most of Chinese projects in the Horn of Africa are in Ethiopia, being the largest country in the region (Pieper 2018).

Ethiopia plans to extend the Djibouti-Addis Railway into a 3,000-mile rail network that will stretch to Sudan, South Sudan, and Kenya. The line will be joined to Kenya by the Lamu-South Sudan-Ethiopia (LAPSSET) Railway. China is also renovating the Port Sudan-Khartoum Railway. Furthermore, it is constructing the Karuma Hydropower Project in Uganda.

China also built the Addis Ababa Light Rail Transit (AA-LRT) with two lines of about 34 km long. It carries about 60,000 passengers per day and has eased city transportation in Addis Ababa. China is also financing, constructing, and running industrial parks in Ethiopia. The African Union (AU) headquarters in Addis Ababa was fully funded and built by China.

At both ends of the Suez Canal where the One Belt One Road leaves Africa for Europe, China is financing and constructing projects at ports on the coast of the Red Sea and in Suez Port on the coast of the Mediterranean Sea. In the Red Sea ports of Nuiweiba and Safaga two container transshipment terminals are being built. The multipurpose terminal in Safaga is to receive containers and non-containerized cargo, integrating it with the free trade zone in the two ports. Another container terminal is to be established at the port of Abu Qir. A cruise port, marina, business center, and entertainment complex is to be established at the Egyptian Red Sea resort city of Sham el Skeikh at the cost of $600 million.

In the Suez Canal Economic Zone (SCZ), China is establishing an industrial, trade, and logistic center. The *yuan* will become one of the major currencies to be used in all sectors of the Suez Zone, unlike as of now when the Chinese currency is limited to use in vessels and shipping services only.

However, the largest Belt and Road Initiative project in Egypt is the construction of a new Egyptian capital, New Cairo, between the Nile and the Suez Canal, 25 miles east of Cairo. This new Egyptian capital city is to cost about $45 billion and to accommodate between 5 and 6.5 million people, covering about 700 km². It will be a modern city with upmarket residential district, an industrial zone, schools, a university, and recreational centers.

Other Chinese port projects along the African coast of the Mediterranean Sea include Bizerte Port in Tunisia. China is to open a car plant in Tunisia for exports in the Mediterranean region as well as in Africa. A Chinese company specialized in assembling train cars and locomotives will set up a production unit in Tunisia for exports to other African countries.

In Algeria, China has financed and constructed the east-west Autoroute Highway. This is a 1,200 km road running across the northern tip of Algeria between the Moroccan and Tunisian borders.

China is financing the Mohammed VI Tangier Tech City in Morocco at the cost of $1 billion, covering an area of 200 hectares in addition to a residential area, and railway and motorway networks. The Tech City is to create thousands of jobs and transfer advanced technology. Among the first industrial projects are to be electric buses and aeronautical components.

South of the Maritime terminal of Mombasa, along the east coast of Africa, in addition to Bagamoyo Port, China has projects at Nacala and Beira in Mozambique. China, together with the African Development Bank, and the Development Bank of Southern Africa are financing the Malawi-Zambia Railway, which will link to the Mozambique ports of Nacala and Beira, and to the Tanzanian Port of Dar es Salaam, and hence to the Central Multimodal Transport Corridor. This project is part of the PIDA Beira-Nacala Multimodal Transport Corridor. It will also link other PIDA programs in Southern Africa such as the North-South Multimodal Transport Corridor and the Southern Africa Hub Port and Rail Program. From the Zambian Copperbelt, the railway will be extended to the north-western part of the country, to the Angolan border.

Given the present lineup of the Chinese and PIDA railway projects in the continent, Africa will be linked up between the Atlantic and Indian Oceans by the Lamu-Douala/Kribi railways; Mombasa/Dar-es-Salaam to Banana in the DRC Northern and Central Corridors, and in Southern Africa at Walvis Bay on the Atlantic coast of Namibia to the eastern coast ports of South African.

China is financing Zambia's cement factory at the cost of $500 million. The project will be undertaken in two phases. China also donated about $140 million for the building of Zimbabwe's new parliament at Mount Hampden about 17 miles from Harare.

China is building a modern city in South Africa to house over 100,000 people. Modderfontein New City is a 13 million square miles commercial, retail, warehousing, office, residential, recreational city located 20 km northwest of Johannesburg.

Belt and Road Initiative projects in Madagascar include a Chinese-run Special Economic Zone (SEZ); the construction of a new highway between Antananrivo and Toamasina; and the development of a network of closed-circuit cameras to improve security in Antananarivo. China is also constructing a deepwater port in the bay of Narinda on the west coast of the country. Another special project China is undertaking in Madagascar is a 20 km tarred road, equipped with road safety facilities, linking egg producers to the capital city.

Along the western coast of Africa, China has many port and other infrastructure projects, some of which are already functioning, while others are still under construction. These include the ports of Dakar in Senegal, Tema in Ghana, and Libreville in Gabon.

The 1,344 km Benguela Railway traverses Angola from its Atlantic port of Lobito to its eastern border town of Luau, linking Angola to the Copperbelts of the DRC and Zambia. This linkage connects the Atlantic coast of Africa to the Indian Ocean via the ports of Dar es Salaam, Nacala, and Beira. China and Angola have also cooperated on building a large hydropower plant. The Caculo Cubaca Hydropower Plant's planned installed capacity is 2,172 MW. It will create about 10,000 jobs for the Angolans during the peak construction period. The Chinese company is to train both management and technical Angolans to run the plant.

A Chinese firm is undertaking a direct investment in a Special Economic Zone (SEZ) in the Congolese port city and oil industry hub of Pointe Noire, which has rail and road links with the capital Brazzaville. Pointe Noire is linked to the PIDA Pointe Noire-N'Djamena Multimodal Transport Corridor, the Central African Hub Port and Railway Program, the Douala-Bangui-Douala-N'Djamena Multimodal Transport Corridor, and the Kinshasa-Brazzaville Bride, Road and Rail Project and the Ilebo Railway that will link to Lubumbashi in the DRC mineral-rich Katanga region.

Another large Chinese funded project in Central Africa in the Kribi Port in Cameroon. This port will be the trade center for the entire region, serving landlocked countries such as Chad and the Central African Republic (CAR). It will add tremendous capacity to the smaller Douala Port, which currently serves the region. It will be linked to Lamu via CAR and South Sudan by LAPSSET. Within Cameroon, the port will boost the mining sector, given the iron ore, bauxite, and other mineral located in the region. The port is capable of docking vessels of up to 100,000 tons.

The 1,400 km Lagos-Calabar Coastal Railway along the Atlantic coast of Nigeria extends the PIDA Abidjan-Lagos Coastal Transport Corridor eastwards along the West African coast. Westwards from Abidjan, PIDA has the Praia-Dakar-Abidjan Multimodal Transport Corridor. The West Africa Hub Port and Rail Program of PIDA also connects all these projects across the coast of West Africa. These projects are connected to the interior of West Africa by PIDA's Abidjan-Ouagadougou-Bamako Multimodal Transport Corridor, and the Dakar-Bamako-Niamey Multimodal Transport Corridor.

Nigeria is also connecting its coastal projects with its interior. Hence, other China-Nigeria infrastructure projects include the double track, Standard Gauge Lagos-Ibadan Railway (312 km), Lagos-Kano Standard Gauge modernization project, the Abuja-Kaduna Standard Gauge Rail Line (186 km).

City infrastructure projects in Nigeria supported by China include a 45 km light railway from the Abuja International Airport to the city's Central Business District. China is supporting Lagos City and state to improve Lagos's urban transport network by constructing a new rail system comprising of seven lines. It will carry 400,000 passengers per day with a full capacity of 700,000 when the route is fully operational. This will go a long way in addressing the high volume of commuter traffic in a densely populated city. China is also building the Edo State Refinery in Nigeria at a cost of about $2 billion.

The Economic Community of West African States (ECOWAS) signed an agreement with China in March 2018 for China to build the headquarters of ECOWAS at Abuja at a cost of $31.6 million.

The BRI has contributed to some infrastructure development in Ghana, including Ghana Gas and Port Expansion Projects. More projects have been planned. In 2017, Ghana agreed to a deal with the Chinese Government for a loan aimed at further exploitation of the country's vast bauxite deposits. This is to involve an integrated aluminum industry, consisting of the development of bauxite mines and an aluminum refinery. Another Chinese loan to Ghana is to support various components of a massive infrastructure development spanning the mining, industrial, and railway fields. This will include the construction of the Eastern and Central Railways, with extension to the north of the country. It will also embrace a number of ports, some inland, and a road network. Ten industrial parks and four internet exchanges will be established in various parts of the country. A gold refinery is to be established in the country to process gold exports, as well as the production of jewelry, gold coins, medals, and other gold products. An oil palm processing plant is to be built, which will also produce soap, detergents, cooking oil, body cream, and other commercial products. China has expressed interest in developing the cotton industry in Ghana.

China is constructing a $191 million bridge over the Abidjan lagoon, the commercial hub of Cote d'Ivoire. It is also building a 60,000-capacity stadium in Abidjan. A major Chinese project in Cote d'Ivoire is the 4 km Soubre Hydroelectric Dam that will add 275 MW to the national power grid. After the completion of this dam, China plans to build three more hydroelectric plants that will add a total of 500 MW to the national grid. Chinese companies have obtained contracts and built soccer stadiums, a port expansion, drinking water facilities, and a coastal highway between Abidjan and the resort town of Grand Bassam.

China is constructing a road linking Dakar to Touba, the second largest Senegalese city. China is also constructing a railway between Dakar and the Malian city of Kididra. This is a part of the PIDA Dakar-Bamako-Niamey Multimodal Transport Corridor. Another Chinese project in Senegal is an Industrial Park in Diamniadio, a suburb of Dakar. The project will employ about 5,000 Senegalese and add value to Senegalese cotton as raw material. Senegal was the first stop of President Xi Jinping when he visited Africa in 2015. Senegal was the first West African country to sign up on the Belt and Road Initiative.

Concluding remarks

African economies remain poorly integrated: links in regional roads, rail, ICT, and power infrastructure networks are missing or weak; capacity at ports is constrained; and access to African airways is restricted. Sub-optimal use of existing assets also results from "soft infrastructure" constraints. Poor regulation on monopolies, together with the collusive behavior of authorities, make pricing in the ICT sector uncompetitive thereby affecting the affordability of services, and lowering trade volumes.

Integrating infrastructure can deliver economies of scale in production and support spatial integration, enabling market efficiency and trade, and supports the mobility of production factors. Augmenting the production base will facilitate the participation of African economies in global value chains and promote the development of regional ones. In addition, it integrates marginalized populations and broadens scope for participation in the development process.

Accelerated development demands a collective action plan to ensure the infrastructure is developed efficiently. This is where regional cooperation is a must for faster and harmonious development, exploiting economies of scale. Coherent implementation of PIDA will have profound impact on the transformation of African economies and the achievement of Agenda 2063. Inadequate infrastructure in African countries partly explains their low intra-African trade and integration. It contributes to low levels of productivity and low share of African exports in the world market. PIDA projects will deepen and solidify African integration as intra-African trade will increase, facilitating the spread of the development process from the regional development poles to their neighbors.

Ultimately, the success of the program rests on the shoulders of the leadership of the African Union Assembly, both collectively and individually. Hence, the functions of Heads of State and Government serving as champions for the program's projects must be taken very seriously. In fact, all Heads of State and Government must set the tone, keep the momentum alive, and provide critical national, regional, and continental leadership by working together and showing an unwavering commitment to integrated policies, projects, and goals. They must create an enabling environment for all the stakeholders, public or private, domestic or foreign. They must see to it that projects located in their territories are accelerated and synchronized with the implementation of projects in neighboring countries. They should ensure that regional priority commitments filter down through top executing agencies and ministries and ensure that the soft governance issues such as harmonization, facilitation, monitoring, and evaluation are timely addressed. Without serious and genuine commitment to African development, any political rhetoric about the *"welfare of our people"* is meaningless.

Leaders of countries in perpetual conflicts must be reminded to realize that they are pulling the continent down. Fragile countries in transition should be assisted to fast recovery. With the completion of political decolonization, economic development becomes the priority of any African government and leader. The larger African countries must provide leadership.

Overall, the major operational constraints on the implementation of PIDA projects are project preparation and project financing. Greater efforts should be made to reduce the reliance of African development on foreign aid. The exploration of alternative financing methods is to be enhanced. African resource-exporting countries should lend their surplus export earnings, earned during resource booms, to a soft loan African Fund, to be utilized in financing joint African programs and projects.

While the Belt and Road Initiative (BRI) has involved financing various types of projects in Africa, its main economic impact on the continent will depend on the extent to which its helps Africa narrow its infrastructure deficit. Many BRI infrastructure projects are parts of PIDA's projects in different countries. China is meeting a large part of PIDA's financial requirements. Properly and efficiently utilized, these resources can greatly reduce Africa's infrastructure deficit and improve connectivity and integration, consequently leading to increase in intra-African trade and economic growth.

Notes

1 The New Partnership for Africa's Development (NEPAD) was established in 2001 by the Organization for African Unity (OAU), the precursor of the African Union (AU), as the socio-economic body charged with accelerating economic cooperation and integration among African countries. The NEPAD Planning and Coordinating Agency (**NPCA**) is NEPAD's implementing secretariat, which works together with the African Union Commission (AUC) as planners and coordinators of the African Economic Transformation Agenda of the African Union.
2 In 1971, the United Nations Economic Commission for Africa (UNECA) drew a plan for Trans-African Highways (TAH). These included the Cairo-Dakar Highway, Dakar-Ndjamena Highway, Ndjamena-Djibouti Highway, Dakar-Lagos Highway, Lagos-Mombasa Highway, Beira-Lobito Highway, Algiers-Lagos Highway, Tripoli-Windhoek-(Cape Town) Highway, and the Cairo-Gaborone (Pretoria-Cape Town) Highway. For details, see the African Development Bank (AfDB) and the UNECA (2003).
3 For details on the Abuja Treaty, see Chapter 1.
4 The Community of Central African States (ECCAS), the East African Community (**EAC**), the Southern African Development Community (**SADC**), and the Economic Community of West African States (**ECOWAS**) have drawn up Infrastructure Master Plans.
5 The discussion in relation to the strategy of regional development poles is limited to PIDA's transport, energy, and ICT programs only as they would impact on most African countries, unlike the trans-boundary water programs whose impacts will be limited to the countries within the specific river basins.
6 In addition to SOFRECO, also see www.au-pida.org. This website and PIDA's annual progress reports contain both historical and current data on PIDA projections and implementation.
7 Refer to note 6 above.
8 For various details on the PIDA programs, see PIDA *Progress Reports 2015–2017*. The Yamoussoukro Decision of 1999 was made by African Ministers of Transport to open their airspaces to African airlines so as to develop an intra-African air traffic network.
9 Africa's Agenda 2063 is a perspective plan of fifty years from 2013, in which Africa will be transformed into a modern prosperous continent based on regional and continental integration. For details, see African Union Commission. 2015. *Agenda 2063: The Africa We Want*. Addis Ababa: AUC.
10 The ACEIR was conceptualized as an inter-disciplinary regional infrastructure development and management-focused center of excellence. It comprises regulatory practitioners, professors, and researchers from global universities and research institutes with PIDA staff members driving and coordinating the work programs.

11 The Belt and Road consist of the historical overland Road from China to Europe (**the Belt**), and a new maritime "Road" that links China to the countries of Southeast Asia, the Gulf countries, East and North Africa, and on to Europe (**the Road**). In 2013, China proposed **the Belt and Road Initiative (BRI)** to improve connectivity and cooperation on a transcontinental scale. The scope of the initiative extends worldwide. It is not limited to the countries along the overland and maritime routes only. The BRI is also referred to as the **One Belt One Road Initiative**.

12 The various projects discussed below are listed more than once in the online sources on the BRI listed in the bibliography.

13 Although China finances its African projects at African national level, the infrastructural projects are either national portions of PIDA projects or complement PIDA's projects. Both types of projects boost Africa's infrastructure and its connectivity.

Bibliography

African Development Bank (AfDB) and United Nations Economic Commission for Africa (UNECA). 2013. *Review of the Implementation Status of the Trans African Highways and the Missing Links: Vol. 2: Description of Corridor.* Addis Ababa: UNECA.

African Union Commission (AUC). 2015. *Agenda 2063: The Africa We Want.* Addis Ababa: African Union Commission.

Edinger, Hannah and Jean-Pierre Labuschange. 2019. "China's Role in African Infrastructure and Capital Projects." https://www.2deloitte.com/us/en/insights/industry/public-sector/ (Accessed July 18, 2019).

Infrastructure Consortium for Africa (ICA). 2013, 2014, 2016, 2017. *Annual Report: Infrastructure Financing Trends in Africa.* Abidjan: AfDB.

Kambanda Callixte. 2013. *Power Trade in Africa and the Role of Power Pools.* Abidjan: AfDB.

Leautier, Frannie A., Michael Schaefer, and Wel Shen. 2015. "The Port of Bagamoyo: A Test for China's New Maritime Silk Road in Africa." www.thediplomat.com/2015/12/the-port-of-Bagamoyo-a-test-for-chinas-new-maritime-silk-road-in-africa/ (Accessed July 20, 2019).

NEPAD, AUC, and AfDB. 2015, 2016, 2017. *Programme for Infrastructure in Africa: PIDA-PAP Implementation Progress Report, Vol. I.* Addis Ababa: and Midrand (South Africa): AUC and NEPAD.

NEPAD, PIDA, UNECA, and Africaninvestor (Ai). 2017. *AU-NEPAD Continental Business Network (CBN) 5% Agenda Report: Mobilizing Domestic Pension and Sovereign Wealth Fund Capital for PIDA and Other African Infrastructure Projects Through Institutional Investor Public Partnerships (IIPPs).* Addis Ababa: and Midrand (South Africa): AUC and NEPAD.

Niyimbona, P. 2005. *The Challenges of Operationalizing Power Pools in Africa.* Addis Ababa: UNECA.

O'Dowd, Emily. 2016. "Special Report: How Five Major African Rail Projects Are Supported by China." https://www.smartrailworld.com/five-major-african-projects-supported-by-china (Accessed July 12, 2019).

Pheiffer, Evan. 2017. "Top-10: Africa Infrastructure Projects in 2018." www.thebusinessyear.com/top-10-china-infrastructure-projects-in-africa-2018/focus (Accessed July 14, 2019).

Pieper, Diemar. 2018. "Geopolitical Laboratory: How Djibouti Became China's Gateway to Africa." www.globalsentinelng.com/2018/02/09/djibouti-become-chinas-gateway-africa/ (Accessed July 14, 2019).

SOFRECO. (n.d.). *Study on Programme for Infrastructure Development in Africa: Africa's Infrastructure Outlooks 2040.* Midrand (South Africa): NEPAD.

———. (n.d.). *Study on Programme for Infrastructure Development in Africa (PIDA) Phase III: Energy.* Midrand (South Africa): NEPAD.

Sy, Amadou N. R. 2017. *Leveraging African Pension Funds for Financing Infrastructure Development.* Washington, DC: Brookings Institution.

Tubei, George. 2018. "10 Massive Projects the Chinese Are Funding in Africa- Including Railways and a Brand-New City." www.businessinsider.com.za/here-are-150-million-rand-products-in-africa-funded-bychina-2018-9 (Accessed July 20, 2019).

UECA and AUC. 2012. *Financing for Infrastructure Development in Africa (PIDA).* Addis Ababa: UNECA.

United Nations Economic Commission for Africa (UNECA). 2002. *Decision Relating to the Implementation of the Yamoussoukro Declaration Concerning the Liberalization of Access to Air Transport Markets in Africa.* Addis Ababa: UNECA.

———. 2000. *Report of the First Meeting of the Monitoring Body of the Yamoussoukro Decision.* Addis Ababa: UNECA.

———. 1999. *Decision Relating to the Implementation of the Yamoussoukro Declaration Concerning the Liberalization of Access to Air Transport Markets in Africa.* Addis Ababa: UNECA.

———. 1988. *Declaration of Yamoussoukro on a New African Air Transport Policy.* Addis Ababa: UNECA.

World Bank. 2019. *Belt and Road Economics: Opportunities and Risks of Transport Corridors.* Washington, DC: World Bank.

Xinhua. 2018. "Belt and Road Initiative Drives Africa's Integration, Economic Growth." www.xinhuanet.com/english/2018-06/29-137287936.htm (Accessed July 24, 2019).

———. 2017. "Backgrounder: Major-Africa Infrastructure Cooperation Projects." www.xihuanet.com/englisg/2017-03/26c_136158456.htm (Accessed July 24, 2019).

———. 2016. "10 Mega Infrastructure Projects in Africa Funded by China." March 22. www.africanglobe.net/business/10-mega-infrastructure-projects-africa-funded-china/ (Accessed July 24, 2019).

9 Summary, conclusion, and policy implications

Overall summary and conclusions

Since the beginning of the twenty-first century, most African countries have shown strong economic growth. Although this performance was largely attributed to oil and mineral production and export, the countries that recorded the fastest rates of growth included those with neither petroleum nor mineral wealth. However, in spite of the impressive growth performance unemployment, poverty, and inequality remained high. This is largely because the sources of African economic growth have changed very little since independence, with agriculture and mineral resources being the main drivers of production and exports. For self-sustaining growth, African economies must be diversified and transformed by both production and exports. Such a transformed pattern of growth will ensure that the benefits are widely shared in order to reduce poverty, reduce inequalities, and raise the standards of living of all sectors of society.

The share of manufacturing should rise from about 10 percent to around 25 percent. Services should be transformed from the distributive trades to knowledge-intensive activities that are needed to support sophisticated economies. Services in the informal sector, which employ most of the low-income jobs in the urban areas, must be modernized. The share of manufactured exports should be increased substantially and the composition of imports shifted towards capital goods, industrial intermediate goods, and components.

Strong growth should be driven by strong domestic demand for goods and investment. Adding value to Africa's natural resources creates jobs by investing in agro-processing industries, mineral processing, and manufacturing of the processed products. Investment in infrastructure is also vital. Better roads, dams, and hydropower should translate into increased electricity consumption by industry and the people. More efficient transportation will reduce transaction costs, raising productivity and competitiveness, thus improving living standards. Human capital must be upgraded by expanding quality education at all levels. Health systems must be expanded and strengthened. Indigenous entrepreneurs must be developed in all sectors and not just in trade. Greater emphasis must be placed on science and technology. Agriculture must not be forgotten as it is the basis of any development. Countries have moved up the technology ladder first by developing agriculture and value addition through agricultural processing. Rural areas must be developed and farming tools, irrigation, rural roads, extension services, seeds, fertilizers, and many other farm inputs must be made available and at affordable prices to the peasants. Research and development and technological transfers and development must be promoted.

Africa's huge untapped natural resources, youthful population, high rate of urbanization, and the rising middle class will play major roles in the continent's growth and development. With an aging population in the west and rising wages in Asia, Africa could offer competitive wages. But Africa's demographic potential of a young population and fast-growing labor force has to be offered comprehensive, innovative skills and knowledge to make them an asset rather than a liability for growth and development.

Drought, security, and political instability are also major stumbling blocks to Africa's development. While poverty, inequalities, and unemployment contribute to political instability, political stability would increase with economic development and prosperity for all.

Growth of factor supplies in key industries is a critical feature in determining the speed and scope of the growth and transformation process. Therefore, there is need for continuous technological flexibility as well as updating of skills and training. Capital goods are more responsive to the need for changes in technology. Continuous reliance on imported capital goods may be frustrated by shortages of foreign exchange. With domestic manufacturing of capital goods, domestic savings can more easily be translated to capital goods which are readily available in the domestic market. Hence, the necessity for locating capital goods industries in Africa accompanied by the development of *trans-Africa infrastructure*, especially transportation networks. This will minimize the need for foreign exchange for overseas importation of essential development inputs. Research and development (R&D) facilitates the economy's flexibility in adjusting to the industries of the future as the economy and per capita income grow and demand patterns change.

Diversification and manufacturing are essential for integrated and self-sustaining economic development. Among the diverse manufacturing subsectors, capital goods manufacturing is the most dynamic. It has strong backward and forward linkages to the rest of the economy. It supplies inputs to various subsectors of industry as well as to agriculture and the services sector. Manufacturing has higher capacity to absorb labor and has higher and rising productivity. The major shortcoming of most African countries is their small size in terms of resources and domestic markets, which are necessary for the establishment of capital goods industries.

Many African leaders, aware of the small sizes of their countries, have advocated for African unity and/or regional integration as the appropriate development strategies. However, their legal and political conceptions of sovereignty have superseded their vision of economic necessity for larger political units. If African leaders persist with the view of narrow and legalistic sovereignty, the continent will continue to be subservient in the increasingly globalizing international economy as the realization of the goals of regional and eventual continental integration will be hard to achieve. Consequently, poverty, inequality, and unemployment will persist or even grow worse, particularly with a large youthful population and faster rates of population growth and urbanization.

Most African economies can hardly be transformed within the existing domestic structures, although a few large ones can. There are a few large African countries with huge resources and large potential domestic markets that can go a long way in establishing self-sustaining manufacturing sectors from which industrialization can diffuse to the neighboring countries. Given the slower rate of regional integration, these large single political entities could be developed into *major regional development poles* from which industrialization can spread to the smaller countries in the rest of the continent. The large political entities include, *but are not limited to*, the Democratic Republic of Congo (DRC), Ethiopia, Nigeria, and South Africa.

The Democratic Republic of the Congo (DRC)

The almost perpetual instability in the *Democratic Republic of Congo (DRC)* has frustrated any meaningful economic progress in the country in spite of its tremendous natural and human resources. However, since the official end of the major DRC wars in 2002, the country had made commendable progress with regards to economic fundamentals until President Kabila reneged on holding constitutionally mandated national elections in 2016. The mining sector, which drives the economy, showed strong growth. The government improved economic policy and made impressive progress. However, widespread corruption and inadequate improvement in governance prevented resource wealth from benefiting other sectors of the economy and the bulk of the population.

Economic growth has been highly contingent on expansion of the mining sector and improvement in infrastructure, particularly transport and energy. However, institutional reforms to boost efficiency and consolidate macroeconomic stability would have the most profound impact on future economic growth. Diversification of the economy would greatly decrease the country's vulnerability to external shocks in natural resources markets.

Having endured conflict and civil strife in the past, a new era of growth and prosperity could see the Democratic Republic of Congo (DRC) become a major economy. The planned $80 billion Grand Inga Dam will be massive, producing over 44,000 megawatts when completed. It will be capable of literally lighting up most of the continent. Currently, the world's largest hydropower plant is the Three Gorges Dam across the Yangtze River in China, delivering 22,500 megawatts.

Nigeria and South Africa, plus the countries between them and the DRC, could join the DRC in investing in the Grand Inga Energy Complex to resolve their long-term energy constraints. Developing of the DRC's infrastructure (roads, railways, rivers, and communications) will improve economic and living conditions not only in the Congo, but in large parts of Africa, especially in the neighboring counties of the DRC.

While the country is very wealthy in natural endowments, especially mineral resources, it is imperative to diversify beyond this wealth alone to propel the DRC to a state that can establish a sustainable and self-sustaining economy and compete economically on global scale. But to achieve this, efforts to provide quality healthcare, education, electricity, and infrastructure to meet the every-day needs of the bulk of the population should serve as the greatest task for the leadership of the country. Raising the general living standards of the population sets a stable base for self-sustaining development.

However, given its significance, the mining sector will have to play the great-est part in the industrialization, diversification, and sustainability of develop-ment in the DRC. The proceeds of mining must be shared by all levels of government – local, provincial, and central – and invested in the Congolese people. The three levels of government should focus on various facets of devel-opment programs and projects. While the central government may focus on national economic transformation, the lower levels of government should con-centrate on raising the standards of living of the local populations in their areas of jurisdictions. For the lower levels of government to fulfil their functions, they should be empowered with political and economic powers. Resource sharing by the three tiers of government must be institutionalized, with regular peri-odic reviews.

Ethiopia

Ethiopia experienced rapid and stable economic growth for over a decade since the beginning of the twenty-first century. This growth was concentrated in agriculture and services. It was driven by substantial public infrastructure investment. Recent growth was also noticeably stable, as the country avoided the volatility from spells of drought and conflict that had plagued growth in the past.

Although the transformation towards a more manufacturing and industrially oriented economy is the ultimate goal, the agricultural sector continues to be the most dominant component of the Ethiopian economy. As such, transforma-tion of the agriculture sector is central in Ethiopia's reaching middle-income country level by 2025. While many opportunities exist to accelerate growth and transformation in the sector, there are also many challenges that must be overcome.

Ethiopia can become globally competitive in the apparel, leather products, and agribusiness industries, and compete with imports in the wood and metal products. The facilitating factors include very low wages combined with high trainability of workers; potential access to competitive sources of key inputs; access to a state-of-the-art container port in Djibouti; a large and growing domestic market and proximity to large export markets; and duty-free access to EU and US markets.

The Agricultural Transformation Agenda addresses the various constraints limiting agricultural development and has instituted long-term measures that should continue to sustain agricultural development. Developing industrial parks and collateral markets are important for all manufacturing subsectors. This policy approach proposes active government support to light manufacturing through means such as targeted policy reforms as well as the provision of public goods such as *plug-and-play* industrial zones, technical assistance for entrepreneurs and workers, control of cattle diseases, and information on costs for potential foreign investors.

In spite of the currently insignificant heavy industry in Ethiopia, the agricultural-led industrialization strategy, together with the strategies of agricultural transformation and electrification will lay a firm foundation for heavy and general industrialization of Ethiopia. With human development and rising incomes of the large population, Ethiopia should be able to establish a self-sustaining industrial economy in the foreseeable future. This is especially so given the country's ability to maintain a high rate of sustained economic growth for about two consecutive decades.

Although Ethiopia has huge areas of arid land, it also has many large rivers. It can irrigate large areas and generate large amounts of hydroelectric power, some of which can be exported.

Moreover, its mineral potential has hardly been tapped. Its program of greatly expanding graduate programs in its universities will enhance the development of the country's huge youthful human resources. With its fast-growing population and large arid lands, industrialization is imperative for Ethiopia, as an industrial economy has greater capacity to sustain a large population. Developing the country's mineral wealth, especially metal mining, will enhance the country's rate of capital goods manufacturing.

Like many facets of Ethiopian development, a large part of every sector relies heavily on foreign financing. Over time, this reliance needs to be minimized and domestic financing substantially raised. Such a strategy will enable Ethiopia to independently prioritize its pattern of development. A distinguishing feature of Ethiopian rapid growth since 2000 is that it did not follow the prescriptions of the Bretton Woods institutions followed by most African countries during the same period. Ethiopian growth depended on a home-made model.

For equitable development, the process must cover various social and geographic sectors in the country. The regional distribution of industrial parks will spread opportunities to various parts of the country. Efforts must be made to facilitate various nationals to acquire the necessary skills and capital so that all groups can fully participate in the development of their country. This measure will be critical in the sustainability of the transformation process. Political leaders should also address political dissatisfaction as this can have serious negative effects on the country's economic progress.

Enhancing productivity growth, the demographic transition, and a large domestic market offer important potential. Continued infrastructure development remains one of Ethiopia's best strategies to sustain growth, but it would need new mechanisms to finance it instead of continued dependence on foreign financing. While making political reforms, the new political leaders should count the recent good economic performance as a positive national achievement to be sustained.

Nigeria

Nigeria is potentially a major economy. With a huge population, tremendous natural resources, large and diverse human capital, and abundant finance from its petroleum proceeds, Nigeria has all the ingredients of becoming one of the major world economies. It has the capacity to serve as a growth and development pole in western Africa and beyond. It should have gained enough experiences from its past efforts at establishing capital goods industries.

Before the oil industry came to dominate the Nigerian economy, the country produced its own food supplies and exported large quantities of cocoa, cotton, cattle, hides and skins, groundnuts, palm oil, and palm kernels. Reemphasis on the development of the agricultural sector would raise incomes, reduce poverty and inequalities, expand the domestic market, and further enhance the national efforts to build a self-sustaining industrial economy.

With a large population and a growing middle class, Nigeria has a big home market. This market is constrained by limited connective infrastructure, thereby reducing producers' and firms' ability to reach wider markets. This lack of connectivity dampens economic collaboration and cooperation among the country's regions, which limits the country's potential for rounded self-sustaining transformation.

Power infrastructure has been one of the major challenges facing Nigeria's economy. Finding a sustainable solution to the power problem will raise productivity of all sectors of the Nigerian economy considerably, especially the manufacturing sector. In the medium run, able states should be free to generate their own power, rather than depending on the federal government. The long-term solution is to establish an efficient power system, including joint investment and sourcing of power from the Grand Inga Power Complex of the Democratic Republic of Congo (DRC).

Also, the Standards Organization of Nigeria (SON) should be adequately funded and equipped with standard laboratories for products testing and subsequent certification. This is because for a locally made product to be accepted in the international market, the product must meet specific quality certification in export market standards. Although changing, local market attitudes to national manufactures is still a problem. Even though some locally made products are far better than imported goods, many local consumers prefer imports.

Financing domestic auto purchases will support the Nigerian car manufacturing efforts. The auto industry is based on a large domestic market. This necessitates the development of domestic credit so that many locals, especially the middle income, can afford the national manufactures. Easier financing of local auto makers will improve their domestic sales relative to imports. Therefore, the development of an appropriate domestic credit system is important.

Oil prices continue to dominate Nigeria's growth pattern. National economic growth remains anemic during poor oil prices years. However, other sources of development financing are developing. In 2016, net remittances to Nigeria, about 4 percent of GDP, were more than double government oil revenue. There are millions of Nigerians in the diaspora. Tapping this source of Nigerian capital will substantially raise domestic savings and capital.

Nigeria's federal structure gives significant autonomy to the states. While the federal government can pursue the global national goal, together with coordinating the plans of various states, state and local governments can mainly focus on the immediate and short-run needs of the population.

Economic diversification and inclusive growth are crucial for long-term economic transformation. Infrastructural development will integrate the national market. The key challenge for policymakers at the federal and state level is to identify interventions that are best suited to realize development potential of subnational regions and integrate domestic markets. Furthermore, for Nigeria to tap its spatial drivers of development, policymakers are directing their efforts towards investments that reinforce clusters and economies of scale and optimize the connectivity between rural areas and the major urban markets.

In addition to enhanced connection, targeted efforts would be needed at the state level to lever economies of scale and agglomeration. The "cluster" concept in the federal government's National Industrial Policy for 2007–2011 made room for establishing special economic zones (SEZs) and Nigeria's Economic Recovery and Growth Plan (2017–2020) emphasizes the need for greater subnational interventions that are best suited to realize the development potential of individual states and regions.

The 2007 Nigeria Industrial Development Strategy tries to promote scale economies in infrastructure provision by only allowing one industrial park in each of the geo-political zones to pool resources for providing high quality infrastructure. States have independently set up industrial parks without being able to fully deliver the required infrastructure such as roads, reliable power, water, and sanitation and provide necessary facilities to allow businesses to invest and operate. Strengthening inter-government coordination in the development of industrial parks and related interventions will have more positive effects on national development. Agglomeration economies from well-managed urban development alongside gains from inter-regional cooperation can enhance productivity and spur economic diversification.

Upgrading road quality along these corridors can boost overall economic efficiency. However, the bottlenecks in inter-regional connectivity in Nigeria stem from more than merely the condition and expansion of the hard infrastructure. Poor security conditions and rent seeking along many routes are a prevailing problem. In addition, poor fleet operations and managements, as well as the lack of coordination in logistics, further exacerbate the challenges in improving connectivity. Inherent operational inefficiency raises the costs of goods and services: vehicles are extremely aged or in poor condition, which is exacerbated further by inefficient operations such as a high percentage of empty return trips. Empty running is a huge drain on fleet efficiency and network usage.

Nigeria has plenty of national entrepreneurs, both individual and institutional. Given the necessary infrastructure, especially in the fields of ample and efficient electricity supply and road and railway networks, can considerably enhance the country's economic transformation. Nigeria's Economic Recovery and Growth Plan (2017–2020) emphasizes the need for greater subnational coordination and outlines incentives to ensure that the federal and state governments work towards the same goals. Consistent implementation of such policies will propel Nigeria's transformation to higher levels.

South Africa

South Africa is already industrialized. But it remains a dual economy with one of the highest inequality rates in the world, perpetuating both inequality and exclusion. The legacy of apartheid still retards further development and transformation of the South African economy. An inequitable industrial economy cannot grow fast since the segmentation of society is translated into many smaller economies within an economy. With prevalent poverty and unemployment, the domestic market is considerably constrained. The dynamism of an industrial economy is substantially reduced by the constrained domestic market. An industrial market economy is very dependent on a rapidly growing mass domestic market. The rich do not provide a massive domestic market, but a substantial rising middle-income class does.

The market of the rich is already saturated. Moreover, the consumption pattern of the rich is largely satisfied with luxuries from anywhere in the world. Hence, to accelerate growth, investing in the victims of apartheid will sustain the general economic development of South Africa. Hence, land reform and mass education and training will speed up economic growth and development in South Africa. Such measures might actually be more important than continuing to prioritize giving incentives to the entrenched business interests.

The country faces structural constraints that also limit economic growth, such as skills shortages, declining global competitiveness, and frequent work stoppages due to strike action. The government faces growing pressure from urban constituencies to improve the delivery of basic services to low-income areas, to increase job growth, and to provide university-level education at affordable prices. Land reform remains a burning issue.

Unstable electricity supplies retard growth. Eskom has built new power stations and has installed new power demand management programs to improve power grid reliability. It is revamping South Africa's nuclear power generating capabilities. South Africa is cooperating with the Democratic Republic of the Congo and other regional countries to implement the Inga III Power Project.

South African manufacturing continues to be heavily dominated by resource-processing sectors that are capital and energy intensive. A structural shift towards higher growth in more value-adding and higher labor-absorbing manufacturing sectors is essential for South Africa to shift to a development path that generates more growth and higher levels of employment.

Unlocking further growth and employment potential of services requires the revitalization of the manufacturing sector so that real national income can be raised. This occurs predominantly through the stimulatory effect on real national income and the associated derived demand that is then generated for the bulk of non-tradable services. Rising national income as the driver of services growth and employment is fundamentally more sustainable than when the growth of services is fueled by increases in household debt levels.

The South African manufacturing sector, although relatively diversified, is dominated by a few large subsectors, specifically chemicals, metals, and machinery, as well as food processing. The chemicals and food processing sectors expanded their respective shares of manufacturing value added since 1994, while those of metals and machinery have remained relatively unchanged.

While many manufacturing subsectors are domestic market orientated, others rely heavily on export markets. Competitiveness is, thus, critical to their success. Consequently, several factors affect subsector performance over time, including domestic and external demand conditions, currency movements, input costs and pricing practices, technological upgrading, policy support, infrastructure and logistics, and regulatory aspects and tariff protection, as well as competition issues. At subsector level, the largest gains in real value added during the 1994 to 2012 period among the manufacturing industries were recorded for petroleum products, motor vehicles, parts and accessories, machinery and equipment, basic chemicals, and electrical machinery.

Besides the demand-side stress, the manufacturing sector also has to deal with substantial cost pressures. Other challenges include electricity shortages, currency volatility, skills constraints, and a poor rate of productivity improvement. The volatility of the rand has also added to the malaise. However, the sector has experienced short periods of relative strength, with some subsectors having registered good growth between 2004 and 2007 as a result of robust export demand backed by solid domestic demand.

According to the Department of Trade and Industry (DTI), there was no single contributing factor that could be identified as being responsible for the decline of manufacturing in South Africa. Instead, the decline was a result of a range of factors that had to be dealt with collectively if the country wanted to raise the levels of diversified manufacturing and employment.

To greatly improve the growth of GDP, and particularly of manufacturing, a number of measures need to be undertaken. Education needs to be transformed to train people for highly skilled manufacturing jobs. The country needs to evolve from being a producer and exporter of primary products to becoming producers of value-added products. The landless need to have their own farms, with appropriate farm support services tailored to their capacities.

The South African government has planned to spend billions of rand over the next few years to help manufacturers upgrade their factories, improve products, and train workers. Additionally, the South African government has instituted two key national strategies that affect the manufacturing sector. These are the *New Growth Path* and the *Industrial Policy Action Plan II (IPAPII)*. The New Growth Path is a framework that seeks to address the issues surrounding unemployment, inequality, and poverty through strategy implementation relating to job creation and aims to create five million jobs by 2020 by attempting to restructure the South African economy to improve performance in relation to labor intensive technology and an improved growth rate. The Industrial Policy Action Plan (IPAP) aims to ensure that stronger cohesion exists between macro- and micro-economic policies that relate to exchange and interest rates, inflation, and trade balance requirements.

Two major factors that could have boosted productive capacity and domestic market and hence economic growth in South Africa are a post-apartheid baby boom and land reform. The post-apartheid baby boom has been completely missed out because of the HIV/AIDS pandemic that befell the country in the immediate post-apartheid period. Rapid growth of population since the end of apartheid would have increased the size and altered the age structure of the population.

These would probably have increased the rate of economic growth as well as the structures of demand and growth. A major land reform that benefits the majority of the poor landless could substantially raise incomes with significant multiplier effects on the rest of the economy, particularly on the consumer goods subsectors of manufacturing and services. This would increase economic growth, particularly in the labor-intensive sectors.

The South African government is aware of the immense challenges it needs to overcome in order to accelerate progress and build a more inclusive country. Although it has done so much, a lot still remains given the magnitude of the initial problem. Increasing and broadening the domestic South African market may re-accelerate the rate of growth of manufacturing in South Africa. Raising the living standards of the poor and greatly reducing inequalities will contribute to such an eventuality.

Intra- and inter-Africa regional infrastructure

For the *Regional Development Poles Strategy* to succeed so that development from the regional development poles can readily diffuse to the other countries, the various African countries will have to be linked with various networks of infrastructure in the form of roads, railways, airlines, ICTs, electricity, and ports. Programs and projects for realizing these goals of infrastructural linkages are already being undertaken at continental level, through the Program for Infrastructure Development in Africa (PIDA). Regional Economic Communities (RECs) are also implementing their own infrastructural projects.

PIDA aims at transforming African infrastructure during the period 2012–2040. It consists of trans- and intra-Africa transport, electricity, ICT, and water development programs and projects. By improving access to integrated regional and continental infrastructure networks, PIDA will allow countries to meet forecast demand for infrastructure services and boost their competitiveness by increasing efficiencies, accelerating growth, and facilitating integration into the world economy, unleashing intra-African trade, and improving living standards.

Weak infrastructure and regulatory impediments are some of the main factors leading to high manufacturing costs in Africa. This means that production costs in Africa could fall quite rapidly relative to competitor countries if these basic infrastructure and regulatory constraints are addressed. PIDA has started to address these constraints.

To accelerate PIDA, African leaders should focus on training of plenty of the relevant human resources and mobilize the necessary finances for undertaking the various programs and projects at various levels of implementation. These trans-Africa projects must be viewed as integral parts of the national projects and hence should be given equal weight to the national projects in their execution.

The belt and road initiative

China, under the Forum on China-African Cooperation and the Belt and Road Initiative, is greatly contributing to meeting the wide PIDA financial gap. Although China's financing is undertaken at the national level, it is up to the African governments to ensure that these national infrastructure projects are aligned with Africa's regional strategies consistent with PIDA programs.

The political consequences of such massive dependence on external funding is unknown. However, if productively utilized, these resources will greatly help African economies integrate and industrialize, thus giving Africa substantial weight in the international arena. With thriving economies, Africa should be capable of taking care of itself, and at the same time, meet its international obligations.

It is hoped that China will hold to the words of President Xi Jinping that the China-Africa relationship is based on *sincerity, real results, affinity, and good faith*. Such a basis of international cooperation is a way forward for a peaceful international system. In any case, Africa is too big to fit securely into any power's pocket.

Final concluding remarks

Although the four economies in the study have similarities, they also face different problems. Consequently, many of their policy priorities will differ. But whatever their nature of problems, they call for the state to play an important role in guiding each economy in its own way. Where capital industries are nonexistent, the state should spearhead the development of the metal industries, especially at their early stages. But the criteria for project selection should be based on economic feasibility such that a project must yield some minimum positive rate of return. Developmental states, such as China, Japan, and South Korea, have been able to achieve industrialization through direct state intervention in the process.

Raising the level of living of the population through agricultural and small-scale nonfarm projects, as well as other local development activities, will contribute to equitable development and reduce poverty, inequalities, unemployment, and instability. A large but poor and segmented population is not a viable domestic market that can sustain high rates of growth of manufacturing, as the different segments of society have different demand patterns.

Rising per capita incomes of most of the population are also important to enhance the domestic market as well as to promote labor and general stability in the country. Therefore, there is necessity for promoting employment and equitable development and incomes. This will broaden the domestic market and the capacity to absorb the resulting increasingly large and diversified domestic output.

Large regional projects and programs in transport, ports, electricity, and ICT should be jointly developed given their region-wide impacts. For example, joint effort by the DRC, Nigeria, and South Africa, plus the countries between them, could speed up the development of the Grand Inga Power Complex in the DRC. This could have tremendous consequences on the efficiency and productivities for the economies in the sub-regions. Electricity interconnectors and national power plants, with export capacity, are regional assets that support energy access programs.

The joint development of the Grand Inga Power Complex will also contribute greatly to sustainable development. Instead of South Africa depending on coal-powered electricity and Nigeria on oil-powered electricity, they could be supplied from Inga with clean hydropower. This would reduce pollution considerably and enable the DRC to raise the living conditions of its peasants who live at subsistence level and depend very much on the Congo forests and wildlife. Such policies will contribute to sustainable development on a wider scale in Africa.

ICT broadband networks should be developed and interconnected regionally. International submarine cables and satellites should be jointly developed, and inland extensions of networks interconnected to neighboring countries. The interconnections should not only link capital cities but must also be extended to the regions of the various countries.

The sooner African leaders at various levels realize that the viability of the development of their countries is greatly interconnected, the sooner the African economies will be transformed. The transformation of neighboring economies depends on developmental states that are fully aware of their relative potentials as well as having independently deep and comprehensive understanding of the evolving complex international environment and each neighbor's comparative advantage. This largely depends on the type of education Africa impacts on its youth.

The role of the state is crucial in the early stages of industrialization. No country has industrialized without the state playing a major role, directly or indirectly, especially in the case of heavy industry. The bulk of manufacturing in Africa consists of three types of product categories: the *processing of primary products*, including agro industries, *consumer goods*, and *labor-intensive industries* producing for export. To progress to the level of massive capital goods manufacturing, countries such as the Democratic Republic of Congo, Ethiopia, and Nigeria will have to protect their markets, using the argument of infant industry. This is what most industrial economies used during their early periods of industrialization. Even countries industrializing today practice protection of their markets.

Trade boycotts against apartheid helped South Africa expand and consolidate its industrialization. Countries comparable in size to the DRC, Ethiopia, Nigeria, and South Africa, such as Brazil, Thailand, and Turkey, among others, have used tariffs and local content requirements to protect their markets. These countries rely on their substantial domestic markets to absorb their own domestic manufactures until they mature to be able to withstand competition from established foreign manufactures.

Appendices

Appendix 1 Basic indicators of African countries, 2015

Country	Area ('000 km²)	Population		GDP (in $ PPP)		Life Expectancy	Education (% Enrolment)			
		Total (million)	Density (per km²)	Thousands	Per capita	Years	Pre-Primary	Primary	Secondary	Tertiary
Algeria	2,381.7	39.9	16.7	582,598	14,250.0	60.7	..	116.2	..	36.9
Angola	1,246.7	27.9	22.3	184,438	3,589.4	52.7		..	..	9.3
Benin	112.8	10.6	93.8	22,955	2,110.0	59.7	23.9	129.0	56.8	15.4
Botswana	566.7	2.2	3.9	35,763	16,010.0	64.5	18.3	107.6	..	27.5
Burkina Faso	273.6	18.1	66.2	30,041	1,600.0	58.6	4.1	88.0	33.7	5.6
Burundi	25.7	10.2	397.2	8,228	800.0	57.1	12.6	123.8	42.5	5.0
Cabo Verde	4.0	0.5	132.2	3,766	6,070.0	73.4	73.7	109.9	92.9	21.7
Cameroon	472.7	22.8	48.3	72,896	3,140.0	55.9	37.8	117.1	58.1	17.5
CAR	623.0	4.5	7.3	2,927	670.0	51.4	..	..	..	..
Chad	1,259.2	14.0	11.1	30,481	2,110.0	52.4	0.8	101.4	..	3.4
Comoros	1.9	0.8	417.7	1,105	1,510.0	63.6	20.5	103.2	60.4	8.9
Congo, DR	2,267.1	76.2	33.6	60,482	740.0	59.0	4.2	107.0	43.5	6.6
Congo, Rep	341.5	5.0	14.6	29,423	5,840.0	62.9	7.2	93.6	43.9	9.2
Cote d'Ivoire	318.0	23.1	72.7	79,361	3,360.0	51.9	4.7	66.3	47.1	..
Djibouti	23.2	0.9	40.0	2,876	..	62.3	30.0	103.9	86.1	36.2
Egypt	995.5	93.8	94.2	999,638	10,720.0	71.3	57.8	79.1	..	..
Equ. Guinea	28.1	1.2	41.9	25,386	19,440.0	58.0	13.2	49.6	30.5	2.6
Eritrea	101.0	..	..	..	..	64.1	30.4	102.1	35.2	8.1
Ethiopia	1,000.0	99.9	99.9	161,571	1,630.0	64.6	38.0	91.6	..	..
Gabon	257.7	1.9	7.5	34,523	16,430.0	64.9	..	109.9	..	16.2
Gambia	10.1	2.0	195.4	3,155	1,640.0	60.5	38.0	91.3	35.2	..
Ghana	227.5	27.6	121.2	115,137	4,060.0	61.5	120.8	109.9	61.4	16.2
Guinea	245.7	12.1	49.2	15,213	1,170.0	59.2	..	91.3	38.8	10.8
Guinea–Bissau	28.1	1.8	63.0	2,680	1,510.0	55.5	..	..	..	..
Kenya	569.1	47.2	83.0	141,951	2,990.0	62.1	76.2	109.0	..	..
Lesotho	30.4	2.2	71.6	5,585	3,390.0	50.0	34.0	105.5	53.3	9.8
Liberia	96.3	4.5	46.7	3,766	720.0	61.2	156.1	93.9	37.3	..

Mali	1,220.2	17.5	14.3	42,737	1,980.0	58.5	4.1	75.8	41.3	..
Mauritania	1,030.7	4.2	4.1	15,425	3,690.0	63.2	10.6	102.5	30.6	5.6
Mauritius	2.0	1.3	622.0	24,596	19,940.0	74.4	103.9	103.0	95.7	36.7
Morocco	446.4	35.8	78.0	273,358	7,610.0	74.3	56.9	114.7	..	28.1
Mozambique	786.4	28.0	35.6	33,177	1,170.0	55.4	..	105.8	32.4	6.4
Namibia	823.3	2.4	2.9	25,606	10,520.0	64.9	21.4	111.4	..	..
Niger	1,266.7	19.9	15.7	18,975	950.0	62.0	7.4	72.5	20.7	..
Nigeria	910.8	181.2	198.9	1,091,698	5,900.0	53.0	..	93.7	55.7	..
Rwanda	24.7	11.6	471.4	20,418	1,780.0	64.5	18.0	132.6	36.7	7.9
Sao Tome & Principe	1.0	0.2	203.7	594	3,130.0	66.5	51.2	113.6	84.9	13.4
Senegal	192.5	15.0	77.8	36,776	2,380.0	66.8	14.9	82.2	49.6	10.4
Seychelles	0.5	0.9	203.1	2,534	25,670.0	73.2	90.5	102.3	81.6	14.3
Sierra Leone	72.2	7.2	100.3	10,264	1,380.0	51.3	10.2	127.6	43.3	..
Somalia	627.3	13.9	22.2	..	..	55.7	..	..	..	..
South Africa	1,213.1	55.0	45.3	723,516	12,900.0	57.4	77.4	99.7	98.8	19.4
South Sudan	644.3	11.9	..	22,829	1,700.0	56.1	10.0	64.1	9.5	..
Sudan	1,861.5	38.6	22.1	167,909	4,150.0	63.7	42.0	70.4	42.7	16.3
Swaziland	17.2	1.3	76.7	10,845	7,980.0	48.9	..	112.8	66.0	5.3
Tanzania	885.8	53.9	60.8	138,461	2,740.0	65.5	31.8	81.7	32.3	3.6
Togo	54.4	7.4	136.4	10,663	1,310.0	60.1	17.5	121.8	..	10.6
Tunisia	155.4	11.3	72.6	126,598	11,090.0	75.0	43.9	114.2	88.2	34.6
Uganda	200.5	40.1	200.2	71,246	1,770.0	59.2	11.6	109.9	23.2	4.8
Zambia	743.4	16.1	21.7	62,458	3,800.0	60.8		103.7	..	..
Zimbabwe	386.9	15.8	40.8	27,985	1,930.0	59.2	42.4	99.9	47.6	8.4
World	129,733.2		56.7	113,653,547	15,669.1	72.0	48.6	104.3	76.4	35.7
Low Income	13,382.2		48.0	1,049,836	1,601.5	62.0	20.8	102.8	39.3	7.6
Lower Middle Income	23,154.4		128.3	18,803,606	6,432.5	67.0	32.3	104.3	68.3	23.1
Upper Middle Income	58,179.0		44.0	41,065,001	15,874.1	75.0	76.1	105.8	94.1	46.9
High Income	35,501.7		33.8	53,062,628	46,230.0	81.0	82.5	102.6	106.6	73.7

CAR = Central African Republic, Congo, DR = Democratic Republic of Congo, Equ. Guinea = Equatorial Guinea

Source: World Bank, *World Development Indicators.*

Table A2 (a) PIDA-PAP: Transport sector

No	Program	Countries	REC(s)	Region
1	Trans-Africa Highways Completion and standardization by 2030	Africa	Continental	Continental
2	Single African Sky Phase 1	Africa	Continental	Continental
3	Yamoussoukro Decision Implementation	Africa	Continental	Continental
4	Smart Corridor Phase 1	Africa	Continental	Continental
5	Northern Multimodal Corridor	Kenya, Uganda, Rwanda, Burundi, South Sudan, DRC	COMESA/EAC	Eastern
6	North-South Multimodal Corridor	South Africa, Botswana, Zimbabwe, Zambia, Malawi, Mozambique, DRC	COMESA/EAC/SADC	Eastern/ Southern
7	Djibouti-Addis Corridor	Djibouti, Ethiopia	COMESA/IGAD	Eastern
8	Central Corridor	Tanzania, Uganda, Burundi, Rwanda, DRC	COMESA/EAC/ECCAS	Eastern Central
9	Beira-Nacala Multimodal Corridors	Mozambique, Malawi, Zimbabwe	COMESA/ SADC	Southern
10	Lamu Gateway Development	Kenya, Ethiopia, South Sudan, Uganda, Burundi, Rwanda, DRC	COMESA/EAC/SADC	Eastern
11	Southern Africa Hub Port and Rail Program	SADC Members	SADC	Southern
12	Abidjan-Lagos Coastal Corridor	Cote d'Ivoire, Ghana, Togo, Benin, Nigeria	ECOWAS	Western
13	Dakar-Niamey Multimodal Corridor	Senegal, Mali, Burkina Faso, Niger	ECOWAS	Western

#	Project	Countries/Members	REC	Region
15	Abidjan–Ouagadougou–Bamako	Côte d'Ivoire, Burkina Faso, Mali	ECOWAS	Western
16	West Africa Hub Port and Rail Program	Members of ECOWAS, PMAWCA	ECOWAS	Western
17	West Africa Air Transport	Members of ECOWAS	ECOWAS	Western
18	Pointe Noire, Brazzaville, Kinshasa, Bangui, Ndjamena Multimodal Corridor	Congo, DRC, CAR, Chad	ECCAS	Central
19	Kinshasa, Brazzaville Bridge, Road, and Rail and Rail to Ilebo (connect to Lubumbashi)	Congo, DRC	ECCAS	Central
20	Doula–Bangui/Doula–N'djamena Corridor	Cameroon, CAR, Chad	ECCAS	Central
21	Central Africa Inter-Capital Connectivity	Cameroon, Chad, CAR, Congo, DRC, Gabon, Burundi, Angola	ECCAS	Central
22	Central Africa Air Transport	ECCAS Members	ECCAS	Central
23	Central Africa Hub Port and Rail Program	Cameroon, Chad, CAR, Congo, DRC, Gabon, Burundi, PMAWCA	ECCAS	Central
24	Trans-Maghreb Highway	Morocco, Algeria, Tunisia, Libya, Egypt	AMU	Northern

Source: PIDA, *Annual Reports 2015–2017.*

Table A2 (b) PIDA–PAP: Energy sector

No.	Description	Description	Countries	REC(s)	Region
1	Great Millennium Renaissance Dam	5,250 MW HEP supply Ethiopia and export	Ethiopia Nile Basin	COMESA/IGAD	Eastern
2	North–South Transmission Corridor	8,000 line: Egypt, Sudan, South Sudan, Ethiopia, Kenya, Malawi, Mozambique, Zambia, Zimbabwe, South Africa	Ethiopia, Kenya, Tanzania, Malawi, Mozambique, Zambia, Zimbabwe, South Africa	COMESA/EAC/ SADC/ IGAD	Eastern/ Southern
3	Mphamda-Nkuwa	1,500 MW HEP for export on the SAPP	Mozambique, Zambezi Basin	SADC	Southern
4	Lesotho HWP Phase II Hydropower Component	Power Supply to Lesotho and South Africa	Orange-Senque River Basin	SADC	Southern
5	Inga III Hydro	4,200 MW, eight Turbines	DRC Congo River	ECCAS	Central
6	Central Africa Interconnection	3,800 km line through the DRC to South Africa and northward	DRC, South Africa, Angola, Namibia, Botswana, Gabon, Equa. Guinea, Cameroon, Chad	ECCAS/SADC	Central/ Southern
7	Sambagalou	128 MW HEP, 930 km line from the mouth of the Gambia River	Gambia, Guinea, Guinea-Bissau, Senegal	ECOWAS	Western
8	West Africa Power Transmission Corridor	2,000 km (1,000 MW) line along the coast from Ghana to Nigeria	Guinea, Guinea-Bissau, Gambia, Sierra Leone, Liberia, Cote d'Ivoire, Ghana	ECOWAS	Western

No.	Name	Description	Countries	REC	Region
9	North Africa Transmission	2,700 km from Morocco to Egypt	Morocco, Algeria, Tunisia, Libya, Egypt	UMA	Northern
10	Kaleta	117 HEP	Guinea, OMVG	ECOWAS	Western
11	Batoka	1,600 MW for SAPP	Zambia, Zimbabwe, Zambezi Basin	COMEASA/SADC	Southern
12	Ruzizi III	145 MW	DRC, Burundi, Rwanda	COMEASA/EAC	Eastern
13	Rusumo Falls	61 MW HEP	Burundi, Rwanda, Tanzania, Nile River Basin	COMEASA/EAC	Eastern
14	Uganda–Kenya Petroleum Products Pipeline	300 km pipeline lower cost for petroleum products	Uganda, Kenya	COMEASA/EAC	Eastern
15	Nigeria–Algeria Pipeline	4,100 km gas pipeline for export to Europe	Nigeria, Niger, Algeria	UMA/ECOWAS	Northern/Western

Source: PIDA, *Annual Progress Reports* (2015–2017).

Table A2 (c) PIDA-PAP: Trans-boundary water resources sector

No	Project Description	Countries	REC(s)	Region
1	Palambo: Regulation dam to improve navigability of Obangui River with added HEP component	Congo River Basin	ECCAS	Central
2	Fomi: HEP in Guinea with Irrigation water supply for Mali and regulation of the Niger River (nine countries)	Niger River Basin	ECOWAS	Western
3	Multisectoral Investment Opportunity Studies: Identification and preparation of investment programs in the basin	Okavango River Basin	SADC	Southern
4	Lesotho HWP Phase II–Water transfer component: Water transfer to supply water to Gauteng Province in South Africa (the Johannesburg–Pretoria–Area)	Orange–Senque River Basin	SADC	Southern
5	Gourbassy: A multipurpose dam located in Guinea for the regulation of the Senegal River (four countries)	Senegal River Basin	ECOWAS	Western
6	Noumbiel: A multipurpose dam with HEP generation component for Burkina Faso and Ghana	Volta River Basin	ECOWAS	Western
7	Nubian Sandstone Aquifer System: Implementation of a regional strategy for use of the aquifer system	Nubian Sandstone Aquifer System	UMA	Northern
8	North-West Sahara Aquifer System: Prefeasibility studies for improved use of aquifer	North Western Sahara Aquifer System	UMA	Northern
9	Lullemeden Aquifer System: Prefeasibility studies for improved use of aquifer	Lullemeden and Taoudenezrouft Aquifer System	UMA	Northern

Source: Annual Progress Reports (2015–2017).

Index

For Product Safety Concerns and Information please contact our
EU representative GPSR@taylorandfrancis.com Taylor & Francis
Verlag GmbH, Kaufingerstraße 24, 80331 München, Germany